AF735020

International Energy Agency

International Energy Agency

Imad Antoine Ibrahim
Tivadar Ötvös
Alina Gilmanova
Enrica Rocca
Christelle Ghanem
Martyna Wanat

This book was originally published as a monograph in the International Encyclopaedia of Laws/Intergovernmental Organizations.

Founding Editor: Roger Blanpain
General Editor: Frank Hendrickx
Volume Editor: Jan Wouters

Wolters Kluwer

Published by:
Kluwer Law International B.V.
PO Box 316
2400 AH Alphen aan den Rijn
The Netherlands
E-mail: international-sales@wolterskluwer.com
Website: lrus.wolterskluwer.com

Sold and distributed by:
Wolters Kluwer Legal & Regulatory U.S.
7201 McKinney Circle
Frederick, MD 21704
United States of America

ISBN 978-94-035-3014-7

e-Book: ISBN 978-94-035-2953-0
web-PDF: ISBN 978-94-035-2954-7

The Authors

Imad Antoine Ibrahim is a Research Assistant, at the Center for Law and Development (CLD), College of Law, Qatar University, Doha, Qatar. He is also a Research Associate at gLAWcal – Global Law Initiative for Sustainable Development, Essex, United Kingdom and Non-Resident Research Fellow at the Center for Innovation in Gas Research and Utilization (CIGRU) & Institute of Water Security and Science (IWSS), West Virginia University, United States. He has been working on global environmental issues from a legal perspective and their interplay with other fields such as emerging technologies for the last five to six years where he spent three of them working on European commission projects in China on topics related to climate change, energy, and environmental protection. He is currently involved in several projects related to natural resources management from a legal perspective and their interconnection with emerging technologies such as Artificial Intelligence and Big Data in places such as South Africa, MENA region, Central Asia, and China. Previously, he was Visiting Researcher at the Environmental Law Institute (ELI), Washington, DC, United States; Junior Fellow at the Global Research Network Think Tank, United Kingdom; Early Stage Researcher at the Dutch Research Institute for Transitions (DRIFT), Rotterdam, the Netherlands; Resident Research Fellow at the Center for United Nations Constitutional Research – CUNCR, Brussels, Belgium; Energy Policy Expert at the Lebanese Oil & Gas Initiative – LOGI, Beirut, Lebanon, EU Commission Marie Curie Fellow at Tsinghua University School of Law, THCEREL – Center for Environmental, Natural Resources & Energy Law, at the CRAES – Chinese Research Academy on Environmental Sciences in Beijing (China) and at the Business School, Research Center for Climate Change and Trade and at Beijing Normal University. He also worked as a researcher in several European and Italian institutes and universities such as the University Institute for European Studies (IUSE) and Università degli Studi del Piemonte Orientale, Novara. Imad was a trainee lawyer at the Jad Law Firm reviewing international conventions related to conventional energy. He holds a PhD in Law from the Institute of Law, Politics and Development (DIRPOLIS), Sant'Anna School of Advanced Studies, Pisa, Italy; a

Master's in European Interdisciplinary Studies, from the College of Europe, Bruges, Belgium, and a Bachelor in Law from the Lebanese University 'Filiere Francophone de Droit', Beirut, Lebanon.

Tivadar Ötvös is a Research Associate at gLAWcal – Global Law Initiative for Sustainable Development, Essex, United Kingdom, and currently working as an Associate at Baker McKenzie, Budapest, Hungary. Previously, he was an EU Commission Marie Curie Fellow at Tsinghua University School of Law, THCEREL – Center for Environmental, Natural Resources & Energy Law, at the CRAES – Chinese Research Academy on Environmental Sciences in Beijing, China and at the Business School, Research Center for Climate Change and Trade and at Beijing Normal University, Beijing, China, dealing with topics related to sustainable development, energy policy and competition law. Throughout his studies, he successfully acquired a PhD in Civil Law, as well as an LLM and LLB at the Pavol Jozef Šafárik University, Košice, Slovakia. He also finished an LLM programme focusing on competition law and economic analysis at the College of Europe, Bruges, Belgium.

Alina Gilmanova is currently a postdoc researcher at the Key Laboratory of Solar Thermal Energy and Photovoltaic System, Institute of Electrical Engineering (Chinese Academy of Science), Beijing, China. Her postdoctoral research focuses on the concentrated solar power policy analysis. She holds a PhD in Social Science from the University of Campinas, UNICAMP (Brazil) where she wrote a thesis on solar energy policy in Brazil and China. Moreover, she has a degree in finance from Russian Public Service University and an MA in International Development from the Pierre Mendès University in Grenoble. Alina is a native Russian speaker, fluent in English, French, Portuguese and has an intermediate level of Mandarin language.

Enrica Rocca is a Research Associate at gLAWcal – Global Law Initiatives for Sustainable Development, Essex, (United Kingdom). She is currently teaching Law and Economics at 'La Rosa Bianca' Institute, Italy. Ms Enrica Rocca has obtained her Master's in European and Transnational Law from the University of Trento, Italy. Between September and October 2015, she spent a research period at the Centre of Energy and Sustainable Development of the College of Law, West Virginia University (US) to deepen her knowledge on hydraulic fracturing, the topic of her final dissertation. In 2016, she was an EU Commission Marie Curie Fellow at Beijing Normal University, Beijing,

China, working for the project *POREEN* (Partnering Opportunities between Europe and China in the Renewable Energies and Environmental Industries), under the 7th Framework Programme for Research in the Socio-economic Sciences and Humanities (SSH). Since 2017, she has also been working for Labsus, the Laboratory for Subsidiarity, which focuses on the principle of Subsidiarity, Cooperation and Active Citizenship.

Christelle Ghanem is a Lebanese lawyer admitted at the Beirut Bar Association since 2016 and was working at Al Jad Law Firm, Beirut, Lebanon at the time of drafting this monograph. She holds a Bachelor in Law (2014) and an LLM in Business Law (2015) from Saint Joseph University in Beirut, Lebanon. Her educational background granted her a thorough knowledge of French and Lebanese laws with an overview of the common law system. Throughout her professional career, she worked with a local Lebanese law firm in association with an international law firm and a group of companies' legal department, and she was able to develop a proficiency in various fields of legal practices in several jurisdictions in Europe and the MENA region. She particularly acquired an expertise in energy law and petroleum regulations. She was involved in advising international oil companies in energy-related matters and several aspects of the petroleum industry value chain, as well as closely assisted in projects related to electricity supply. Christelle today advises actively local, regional and international clients concerning wide matters related to, *inter alia*, energy and oil and gas laws, business transactions, banking and finance, mergers and acquisitions, employment queries, corporate issues, and dispute resolution.

Martyna Wanat is a lawyer and policy analyst with five years of experience in the international environment. She has worked with the biggest regional and international organizations, including the Council of Europe, OECD, and United Nations agencies. She also holds the position of Associate at KCMB Consulting. Martyna specializes in public policy, sustainable development, and public governance. Before starting the consultancy work with international and other non-profit organizations, she had worked in government agencies, NGOs, foundations, and academia. Martyna holds Master's in Law from the Adam-Mickiewicz University in Poznan, Poland, with a major in Public Law, as well as double LLB and LLM in German and Polish Law from the European University Viadrina in Frankfurt/Oder, Germany.

The Authors

Table of Contents

List of Abbreviations

2SD	2°C Scenario
AEO	Africa Energy Outlook
AU	African Union
APEC	Asia Pacifica Economic Cooperation
ABD	Asian Development Bank
ASEAN	Association of Southeast Asian Nations
B2DS	Beyond 2°C Scenario
BECCS	Bio-Energy with Carbon Capture and Storage
BNEF	Bloomberg New Energy Finance
BC	Budgetary Committee
BAU	Business As Usual
CCS	Carbon Capture Storage
CCUS	Carbon Capture, Utilization and Storage
CO_2	Carbon Dioxide
CEM	Clean Energy Ministerial
CCXG	Climate Change Expert Group
CTI	Climate Change Technology Initiative
CERM	Co-ordinated Emergency Response Measures
CIAB	Coal Industry Advisory Board
CSP	Concentrating Solar Power
COP	Conference of the Parties
CPS	Current Policy Scenario
BRI	Belt and Road Initiative
EWS	Efficient World Scenario
EPRI	Electric Power Research Institute
EV	Electric Vehicle
EVI	Electric Vehicles Initiative
EREs	Emergency Response Exercises
ERR	Emergency Response Review
ESS	Emergency Sharing System

List of Abbreviations

ETS	Emissions Trading Systems
EBC	Energy Business Council
ECT	Energy Charter Treaty
ECG	Energy Coordinating Group
EE	Energy Efficiency
E4	Energy Efficiency in Emerging Economies
EEMR	Energy Efficiency Market Report
EIA	Energy Information Administration
ETP	Energy Technology Perspective
ETSAP	Energy Technology Systems Analysis Programme
EOR	Enhanced Oil Recovery
EPA	Environmental Protection Agency
ESEFP	Environmental Safety and Economic Aspects of Fusion Power
EPRS	European Parliamentary Research Service
EU	European Union
EXCAP	Exercise in Capitals
FES	Future is Electric Scenario
GECF	Gas Exporting Countries Forum
GCP	Gas, Coal and Power Markets Division
GHG	Greenhouse Gas
GDP	Gross Domestic Product
G20	Group of 20
G7	Group of 7
G8	Group of 8
HELE plants	High-Efficiency Low-Emission Power Plants
IA	Implementing Agreements
IDR	In-Depth Review
ICRP	Initial Contingency Response Plan
IPCC	Intergovernmental Panel on Climate Change
IAEA	International Atomic Energy Agency
IETA	International Emissions Trading Association
IEA	International Energy Agency
IEF	International Energy Forum
IMF	International Monetary Fund
INGO	International Non-Governmental Organizations
IRES	International Recommendations for Energy Statistics
IRENA	International Renewable Energy Agency
ITER	International Thermonuclear Experimental Reactor

Remap 2030	IRENA's Renewable Energy Roadmap
JODI	Joint Oil Data Initiative
OLADE	Latin American Energy Organization
LDCs	Least Developing Countries
LIFEWAY	Linked Indicators for Food, Energy and Water Availability
LNG	Liquefied Natural Gas
LTCP	Long-Term Co-operation Programme
EXMAIN	Main Exercise
MI	Mission Innovation
MODS	Monthly Oil Data Service
MOS	Monthly Oil Statistics
NAEI	National Administration of Energy Industry
NGL	Natural Gas Liquids
NEET	Networks of Expertise in Energy Technology
NPS	New Policies Scenario
NGO	Non-governmental Organization
NEA	Nuclear Energy Agency
OMR	Oil Market Report
OECD	Organisation for Economic Co-operation and Development
OSCE	Organization for Security and Co-Operation in Europe
OAPEC	Organization of Arab Petroleum Exporting Countries
OPEC	Organization of the Petroleum Exporting Countries
PV	Photovoltaics
PAMS	Policies and Measures Database
PPP	Purchasing Power Parity
RTS	Reference Technology Scenario
RIAB	Renewable Industry Advisory Board
R&D	Research and Development
RD&D	Research, Development and Demonstration
PV	Solar Photovoltaics
SPS	Stated Policies Scenario
STEPS	Stated Policies Scenario
Eurostat	Statistical Office of the European Communities
SDGs	Sustainable Development Goals
SDS	Sustainable Development Scenario
TCP	Technology Collaboration Programme
IEP Agreement	The Agreement on an International Energy Program

List of Abbreviations

TFC	Total Final Consumption
TPES	Total Primary Energy Supply
TCEP	Tracking Clean Energy Progress
UNFCCC	Unite Nations Framework Convention on Climate Change
UAE	United Arab Emirates
UN	United Nations
UNCED	United Nations Conference on Environment and Development
UNEP	United Nations Environment Programme
UNSC	United Nations Security Council
UNSD	United Nations Statistics Division
US	United States
WEC	World Energy Council
WEI	World Energy Investment
WEM	World Energy Model
WEO	World Energy Outlook
WTO	World Trade Organization

Chapter 1. Introduction: International Energy Agency in the Context of Global Governance

1. Global governance has emerged in the last few decades as a new mechanism through which problems that are common to many nations can be dealt with through a global collaboration.[1] Unlike the previous centuries and first years of the 1900s where this idea was perceived as impossible or seen with suspicion, global governance nowadays is seen as the norm in particular in the context of globalization and the increasing economic interconnection between the different economies where the costs of non-collaboration are much higher given the increasing benefits of cross-border cooperation.[2] In addition to the economic incentive, numerous challenges that have emerged in the last decades and which are common to many states have also pushed towards the emergence of new models of governance that take into consideration these emerging factors.[3] Indeed, states have noticed that their inability to deal with issues such as global warming can be drastically improved once all the nations pull their resources together for the sole objective of solving the common problem.[4] The idea of global governance emerged from this line of reasoning where the objective is to rather deal with different issues ranging from international trade to environmental problems.[5]

2. In this context, the number of international agreements adopted in particular after the Second World War has increased significantly even though such agreements required a lengthy period of negotiation and most importantly compromises on behalf of states looking to establish them.[6] Moreover, these agreements required constant updating over the years and in many cases amendments to take into consideration the changing contexts, circumstances and the fast technological developments that occurred since then. These elements added further complexities in this context given the constant need for negotiation among the different nations to

1. Thomas G. Weiss, Governance, *Good Governance and Global Governance: Conceptual and Actual Challenges,* 21(5) Third World Quarterly. 795-814 (2000); Miles Kahler, *Global Governance: Three Futures,* 20(2) International Studies Review. 239-246 (2018).
2. Barry Carin & Ramesh Thakur, *Global Governance for a Global Age: The Role of Leaders in Breaking Global Deadlocks* 1-15 (CIGI Policy Brief No. 7; Nov. 2008); Philipp Sebastian Müller, *Politicians of Global Governance,* 1(1) CONfines de relaciones internacionales y ciencia política. 51-66 (2005).
3. Richard Lewis Dixon, *The Challenge & Complexities of Nation-State Sovereignty in the Era of 21st Century Internationalism* 1-68 (American Public University System; 15 June 2011); John Agnew, *The Tragedy of the Nation-State,* 5(4) Territory, Politics, Governance. 347-350 (2017).
4. Richard A. Matthew & Anne Hammill, *Sustainable Development and Climate Change*, 85(6) International Affairs. 1117-1128 (2009); Adam Vaughan, *A Century of Global Warming,* 242 (3228) New Scientist. 1-14 (2019).
5. Thomas G. Weiss, *Thinking about Global Governance: Why People and Ideas Matter* (Routledge, 2011); Jim Whitman, *The Limits of Global Governance* (Routledge, 2005).
6. Aslaug Asgeirsdottir, *Who Gets What?: Domestic Influences on International Negotiations Allocating Shared Resources* 144 (State University of New York Press, 2008); Andrew T. Guzman, *The Design of International Agreements,* 16(4) The European Journal of International Law. 579-612 (2005).

amend or reach new treaties.[7] Still, these factors did not constitute a real obstacle for the adoption of such conventions which reflects the importance granted by the different nations to global governance as a means to solving emerging and pressing problems as well as to dealing with matters such as international trade.[8] Despite the existence of multiple and various interests which normally complicate the process of reaching an agreement or a consensus over a particular topic, nations were able to overcome their differences and ignore their short-term immediate gains to ensure long-term prosperity through collaboration.[9] It is worth mentioning in this regard that the consensus reached in many cases led to the dilution of many important elements that are crucial to dealing with the issue that is being examined.[10] Such dilution was necessary to reaching a consensus for the adoption of the Agreement in the first place given the need to reconcile the interests of the different states that are concerned with the negative consequences of a given treaty.[11] Hence, in many instances, even though an agreement has been reached, this convention did not lead to the expected outcomes or it further delayed the discussions that need to take place as states were not willing to make compromises which prompted the parties to adopt vague declarations and sometimes instruments reflecting this reality.[12]

3. This situation along with many other factors has led to questioning the value of global governance in recent years where citizens and civil society actors have heavily criticized the developments that are taking place in the international sphere, in particular the lack of legitimacy of the existing international institutions.[13] This is why citizens, for instance, have manifested in many situations in the context of international meetings that were held at the headquarters of the international organizations or during the summits that took place disrupting in many cases the work of these organizations.[14] Additionally, nations from the global South have also voiced their discontent with the current international governance system accusing it of favouring developed countries especially as it was set up after the Second World

7. Emily O'Brien & Richard Gowan, *What Makes International Agreements Work: Defining Factors for Success* 1-28 (New York University Center on International Cooperation, September 2012); Paul Meerts, *Diplomatic Negotiation: Essence and Evolution* (Clingendael 2015).
8. David Kennedy, *The Mystery of Global Governance,* 34(3) Ohio Northern University Law Review. 827-860 (2008); M.P. Ferreira-Snyman & G. M. Ferreira, *Global Good Governance and Good Global Governance,* 31 South African Yearbook of International Law, 52-94 (2006).
9. Parag Khanna, *Global Governance and Megadiplomacy,* 18(1) Brown Journal of World Affairs. 25-38 (2011); Wang Youming, *Global Governance versus Harmonious World,* 24 China International Studies. 79-90 (2010).
10. Pedro Roffe, *Reflections on Current Attempts to Revise International Legal Structures: The North-South Dialogue – Clash of Values and Concepts, Contradictions and Compromises,* 9(3) Georgia Journal of International and Comparative Law. 559-574 (1979).
11. Katerina Linos & Tom Pegram, *The Language of Compromise in International Agreements,* 70(3) International Organizations. 587-621 (2016).
12. Guzman, *supra* n. 6 at 579-612; Kal Raustiala, *Form and Substance in International Agreements,* 99(3) The American Journal of International Law. 581-614 (2005).
13. Esref Aksu, *What, Then, Is Global about Global Governance,* 1(2) Chinese Journal of Global Governance. 105-132 (2015); Jim Whitman, *Disseminative Systems and Global Governance,* 11(1) Global Governance. 85-102 (2005).
14. Paolo Davide Farah, *Trade and Progress: The Case of China,* 30(1) Columbia Journal of Asian Law. 51-112 (2017).

War, a period in which Western countries had great advantages while the rules that were written reflect Western perceptions and values.[15] This reality led the different scholars to rethinking the global governance system suggesting ways through which a compromise may be reached to reconcile the shortcomings of this system with its achievements.[16] Indeed, the existence of several issues that emerged during the previous decades does not mean that the global system must be eliminated given the factors requiring the establishment of such system in the first place and which were mentioned earlier.[17]

4. Despite the great problems that are being witnessed worldwide when it comes to global governance where the legitimacy of international organizations is being questioned, such bodies are vital for dealing with different matters that are highly complex and technical and that have a transboundary nature.[18] In that sense, states are no longer the only actors in the international sphere given the need for international governance bodies to regulate fields such as energy, climate change, trade and so on.[19] One may criticize the work that is being done by an international organization, the current lack of efforts by the international community or the weak and vague provisions of a binding international agreement or soft law instruments.[20] However, the existence of international mechanisms, for instance, is an achievement in itself given the amount of efforts put into reaching a consensus among the various nations that have different interests. Hence, the efforts and criticism focused on the elimination of the entire system would be better spent on improving it through constructive criticism while having good faith.[21] Instead of only criticizing the World Trade Organization (WTO) for the sake of scoring short-term political gains, it is rather more beneficial to provide feedback and suggestions on the ways

---

15. Yakub Halabi, *The Expansion of Global Governance into the Third World: Altruism, Realism, or Constructivism?,* 6(1) International Studies Review. 21-48 (2004); John W. McArthur & Eric Werker, *Developing Countries and International Organizations: Introduction to the Special Issue,* 11(2) The Review of International Organizations. 155-169 (2016).
16. Steven Bernstein, *Grand Compromises in Global Governance,* 47(3) Government and Opposition. 368-394 (2012).
17. Jean Pisani-Ferry, *Should We Give up on Global Governance?* 1-17 (Policy Contribution, Issue No 17, October 2018); Miles Kahler, *Regional Challenges to Global Governance,* 8(1) Global Policy. 97-100 (2017).
18. Akira Iriye, *Global Community: The Role of International Organizations in the Making of the Contemporary World* (University of California Press, 2002); Stanley Hoffmann, *The Role of International Organization: Limits and Possibilities,* 10(3) International Organization. 357-372 (1956).
19. Thomas G. Weiss, D. Conor Seyle, & Kelsey Coolidge, *The Rise of Non-State Actors in Global Governance: Opportunities and Limitations* 1-27 (One Earth Future Discussion Paper, 2013); Christoph Schreuer, *The Waning of the Sovereign State: Towards a New Paradigm for International-Law?* 4 European Journal of International Law. 447-471 (1993).
20. Giulio M. Gallarotti, *The Limits of International Organization: Systematic Failure in the Management of International Relations,* 45(2) International Organization. 183-220 (1991); B. S. Chimni, *International Institutions Today: An Imperial Global State in the Making*, 15(1) European Journal of International Law. 1-37 (2004).
21. Commission on Global Security, Justice & Governance; The Hague Institute for Global Justice; The Stimson Center, *Confronting the Crisis of Global Governance: Report of the Commission on Global Security, Justice & Governance* (Research Report, 1 June 2015).

such organization can function in a more efficient and just manner.[22] Instead of also criticizing the international community because of the inability to reverse climate change events through negotiations and binding commitments, it is better to shift the focus towards the national governments that can be supported through different initiatives to protect the environment in particular in developing and least developing countries (LDCs) that are lacking the technical capacity.[23] Hence, global governance institutions must be supported given the fact that we live in an interconnected world where many global problems exist that can only be solved by pooling the resources together despite the problems encountered by these bodies.[24]

5. It is in this context that currently plenty of international organizations are conducting their missions in accordance with the competences and mandates granted to them by the states that are members to these organizations.[25] The International Energy Agency (IEA) like any other organization that was established for tackling the issue of global governance, in this case in the energy sector, has been subject to praise and criticism simultaneously.[26] Nonetheless, no one questions the achievements that have been realized in terms of energy development and cooperation by the IEA as even the majority of those criticizing the IEA do so in good faith given their recognition of the important role the Agency is currently assuming globally.[27] In fact, over the years, this organization proved to be extremely important in the energy field in particular since its establishment.[28] The IEA in the last few decades was capable of keeping up-to-date with the latest energy developments that occurred such as the advent of new energy technologies while taking into consideration other factors that are equally important such as the geopolitical situation surrounding international energy governance and so on.[29] In doing so, the Agency was capable of navigating between all the factors and issues that make energy governance

---

22. Bernard Hoekman, *Proposals for WTO Reform: A Synthesis and Assessment,* 20(2) Minnesota Journal of International Law. 324-364 (2011); Kent Jones, *Green Room Politics and The WTO's Crisis of Representation*, 9(4) Progress in Development Studies (2009).
23. Carolyn Deere-Birkbeck, *Global Governance in the Context of Climate Change: The Challenges of Increasingly Complex Risk Parameters,* 85(6) International Affairs. 1173-1194 (2009); Marcelo Santos, *Global Justice and Environmental Governance: An Analysis of the Paris Agreement,* 60(1) Revista Brasileira de Política Internacional 1-18 (2017).
24. Ian Hurd, *Legitimacy and Contestation in Global Governance: Revisiting the Folk Theory of International Institutions,* The Review of International Organizations. 1-13 (2018); Magdalena Bexell, Jonas Tallberg & Anders Uhlin, *Democracy in Global Governance: The Promises and Pitfalls of Transnational Actors,* 16(1) Global Governance. 81-101 (2010).
25. Dapo Akande, *The Competence of International Organizations and the Advisory Jurisdiction of the International Court of Justice,* 9 European Journal of International Law. 437-467 (1998); Dan Sarooshi, *Some Preliminary Remarks on the Conferral by States of Powers on International Organizations* (Jean Monnet Working Paper 4/03).
26. Ann Florini, *The International Energy Agency in Global Energy Governance,* 2(1) Global Policy. 40-50 (2011).
27. Klaus Mohn, *Undressing the Emperor: A Review of IEA's WEO* (University of Stavanger Business School; Conference: 15th IAEE European Conference 2017).
28. Sijbren de Jong & Jan Wouters, *Institutional Actors in International Energy Law, in* Research Handbook on International Energy Law 18, 23 (Kim Talus ed., Edward Elgar Publishing, 2014).
29. Wilfrid L. Kohl, *Consumer Country Energy Cooperation: The International Energy Agency and the Global Energy Order, in* Global Energy Governance: The New Rules of the Game 195, 195 (Andreas Goldthau & Jan Martin Witte eds, Brookings Institution Press, 2010).

extremely complicated while trying to balance energy needs, the development of new energy technologies with states interests, ecological concerns such as climate change and the impact of energy consumption on global warming.[30] As such, no wonder that the Agency currently plays a vital role in international energy affairs and governance given its ability to navigate between several diverging and competing matters and interests.[31] This role is only expected to grow given the increasing energy demands as a result of population growth where several places in developing countries and LDCs have only received access to electricity, for instance recently while there are still many communities that have no access to electricity or cannot benefit from the existing energy technologies to facilitate their daily life.[32] As such, the IEA has still a long way ahead in order to guarantee energy security of the entire global population while navigating the interests of the different states and geopolitical situations complicating its tasks. Hence, one cannot but admire the great work that has been done by the IEA over the years despite the many obstacles.[33]

6. In this context, this monograph is dedicated to examining all the relevant aspects of IEA's work in the international sphere. Even though it is impossible to summarize the entirety of the IEA's contribution to international energy governance in a monograph given that the Agency has been operating since decades, the monograph will provide an overview of the main developments that took place in these decades. It will also shed light on the internal structure of the IEA and the development of this structure since 1973 given the many events that occurred in the international sphere since then and the ways in which these events have affected the evolution of the IEA, its policies and global energy perspectives. The importance of this monograph lies in the fact that very few studies have been conducted addressing the matters discussed in the following chapters despite the importance of the IEA to international energy governance. Indeed, it was particularly difficult when conducting the research to find relevant materials besides the IEA's website to discuss the different matters that are examined in the chapters given the great technicalities of the issues that are being discussed. Despite this obstacle, the contributors were able to conduct a quality research after spending a huge amount of time seeking the proper information and connecting the dots together. As such, the chapters hereinafter will reflect the in-depth analysis that was conducted over a year and half period where the different contributors have dedicated huge efforts to drafting the different chapters reflecting the various aspects of the IEA and its relevant role in

30. Andrei Konoplyanik, *Energy Security and the Development of International Energy Markets, in* Energy Security: Managing Risk in a Dynamic Legal and Regulatory Environment 47, 73-74 (Barry Barton, Catherine Redgwell, Anita Rønne, Donald N. Zillman eds, Oxford University Press 2004).
31. Sanam S. Haghighi, *Energy Security: The External Legal Relations of the European Union with Major Oil- and Gas-Supplying Countries* 140-141 (Hart Publishing 2007).
32. Tanja Winther, *The Impact of Electricity: Development, Desires and Dilemmas* 1-2 (Berghabn Books 2008); Xia Zuzhang, *Unlocking Financial Resources, in Energy Poverty: Global Challenges and Local Solutions,* in Energy Poverty: Global Challenges and Local Solutions 411, 424-425 (Antoine Halff, Benjamin K. Sovacool, Jon Rozhon eds, Oxford University Press, 2014).
33. Thijs Van de Graaf, *The Politics and Institutions of Global Energy Governance* 85-100 (Palgrave Macmillan 2013).

international energy governance. As for the structure of the monograph, Chapter 2 will examine the historical development of the IEA and its role since its establishment. After that, the contributors will discuss in detail the institutional framework, organs and competences of the IEA in Chapter 3 and then the activities in Chapter 4. Chapters 5 and 6 are dedicated to the topics of IEA financing and data and publications of the organization, while Chapter 7 will tackle the interplay between IEA and other organizations. Finally, Chapter 8 shall provide a brief conclusion based on the analysis conducted in the previous chapters.

Chapter 2. Genesis and Historical Development

7. IEA is an intergovernmental institution operating in the energy sector. It stands out as the leading energy policy forum of the industrial countries.[34] Its work currently revolves around four main fields in particular: energy security, economic development, environmental awareness and worldwide engagement. The IEA, being a global energy authority, focuses on collecting and providing data, analysis, solutions and recommendation to different stakeholders from governments to industries and people as a guidance towards making secure, sustainable and affordable energy choices. This chapter contributes to clarify how the IEA from its outset evolved towards occupying the central position in the global energy governance. It will focus on the related incidents and events that show the stated IEA historical evolution. However, this chapter will not dive in a detailed description of the extensive decisions, strategies and activities undertaken by the IEA throughout the years.

§1. Origins of IEA

8. The IEA was founded in 1974 in response to the 1973 oil crisis also known as 'the first oil crisis'. Its ensuing devastating impacts made urgent for the industrial countries to converge their efforts in order to effectively face the energy challenges and develop a strong collective response to similar oil crises. Countries as well needed to come up with a process of cooperation to fulfil their energy shared interests and objectives. Their will was concretized in 1974 in the Agreement on an International Energy Program ('the IEP Agreement') as detailed below.

I. The 1973 Oil Embargo

9. In October 1973, and in the context of the Arab-Israeli conflict, a war was fought by a coalition of Arab states against Israel. The United States (US), in this so-called 'Yom Kippur War', 'Ramadan War' or 'October War', came in support of Israeli military by delivering weapons and supplies thereto. Consequently, some Arab petroleum exporting countries declared an oil embargo against the US intended to induce policy change and pressure Israel. The boycott was later extended to other Israel allied countries including, *inter alia*, the Netherlands, South Africa, and Portugal.[35] What justifies this embargo is that oil-producing countries were considering oil as a weapon. First, oil reserves were heavily concentrated in their hands. Second, the industrial countries were reducing their oil self-sufficiency and shifting to a growing oil importation. Consequently, they were employing it to gain economic advantages and, whenever possible, to influence political events and

34. Thijs Van de Graaf and Dries Lesage, *The International Energy Agency After 35 Years: Reform Needs and Institutional Adaptability,* 4 The Review of International Organizations. 294 (2009).
35. Richard Scott, *The History of the International Energy Agency* 28 (Organisation for Economic Co-operation and Development, International Energy Agency 1994).

to obtain political objectives in the framework of international relations.[36] Accordingly, the aforementioned embargo was proclaimed by the concerned Arab countries in the aim of pushing the targeted governments to strike stances in their favour. The embargo introduced significant cuts in oil production and was accompanied by a dramatic increase in the oil prices. The high prices remained even after the end of the embargo in March 1974.

10. The reason for this aftermath is that, at that time, the oil-importing countries were vulnerable to any oil supply turbulence and to price shocks. This fact was driven by two circumstances:

(1) Poor management oil policies: during the years preceding the crisis, the industrial countries were increasingly dependent and reliant on oil imported from foreign sources, being inexpensive and abundant commodity, and without any consideration to the energy security. Effectively, oil was being used in a wasteful manner, and no energy conservation measures were being adopted. Moreover, such counties did not seek for any alternative energy sources.
(2) Weak institutional situation: unlike the oil producers who were constituting an economic power due to their unity within the Organization of Petroleum Exporting Countries (OPEC) and the Organization of Arab Petroleum Exporting Countries (OAPEC), the industrial countries were not grouped in any institutional arrangement. Soon it was apparent that individual efforts at the national scale were not enough to deal with the energy challenges. The institutional lack made it impossible for them to cooperate and undertake coordinated energy policies or to collectively cope with any energy supply emergency. The absence of essential data and information contributed to the hardships through the inability of properly understanding the energy markets.

II. Necessity of a Remedial Policy

11. The burdens resulting from the oil embargo and the 1973 oil crisis, and the fact that the industrial countries failed to spread their control on one of the most important goods, if not the most vital commodities, aroused their strong belief of the importance of international cooperation and the necessity of taking collective measures. Consequently, they decided to run over the divergence in their private national perceptions and objectives and move all together towards common corrective energy policies.[37] At first, the reflex action was to pull together by means of the Organisation for Economic Co-operation and Development (OECD). At that time of the crisis, the OECD was the principal economic organization of the industrial countries. Nevertheless, it did not present the convenient characteristics for the needed international solidarity. The structure the OECD[38] could not deal promptly

36. *Ibid.*
37. *Ibid.*
38. The OECD was composed of the Council, the Executive Committee, the Oil Committee and the Energy Committee.

with the troubles generated by the energy crisis. For instance, only the Council was empowered to solely take decisions and act directly in the field of energy. This constitutes, in the presence of variances in the countries' policies and interests, an encumbrance for an effective cooperation. Also, the OECD was not well equipped with developed information systems and support services, which are necessary for any defensive operation launch in the event of any emergency.

III. Towards a New Permanent Institution

12. The industrial countries' policymakers realized that a new institutional base was necessary to establish. In view of the magnitude of the shock, only a permanent institution arrangement could be the key platform for carrying out concerted international actions and for meeting the energy policy challenges.[39] The initiative of a new permanent institution was first taken by U.S. Secretary of State Kissinger in a speech addressed to the Pilgrims Society in London on 12 December 1973. Thereafter, a diplomatic phase commenced in the aim of fulfilling the institutional objective referred to in the aforementioned speech. It led to the Washington Energy Conference, which was followed by the Energy Coordinating Group (ECG) negotiations that were hosted in Brussels. The outcome of the said negotiations was the resolution to establish a new autonomous, independent organization within the orbit of an existing institution.

§2. The Establishment of the IEA

13. Therefore, the IEA was founded in 1974 under the Agreement on the IEP,[40] and it operates under the OECD framework[41] primarily to build on OECD's expertise in the energy sector and to ensure the operation of this institution.[42] Moreover, the purpose was for the new institution to benefit from the administrative support provided by the existing institution to become immediately operational. This would allow the new institution to immerse readily and abruptly into the rescue plan. In addition, as the new institution is endeavoured for mere cooperation and outreach, the latter resolution would avoid any appearance of confrontation with oil-producing countries and would help to widen international cooperation. Although the IEA is considered a part of the OECD, the bargain was to make this integration

---

39. Scott, *supra* n. 35 at 29.
40. The IEP was signed in Paris on November 1974 and was last amended in 2018. The IEP states the founders' objectives and is destined to design the institutional arrangements for implementing the international energy relations. The original founding members of the IEA were Australia, Belgium, Canada, Denmark, Germany, Ireland, Italy, Japan, Luxembourg, the Netherlands, Norway, Spain, Sweden, Switzerland, Turkey, the United Kingdom, and the United States.
41. The IEA was established and lodged within the OECD framework by virtue of the OECD Council decision. It was adopted on 15 November 1974 by unanimity with the exception of abstentions by Finland, France and Greece.
42. European Parliamentary Research Service (EPRS), *International Energy Agency, Origins and Development* 3 (European Parliament 2016).

limited. In fact, and although the IEA could make use of the OECD services, the IEA enjoys under the IEP Agreement a legal personality and retains full autonomy. The IEA sets its own policies, can raise independently its funds and has its independent decision-making structures. No authorization from the OECD is needed for the IEA to carry out any activity or external relations powers. Only the IEA is required to inform the OECD of its programmes of work.

I. The IEP Agreement

14. The founders were careworn to successfully plant the Emergency Sharing System (ESS), which is the main focus of the IEP Agreement. By virtue of this system, burdens are distributed between countries in case of an oil crisis. Hence, the founders were conscious that no country could reasonably be expected to carry out any costly cooperative action, unless it was satisfied that the strongest measures were in place to ensure that the other participants would definitely accept their shares of the overall burden and carry out their commitments under the system. The founders resolved that the use of legally binding provisions would minimize such problems. Systems based on recommendations and declarations do not function properly during times of crisis. In fact, any decision made in conformity with the IEP Agreement is binding upon the IEA members under Article 52 of the IEP Agreement. Yet, the founders preferred not to consider the Council Decision to comprise the IEP Agreement. They were seeking an instrument with an independent juridical standing that could from a legal standpoint confer an absolutely legally binding effect to the terms of the Agreement.

15. As a result, the founders opted to adopt the IEP Agreement in an international treaty. Effectively, a treaty is subject to the Vienna Convention on the Law of Treaties, which Articles 26 and 27 respectively state that 'Every treaty in force is binding upon the parties to it and must be performed by them in good faith' and 'A party may not invoke the provisions of its internal law as justification for its failure to perform a treaty.' The treaty form subordinate to the *Pacta Sunt Servanda* principle is the key guarantee to attain the objectives set out in the Agreement. When the obligations are stated in mandatory terms, all members become on an equal basis compelled to respect fully their commitments. And the performance of each country in carrying out its obligations is essential for the security of the group as a whole.

A. The IEP Agreement Objectives

16. At the outset of the 1973 oil crisis, the founders of the IEP Agreement were above all concerned with ensuring energy security. In summary, they sought for emergency oil self-sufficiency, which reflects short-term means that could respond instantly on an urgent basis to any oil shortage that could occur. Thus, they created the ESS. Furthermore, in the aim of avoiding sharply the vulnerability of nations to oil supply turmoil and mitigating any risks if ensued therefrom, they committed to instal long-term national and cooperative programmes based on the reduction of oil import dependence. Other intended objectives of the founders were reflected in the IEP Agreement and include, *inter alia*: (i) establishing information system on the oil market, (i) getting involved in relations with other energy-consuming and energy-producing countries, and (iii) consulting with oil companies.[43]

§3. The First Ten Years

17. Like in the early years of any emerging new institution, the IEA in its first decade was much preoccupied in organizational matters, the adoption of modes of operation and the development of policy mechanisms and objectives.[44] Accordingly, it adopted a fundamental long-term cooperation decision and the Implementing Agreements (IAs) technique. Apart from this movement, the IEA faced an oil disruption that tested its response capability. The IEA came out successfully with a new response system. With proving a powerful start-up, the IEA was therefore able in the ensuing decades to rely on a strong basis to twinkle in the energy sector.

I. The Emergency Sharing System

18. As a resolution to face immediately threatening risks, the founders instituted the ESS considered as the primary instrument to accomplish the IEA's goal of promoting 'secure oil supplies on reasonable and equitable terms'.[45] The ESS was adapted to emergencies on an urgent and short-term basis. This mechanism was integrated and took the largest part of the IEP Agreement and was extended to four chapters. The ESS imposes two key obligations on the IEA Member States. The first obligation is to be executed during calm, peaceful periods, and it requires the Member States to build up a reserve of oil supplies. This oil stockpiling was fixed initially at the equivalent of sixty days of net oil imports, later raised to reach the current level of ninety days since January 1980. The other obligation was set to be run during times of scarcity in oil supplies. Each Member State shall prepare a programme of contingent demand restraint measures sufficient to reduce oil consumption to meet with the Agency's emergency standards.[46] These measures aim to lengthen the period in which available supplies meet with the consumers' minimum needs. In addition, the system imposes an allocation system that shares the oil reserves equitably between the consumers in times of oil shortage: IEA countries facing a major loss of supply obtain oil from countries in the group that are better supplied, and the latter are obliged to supply those countries in greatest need.

19. The IEA has been supervising the compliance of the members with the emergency reserves commitment. Consequently, members undertook over the years the

43. Scott, *supra* n. 35 at 48.
44. Richard Scott, *The History of the International Energy Agency* (IEA the First 20 Years) 18 (International Energy Agency 1994).
45. de Graaf and Lesage, *supra* n. 34 at 301.
46. Scott *supra* n. 44.

oil stock building commitment with good faith. Their performance led to aggregate oil stock holdings exceeding the total commitment level. Consequently, the members could rely securely upon their own energy resources notwithstanding a significant shortfall in oil supply. However, the ESS' procedure has been proven complex, heavy and weighed by very formal conditions and costly procedures. It requires up to several weeks to be fully activated. Most importantly, the ESS operates during very dramatic disruptions, when at least oil supply shortfalls occur at a rate of 7%, only which the Secretariat declares emergency and activates the ESS.[47] The repercussion of this inconvenience was when with the evolution of time the ESS revealed a deficient effectiveness. The 1979 supply shock was considered as the first test for the effectiveness of the IEA and for the solidarity of the IEA Member States in face of a real supply crisis.[48] However, the ESS has proved to be a failure and questioned the preparedness of the Member States in face of a crisis. Of the main lessons learnt from the 1979 oil crisis was that the threshold set (7%) was high and restrictive, particularly that smaller disruptions could lead to serious economic damage.[49]

20. The IEA founders emphasized in the IEP Agreement on the twofold considerations of short-term and long-term policies. Nevertheless, as they were much strained in addressing the challenges aroused out of the 1973 oil crisis, they dedicated a high priority to the short-term response policy. In this sense, the IEA ESS received the most extensive development of the IEP Agreement. As in the course of the IEP Agreement negotiations there was no great available time to be devoted to the long-term cooperation on energy, this interest came laid on only three Articles out of the seventy-six Articles of the IEP Agreement. Only framework provisions were provided: the countries declare to commit to the reduction of oil import dependence and to coordinate to that end in four particular areas, the conservation of energy, the development of alternative sources of energy, energy Research and Development (R&D) and uranium enrichment. That said, the founders were aware that reduction of the dependency on imported oil could not be achieved unless by virtue of clear express long-term policies. They were so acute to strive for detailed specifications that would give substance to the broad commitment stated in the IEP Agreement and that would therefore truly realize the intended objective. Consequently, they charged the IEA to adopt posteriorly a coherent long-term energy cooperation programme complementary to the long-term policy provisions stated in the IEP Agreement.

21. The IEA promulgated on 30 January 1976 the Long-Term Co-operation Programme (LTCP). This latter is a comprehensive programme designed as premeditated to give effect to the framework provisions of the IEP Agreement. Some of its terms were embraced in a legally binding form and the rest, mainly those related to political commitments, were formulated in terms of declarations and recommendations with no binding effect. The LTCP reflected the commitment of the nations to

47. de Graaf and Lesage, *supra* n. 34 at 301.
48. *Ibid.*
49. *Ibid.*

persevere through national efforts and collaborative strategies towards meeting the goal of reducing the dependence on imported oil. Under cooperation programmes, they commit to share means, efforts and resources in terms of information, knowledge and know-how. The LTCP further entrusted the nations to remove any legislative or administrative obstructions that would impediment the realization of the programme. Among other things, the LTCP proclaimed the conservation of energy through several measures such as reduction of oil consumption, elimination of waste, application of energy price levels to reduce demand. It enhanced the indigenous oil production and determined ceilings on imported oil. Furthermore, the LTCP encouraged new beneficial technologies for the efficient utilization of energy, and it promoted the policy of 'energy diversity' through fostering the oil substitution and stimulating the development of alternative sources of energy. It sets a Minimum Safeguard Price mechanism to ensure that imported oil is not sold in domestic markets below a determined price. It contained the commitment of countries to carry out R&D cooperative projects on many energy facets and new technologies.[50]

22. In order to boost and facilitate the formation of R&D cooperative projects, the participant countries adopted Guiding Principles and annexed them to the LTCP. These Guiding Principles concern, *inter alia*, the identification of projects, the sharing of contributions to projects, the security of financial, technical and scientific resources, the use of equipment and manpower, the organization of research, the exchange of information and measures for the facilitation of investment. Based on the above-mentioned components and also other aspects and approaches highlighted in the LTCP, the latter in the ensuing years could serve as a ground for the IEA to endorse several decisions and interventionist features. Actions and policies were imposed on countries, analytical studies, publications, and public education programmes were also issued in this purpose. All of them were vital to accomplish the wilful objectives and concretize the LTCP.

II. Adoption of Implementing Agreements (IAs)

23. As mentioned in the previous paragraph, the IEA member countries are incited to proceed with cooperative projects and programmes by virtue of the LTCP and R&D provisions. In this regard, the IEA inaugurated the IA as a mechanism for the incorporation, management and operation of the projects. The IA institutes a contractual framework for the participants' relations. They are subject to the general principals of contracts and thus are legally binding upon only the Signatories. This entails a guarantee for the viability of the projects, as each party is obliged to undertake firmly its commitments regarding participation, contribution, funding, etc. The IEA identifies the parties to the projects, determines their contributions, determines their obligations, rights and powers, assigns the tasks, imposes the procedures and rules, defines the liabilities, shares the means and illustrates any necessary arrangement required for the development of the projects. Furthermore, the

50. *Ibid.* at 158.

IAs are open for the participation of IEA non-member countries, for national agencies, public organizations, private corporations, companies and other entities. They make a tool for the outreach activities of the IEA. Effectively the IEA relied immensely on IA, which hence became the keystone for collaboration in joint activities and the vehicle for running the cooperation projects.

III. Other Highlights

24. The first ten years of the IEA showed the accession of a number of countries into the Agency.[51] In 1977, the IEA published its first edition of the *World Energy Outlook (WEO)* which is a flagship publication. This publication is considered as the most 'authoritative source of energy-market analysis and projections'.[52] The *WEO* provides critical analysis and recommendations, and it has been an important product of the IEA and plays a role in informing the public as well as the different concerned parties through the discussions of energy matters.[53] And ever since, the IEA has been playing a critical role in publishing energy-related data.

§4. The Second Ten Years

25. The inadequacy of the IEA to react through the ESS led the IEA to hit an ad hoc approach to extend the security policy to include the management of oil disruption that does not fully fulfil the scenario of the ESS, particularly after the 1979-1981 Middle East crisis, and later the 1990-1991 Gulf crisis.[54] This new approach was based on decisions taken on a case-by-case basis to deal with imminent problems. The upshot of these decisions was the adoption of the Coordinated Emergency Response Measures (CERM) as detailed below. The CERM was adopted in 1984 as a result of negotiations and intensive discussions following the 1979 oil crisis, and in an attempt to reform the emergency mechanism. Like its 1973 predecessor, the 1979 oil shock was associated with events in the Middle East. In 1978, Iran faced months of political and labour unrest and resulted in interruptions in the Iranian oil output and a stop in its oil exports. The decreased global oil supply caused a widespread panic about shortages driving the oil prices high. The situation was exacerbated in 1980 with the outbreak of the Iraq-Iran war leading to a block in the Iraqi exports. Consequently, supplies were falling short of oil demand and prices kept on rising.[55] At no point the oil supply shortage approached a 7% rate. As the

51. The joining countries include Greece (1976), New Zealand (1977), Australia (1979) and Portugal (1981).
52. International Energy Agency, *About WEO* https://www.iea.org/weo/aboutweo/ accessed 8 February 2019.
53. Craig S. Bamberger, *The History of the International Energy Agency 1974-2004* 194 (IEA the First 30 Years), International Energy Agency (1994).
54. Scott, *supra* n. 44 at 71.
55. *Ibid.* at 114.

7% rate is the condition *sine qua non* to trigger the ESS, the latter could not be activated. Though the shortage had been constantly below 7%, the after-effects caused by the crisis have been deemed very detrimental.

26. The scene was alarming, calling for an implementation of a course of actions to avoid the deterioration of the situation. There was a dire need to strengthen measures for stabilization and saturation of the market. In this line, and in the view of the inefficiency of the ESS, the IEA countries were squeezed to develop concrete responsive ad hoc measures. Their aim was to remove pressures on the oil market which lead to higher prices, thereby damaging the world economy. Therefore, they agreed to induce a reduction on oil demand. The oil demand restraint measures were left at the discretion of each member to be adopted in accordance with the country's circumstances. Typically, countries were shifting to rationing measures on transport fuel, residential and commercial lighting, heating and cooling. Also, they adjusted regulatory systems and increased taxes on petroleum products. They switched away from fuel consumption and refrained from abnormal purchases on the spot market. They supported high levels of indigenous oil and gas production. Releasing stocks was regarded as a crucial measure due to its vital role: providing additional supplies to the market, maintaining a balance between oil supply and demand in the world market, reducing the pressure for price increases. Therefrom, stock drawing was deemed the most promising measure that could contribute to the economic well-being. The above measures were manifested through the two following fundamental decisions: 'Decision on Preparation for Future Supply Disruptions' of 10 December 1981 and 'Decision on Stocks and Supply Disruptions' of 11 July 1984.

27. The CERM was subjected to an appraisal test to examine its mechanisms. Subsequently, the IEA adopted in September 1988 the *CERM Operations Manual.* The Manual contains detailed information on the context of CERM consultations, the decision-making process, information requirements, and response development methodology, timetable and monitoring systems. The CERM establishes flexible arrangements and swift decision-making procedures for the adequate responses needed to manage any oil supply shortage. It sets clear procedures for prompt decision on stock draw possibilities, as well as it retains the possibilities for other measures including demand restraint and defines the proceedings thereof. The actions are deliberated after the IEA had effectuated an assessment of the situation based on several material factors, such as, *inter alia*, the causes, magnitude, and impact of the crisis, the world economy and the current available stock levels.

28. It is worth noting that the CERM does not alter or displace existing arrangements. The ESS remains valid and is maintained in place despite the institutionalization of the aforementioned two ad hoc measures. The IEA reserves its freedom to decide which system to activate based on the right required measures. However, at some point it was fair to say that the sharing system has been less likely to be needed than initially anticipated by the founders in 1974, yet, this conclusion is subject to rising net oil imports, which may again change the situation.[56] To date, the CERM was activated on different occasions including in 1991 during the first gulf war, in 2005 after Hurricane Katrina shut down oil production in the US, and in 2011 in response to supply risks from the civil war in Libya.[57]

I. Adoption of a Mandate Expansion

29. In its early years, the IEA was much distracted by its intrinsic mandate of maintaining energy security. Notwithstanding this core mission stipulated in the IEP Agreement, the IEA was urged later to adapt to the changing circumstances in order to remain efficient and relevant. Effectively, environmental and economic issues were booming with having interrelations with energy issues. That being the case, the IEA did not confine its scope of works to energy security. Quite the contrary, it went beyond to focus on environmental protection and economic development. This movement was essential for the IEA to preserve its pivotal position. The environment topic was not much spelled out in the IEP Agreement. It came only in a bashful mention in Article 42.1 (b), in which the IEA is assigned in the frame of development of alternative sources of energy to set cooperative programmes on 'criteria, quality objectives and standards for environmental protection'. With such an extremely decent and modest reference, further broader developments are required whenever any interference in environmental matters is intended.

30. With the passing of years, the IEA shifted in favour of stronger measures on environment and started to integrate the environmental concerns comprehensively into its energy policies and programmes. This movement appeared at the beginning of the 1980s when the IEA launched cooperation with the OECD Environment Directorate. By the late 1980s, the 'interplay between environmental policies and energy policies' became a major focus of the IEA work.[58] The environmental interference came across the entire spectrum of energy areas. It marked, for example, the energy production, conversion, transport and consumption. It introduced reliable technologies and methods to control the environmental impact. It disseminated environmentally acceptable ways for the electricity production, the burning of coal and other energy actions. It also dedicated particular primordial concerns to mitigating global warming and climate change.[59] All the promoted lines of environmental actions were adopted in the policies of the nations. The aim of this evolutionary process was to enhance the protection of the environment as well as to conciliate between both the environmental and energy policies.

---

56. *Ibid.* at 72.
57. European Parliamentary Research Service, *supra* n. 42 at 12.
58. Scott, *supra* n. 44 at 41.
59. It is worth to note that the IEA Secretariat had an active and important role in the implementation of the United Nations Framework Convention on Climate Change (UNFCCC). The UNFCCC was adopted and agreed upon in the Rio De Janeiro Earth Summit in 1992 in Brazil, committing its Signatories to, *inter alia*, substantial reductions in greenhouse gas emissions. For more information, *see* Bamberger, *supra* n. 53 at 219.

31. In addition, the IEA accorded interest to sustainable economic development issues. It involved in ensuring stable energy supplies and promoting free markets to foster economic growth and reduce energy poverty. Market liberalization, deregulation and reform were the most important economic developments in this decade. In spite of this aforementioned mandate enlargement which englobed environment and economic issues within the integrated policies of the IEA, the latter in the previous years has witnessed also an intensification of its energy security policies. Accordingly, the amplified overall activities of the IEA became in a nutshell relied on energy security, environmental protection and economic growth. This has become known as the 'Three Es', which symbolized the IEA general policy. In consecration of this 'Three Es', the IEA announced in 1993 the 'IEA Shared Goals'.

32. The 'IEA Shared Goals' were an update on the dilated IEA policies. They encompassed goals on the environment, diversity, efficiency and flexibility within the energy sector, improved energy efficiency, R&D, undistorted energy prices, free and open trade, cooperation among all energy market participants. These goals empowered the policies of the IEA, which is further looking for non-member countries to subscribe to them for a worldwide benefit.

II. Adoption of an Emergency Response Contingency Plan

33. The Contingency Plan was adopted in the background of the Gulf crisis. In August 1990, in response to Iraq's invasion of Kuwait, a war was fought by a military alliance led by the US against Iraq. In fact, a strong international consensus had been obtained to compel Iraq to withdraw from Kuwait. This coalition of states was further reflected in the decision of the United Nations Security Council (UNSC) to impose on Iraq and occupied Kuwait a financial and trade embargo which includes, *inter alia*, prohibition of buying Iraq and Kuwait's oil. Threat to oil supplies appeared in the horizon. Besides, the IEA was enjoying a great level of preparedness. It had in place the ESS for massive oil disruptions and the CERM for those who do not exceed the 7% threshold. Along with the political alertness, the IEA depth of readiness was vigorous, allowing it to act promptly should any output cut or oil shortfall spark.

34. Throughout the first period of the 1990 invasion, the IEA proceeded with monitoring and assessing the situation, and proceeded with adopting preparatory measures. The IEA established that there was no need to recourse to any emergency response system and the effects of the embargo were not outrageous. Actually, the IEA provided that the OPEC Member States resolved to provide compensatory oil supply to offset the loss of Iraq and Kuwait output to the market, and so the world petroleum market was generally adequately and comfortably supplied due to the increased oil production by OPEC.[60] At no stage of the crisis there were actual or imminent shortages of oil that could justify the activation of the emergency response measures. Stocks on the market were continuously available. Regardless, the crisis

60. Scott, *supra* n. 44 at 138.

did cause problems. Prices were high and erratic; they have effectively doubled within barely a two-month period. These high prices spread fears in the Gulf about imminent rather than actual loss of supplies. In addition, hostilities in the Gulf raised. The IEA further deduced that volatility in the market could occur as a result of a potential temporary shortfall of supply.

35. With this prevalent situation, the countries felt that preparations should be completed on a standby basis to intensify their ability to react. For that reason, they decided to issue precautionary measures regarding energy conservation, fuel switching and supervision of stock building. Acting prudently, the IEA therefore adopted a coordinated energy emergency response contingency plan in anticipation of any possible shortfall in oil supplies. The plan relies on specific commitments in relation to stock draw, demand restraint, fuel switching, and increased indigenous oil production. This combination of measures is preparatory to surge the response capacity of the countries in the event of any oil trouble. If applied, these measures would make available in the oil market a number of barrels of oil per day and so would help to reduce volatility and uncertainty. In fact, on 17 January 1991, the Executive Director of IEA at that time Helga Steeg gave formal notice to all IEA Member States and other participants to activate the Co-ordinated Energy Emergency Response Contingency Plan. The IEA released for the first time in its history emergency oil stocks to the market in an attempt to make available 2.5 additional million barrels of oil per day at a span of fifteen days' time to ensure a steady supply.[61] With this experience, the IEA reinforced more its emergency response measures.

36. Towards the end of the second ten years of its establishment, and by the start of the third ten years, the IEA started to devote more attention to the growing globalization of the energy developments and started working on strengthening its global perspective in different regions. Furthermore, the IEA started promoting enhancing relations with the oil-producing countries as well as relations with the non-members in an attempt to extend the IEA's energy policies beyond its Member States.[62] This concept of cooperation has already been broadly mentioned in the IEP Agreement. All in all, and in this second ten-year period, the IEA proved a process of rapid adaptation to evolving circumstances. It innovated new approaches to energy policy by including new fields in its mandate. In addition, it responded to another crisis again in a new manner.

§5. The Third Ten Years

37. After twenty years in the life span of the IEA, the latter arrived to this era much stronger, experimented and equipped. It thereon did not need at that time much new innovation and adjustments. It could therefore simply apply all its outcomes and benefit from the wide range of experiences it gained. Accordingly, the

61. *Ibid.* at 134.
62. *Ibid.* at 325.

IEA during this period persisted way more in its activities. They were large enough and diffused in all the fields. The IEA was also deemed well equipped with the necessary diversified response plans, fast and flexible enough to face almost any oil trouble.

I. Expansion of Data

38. On the other hand, the beginning of this decade was highlighted by the expansion of the IEA data coverage whereby the IEA data coverage has expanded by 1994 in addition to the OECD members, to over hundred countries. The founders of the IEA have sought since day one to bring and achieve 'transparency' in the international oil market through gathering information from different sources and disseminating oil industry information directed not only to the IEA and its members but also to the industry and the general public.[63] Transparency is achieved by making available 'complete, reliable and accurate information on oil market structures, operation, prices and trends'.[64] In fact, the IEA has gradually developed its general information system to eventually reach a state of acceptance and effectiveness.[65]

II. Cooperative Environment

39. The Energy Charter process has been driven by the arising opportunities in energy trade and investment, particularly in Central and Eastern Europe and the Soviet Union after the end of the Cold War. Therefore, the IEA countries were encouraged to enter into mutually advantageous energy relations with states in those areas. Having said that, the IEA Secretariat played a vital role in providing support, participating in the process, producing a paper outlining investment improvement measures, and making a number of other contributions to the Charter.[66] Eventually, and in December 1994, *the Energy Charter Treaty (ECT) and its Protocol on Energy Efficiency and Related Environmental Aspects* were signed by a number of states including all but five of the IEA countries.[67] One of the important effects of such an event is the attempt of imposing binding legal obligation on the Signatories of the treaty as per international law, as opposed to the soft and non-binding nature of the commitments arising of the IEA.[68] The ECT covers different aspects including, *inter alia*, investment, trade, transit, energy efficiency and dispute settlement.

40. Since 1991, the *International Energy Forum (IEF)* was launched developing the producer-consumer dialogue. By the 2000s, and after its 7th meeting, a permanent secretariat for the IEF was established with a main purpose of facilitating this

63. *Ibid.* at 287.
64. *Ibid.*
65. For more information, *see* Chapter 6 of Richard Scott, *The History of the International Energy Agency* (IEA the First 20 Years), International Energy Agency (1994).
66. Scott, *supra* n. 44 at 204.
67. *Ibid.* at 207.
68. *Ibid.*

producer-consumer dialogue.[69] In 2001, another cooperative initiative called the *Joint Organisations Data Initiative (JODI)* was launched by the IEA and five other key international organizations with the aim of realizing transparent and reliable oil statistics and achieving systematic global data improvement.[70] Another glimpse of cooperation could be said to have potentially been witnessed between IEA and OPEC in 2002 upon IEA's first-ever official visit to OPEC Secretariat at the Vienna headquarters. Historically, OPEC and IEA have differing perspectives on different aspects related to oil and energy particularly that the former was founded by oil-producing countries while the latter mainly by oil consumers. However, the relationship between both institutions has somehow changed with time, particularly after the realization of common interests including, for instance, avoiding very sharp price fluctuations.[71]

III. Response Plans

41. The IEA kept on updating and developing emergency response plans according to the developments and circumstances. This continuous systems review was crucial as it was not possible to predict the nature of the crisis that could surge. The IEA therefore kept on improving them in order to render any disruption if as well occurred less severe and shorter. Two events that marked this decade in which the IEA had to consider emergency response plans to rebut the damages include, *inter alia*, the following.

42. The 'year 2000 millennium bug': prior to 2000, there were concerns over what is known as the 'year 2000 millennium bug'; that is computer programs and hardware risk to fail through computer bugs at the beginning of 2000. These problems were likely to affect negatively the oil industry and cause supply disruptions, and thus the IEA conducted its research and analysis to fully explore and plan for any potential problems.[72] The IEA resolved to opt a response plan that would respond to any loss in oil supplies in the event of computer problems. Consequently, the *Y2K Response Plans* were adopted in December 1999. It provides for, *inter alia*, legally binding commitments related to oil stock drawdown, fuel switching, production measures and oil demand restraint, and aims to respond to any supply disruptions that could result from the year 2000 millennium bug at the early days.[73]

---

69. de Graaf and Lesage, *supra* n. 34 at 308.
70. *Ibid.* It was initially named Joint Oil Data Exercise.
71. Neil Hirst & Yufeng Yang, Next Steps of Modernisation of the International Energy Agency (IEA): Discussion Document (imperial.ac.uk, 2017) https://www.imperial.ac.uk/media/imperial-college/grantham-institute/public/website/Next-Steps-of-Modernisation-of-the-International-Energy-Agency-(IEA)-18-10-17.pdf (accessed on 28 January 2020).
72. Bamberger, *supra* n. 53 at 188.
73. *Ibid. at* 189.

43. The events of 11 September 2001: after the tragic attacks of 11 September 2001 in the US, volatility in oil market was very high and a perception of a potential oil supply disruption mounted. This situation was risking economies in growth to face burdens should any supply trouble happens. The IEA therefore promptly prepared an oil emergency contingency plan to be applied if necessary.[74] The plan relies mainly on drawing on stocks to make additional oil available in the market. It instals a period of consultation prior to the system's activation. It instals also an opt-out clause that allows countries to elect prior to the system activation not to participate in the response plan. Subsequently in 2002, this response plan was revised, and the 2002 *Initial Contingency Response Plan (ICRP)* was adopted instead. The latter mainly removed the opt-out clause in order to increase the solidarity between the countries and further improved the consultation procedures in the aim of assuring a flexible rapid response to any challenges aroused.[75]

§6. The Fourth Ten Years

44. The IEA's activity has been on an increase on different levels, and particularly on monitoring the market and providing its analysis and policy advises to different parties including, *inter alia*, international forums such as the Group of 8 (G8) in 2005.[76] The IEA Secretariat has been providing regular support to the G8 meetings, and it was eventually invited to participate in the 2005 G8 summit in Gleneagles. The IEA was tasked to provide its policy recommendation and roadmaps to achieve sustainable energy, including new technologies and greater efficiency. However, the IEA provided reports not only on fossil fuels but also on sustainability and climate change. The goal was to achieve clean, competitive and clever energy future. Ever since, the IEA has participated in almost all G8 meetings that followed and provided various reports including on energy efficiency (2009 G8 summit) and carbon capture and storage (2010 G8 summit).[77] In this fourth decade following its establishment, the IEA was labelled by two major events that led the IEA to release emergency oil stocks. The first occasion is the Hurricanes Katrina and Rita in 2005, which led to the destruction of oil facilities in the US in the Gulf of Mexico. This has pushed the IEA to apply the CERM mechanism, similar to that applied on the eve of the 1991 Gulf War, and it made available to the market the equivalent of 60 million barrels to ensure oil supplies and to stabilize the market.[78]

45. The Libyan Civil War in 2011 devastated oil production and caused an escalation in oil prices. This oil disruption has led the IEA to release emergency oil stocks whereby the IEA members agreed to release 60 million barrels of oil into the global markets. However, this IEA decision raised some controversies particularly that this oil stock release was deemed as a preventive measure in anticipation of an

74. *Ibid. at* 170.
75. *Ibid. at* 192.
76. European Parliamentary Research Service, *supra* n. 42 at 1.
77. *Ibid.* at 13.
78. de Graaf and Lesage, *supra* n. 34 at 302.

expected shortfall rather than a direct response to an actual shortfall in comparison to previous oil stock release decisions, which count it as a first.[79] As for the IEA's relations in this fourth decade, and in addition to the strategic partners and international bodies it has been cooperating with, the IEA established tight relations with the European Union (EU) particularly given the overlapping membership between EU Member States and the IEA members.[80] The IEA acknowledges the importance and the role of the EU and they both share concerns over energy and climate change. On this account, the EU entrusted IEA with conducting regular reviews on the energy policies of EU countries and providing recommendations. IEA has as well reviewed the energy policies of the whole EU.

46. In 2009, the IEA created its own Energy Business Council (EBC) with the aim of promoting a closer consultation with the energy business community and bringing together the world's largest companies involved with the energy industry as well as policymakers.[81] The first meeting of the EBC was held in March 2009. In the last decade, the IEA has been giving more focus and greater emphasis on renewables and matters related to energy efficiency and climate change, issues that have been attracting the extensive focus of the world. The first edition of IEA's *Medium-Term Market Report on Renewable Energy* was published in 2012, and on *Energy Efficiency* in 2013. Ever since, such reports have been published annually. To reaffirm its interest and concern with the said issues and energy trends, the IEA Energy Ministers recognized that they should work to deliver 'secure, affordable and sustainable energy' when issuing their first Climate Statement on the margins of the 2013 Ministerial meeting.

I. Current Status of IEA

47. Recent years have seen the world dealing and discussing different challenges, including climate change, pollution, and economic energy challenges. The IEA has been seen taking a stance on renewables and clean energy.

48. As a step towards becoming a global energy organization in general, and a global hub for clean energy technologies and energy efficiency, the IEA Association was activated during the 2015 Ministerial meeting. This allowed countries such as China, Indonesia and Thailand to join the IEA as Association countries.[82] Such a step would allow these countries to, *inter alia*, participate in IEA standing groups and committees, participate in technology networks, and participate in joint actions

79. European Parliamentary Research Service, *supra* n. 42 at 12.
80. *Ibid.* at 14.
81. Hirst and Yang, *supra* n. 71.
82. International Energy Agency, *Energy Ministers Set Course for New Era at IEA* (2015) https://www.iea.org/newsroom/news/2015/november/energy-ministers-set-course-for-new-era-at-iea-.html accessed 11 March 2019.

to coordinate security of supply measures.[83] Subsequently, the IEA timeline showcased a series of events proving IEA's efforts in the clean energy and energy efficiency. The IEA played a role during the Conference of the Parties (COP21) Paris Climate Change Agreement. Before the successful conclusion of the Paris Agreement, the IEA provided a number of publications for delegations and observers and country-level analysis, as well as practical ways and measures for successful implementation and its recommendations.[84]

49. In June 2016, the IEA was chosen to host the Clean Energy Ministerial Secretariat (CEM). The CEM is a high-level global forum of many of the world's economies working together to promote policies and programmes, share lessons and best practices and accelerate global transition to clean energy. In September 2016, the IEA hosted the first energy efficiency forum which brings together governments, industries, business and finance and focuses on the relation between renewables and energy efficiency. By November 2017, the IEA launched a new programme called the Clean Energy Transitions Programme backing a EUR 30 million plan to support clean energy transitions, through providing, *inter alia*, technical support to countries that would impact the speed of global transition towards sustainable energy future.[85]

II. Upcoming Future[86]

50. The world is facing everyday energy challenges, and the global energy demand is in continuous increase to record in 2018 an alarming increase by 2.3% marking the fastest pace in this decade.[87] Renewable energy and energy from natural gas largely contributed to the energy produced. However, and despite the growth of renewables and clean energy, Carbon Dioxide (CO_2) emissions are in increase as well which highlights the challenges being faced by the world and requiring immediate action on different levels. Moreover, and although renewable energy has been witnessing a strong annual growth within the past two decades, 2018 witnessed an unanticipated flattening of the growth of renewables which raised the concerns of IEA and the world particularly with respect to meeting the long-term climate goals and the Paris Agreement goals.[88]

---

83. European Parliamentary Research Service, *supra* n. 42 at 12.
84. COP21 (Iea.org) https://www.iea.org/cop21/ accessed 14 April 2019.
85. International Energy Agency, *IEA Launches the Clean Energy Transitions Programme to Support Clean-Energy Development* (Iea.org, 2017) https://www.iea.org/newsroom/news/2017/november/iea-launches-the-clean-energy-transitions-programme-to-support-clean-energy-devel.html accessed 13 April 2019.
86. Hirst and Yang, *supra* n. 71.
87. International Energy Agency, *Global Energy Demand Rose by 2.3% In 2018, Its Fastest Pace in the Last Decade* (Iea.org, 2019) https://www.iea.org/newsroom/news/2019/march/global-energy-demand-rose-by-23-in-2018-its-fastest-pace-in-the-last-decade.html accessed 1 May 2019.
88. International Energy Agency, *Renewable Capacity Growth Worldwide Stalled in 2018 After Two Decades of Strong Expansion* (Iea.org, 2019) https://www.iea.org/newsroom/news/2019/may/renewable-capacity-growth-worldwide-stalled-in-2018-after-two-decades-of-strong-e.html accessed 9 May 2019.

51. In light of the foregoing, and despite all the efforts being put into the transition into clean energy, the statistics show that further developments shall be made on different levels to tackle this continuous increase in energy demand and its consequences, including, among other things, developing all clean energy solutions, improving emissions, encouraging innovation and energy technology.[89]

III. The Importance of the Establishment of the IEA and What Could Have Been the Situation Otherwise?

52. The industrial countries in facing the 1973 oil agitation could have responded by virtue of ad hoc conferences. However, they recognized that such an alternative is the weakest. Even if it succeeds to calm the oil supply disruption, it is not predestined for continuity. Thus, they chose to respond in an institutional approach. This was a smart reaction as by establishing a permanent agency, they would benefit from constant support and a constant readiness to any future potential oil crisis. Actually, the countries were aware that if an oil shock occurred in 1973 for the first time, nothing prevents from a resurgence of another one at any later time. Thus, they instituted the IEA by virtue of which they could engage in much more far-reaching objectives than the simple punctual one of response to oil supply disruptions. Effectively, they evolved the IEA mission by enlarging the scope of its activities to cover a whole spectrum of energy fields as well as environment and economic issues.

53. The choice of a permanent institution has proven to be successful. Throughout the years, other oil crises occurred. In the framework of the IEA, the side effects have been mitigated. Otherwise, without the IEA, severe turbulence would have scrambled. What assured the successful responses is the oil stockpiling. This latter is the cornerstone of the oil insurance system and could not have been met unless in the framework of the IEA, which founding treaty stipulated binding terms in this effect. Even in the coming decades, maintaining this emergency response capability will still prove vital as the global oil market remains vulnerable to a wide range of risk factors including, *inter alia*, natural disasters and geopolitical tensions. In addition, the IEA transferred from a simple oil insurance regime to a key global institution for sustainable energy policies. It adopted long-term preventive measures to oil shocks. It also interfered in very rising eminent subjects like climate change. The importance of the IEA intervention derives from the fact that this intervention is unique. Actually, there is no other strong global energy organization comparable to the IEA at the moment.

54. The IEA continuously gathers information, and today it maintains energy databases that are considered to be the most accurate in the world. It is thus capable to provide analysis and advice on all energy matters to its members. In addition, the IEA is following a process of continuous outreach to non-member countries, mainly those of emerging new powers like China, India and Russia. It is thus striving to

89. International Energy Agency, *supra* n. 87.

stay the centre of gravity in the world energy field and to become the global energy organization. In fact, the global energy consumption of the IEA group grew up from less than 40% in 2015 to more than 70% by 2018.

55. In a nutshell, the IEA acquired a profile of the highest standing that imprinted the world energy area. It gained a depth of expertise and experience unrivalled by any other institution. Without it, we can barely envisage that the results realized could have been achieved through any other means.

Chapter 3. Institutional Framework

§1. Membership

56. Membership of the IEA is bounded with the OECD. In light of the IEA status as an autonomous body to the OECD, the IEA Agreement sets the OECD membership as a prerequisite. The two fundamental elements – (i) commitment to the values of democracy based on rule of law and human rights and (ii) adherence to open and transparent market-economies – demonstrate a like-mindedness of member countries and serve as essential membership criteria.[90] There are currently thirty-seven OECD member countries. The OECD membership does not automatically bring forth the membership to the IEA. It sets additional requirements and a separate procedure. There are currently seven OECD member countries outside the IEA framework (i.e., Chile, Colombia, Iceland, Israel, Latvia, Lithuania, and Slovenia).

I. Requirements

57. A candidate country needs to satisfy four IEA-specific criteria outlined in the IEP Agreement. First, it is required to demonstrate it has crude oil and/or product equivalent to ninety days of the previous year's net imports. It could be owned by either a state or a private stakeholder but must remain immediately accessible for the emergency response.[91] Second, the national legislation and organization must integrate relevant provisions to operate the Co-ordinated Emergency Response Measures (CERM). Third, the country is requested to create a reporting system for all oil companies under its jurisdiction to be enshrined in its legislation and other measures. Last, it needs to introduce a demand restraint programme to reduce national oil consumption by up to 10%.

58. The IEA framework foresees an exception for oil-producing countries provided that they can meet membership criteria. This is of a particular relevance to the status of Norway that joined the IEA in 1974 under a separate Agreement.[92] It does not provide for a membership in a formal sense but allows participating in the IEA work equal to a member.[93] Norway is allowed to waive the oil stockholding requirement and is given a particular role in the emergency response scheme on a voluntary basis.[94] In an oil supply crisis, the country would serve as an alternative

90. OECD, *OECD 50th Anniversary Vision Statement*, https://www.oecd.org/mcm/48064973.pdf (accessed 5 November 2019).
91. European Parliamentary Research Service, *supra* n. 42 at 4.
92. Marek Gadowski, *Międzynarodowa Agencja Energetyczna (MAE), Wybrane zagadnienia organizacyjno-prawne,* 4 Biuletyn Urzędu Regulacji Energetyki, 9, 11 (2011).
93. Katrin Forgó, *Die Internationale Energieagentur, Grundlagen und aktuelle Fragen*, 26 EI Working Papers / Europainstitut, 1, 5 (2000).
94. Thomas W. Wälde, *International Energy Agency,* in Handbook of Transnational Economic Governance Regimes 926 (Christian Tietje and Alan Brouder eds, Brill | Nijhoff, 2009).

source of supply by taking appropriate oil demand restraints and activating additional and substitute oil production capacity.[95]

II. Membership Procedures

59. The membership to the IEA has been concluded through two separate procedures. The first one concerns an initial signature of the IEP Agreement and procedures reserved for Signatories – the founding members of the Agency. Another procedure describes the accession to the IEP Agreement and related procedures.

A. *Initial Signature of the IEP Agreement: Signatories*

60. There are sixteen countries that signed the IEP Agreement in 1974, namely Austria, Belgium, Canada, Denmark, Germany, Ireland, Italy, Japan, Luxembourg, the Netherland, Spain, Sweden, Switzerland, Turkey, the United Kingdom, and the US. All of them were participants of key events preceding the foundations of the IEA such as: Washington Energy Conference, and Brussels Energy Co-ordinating Group shaping up the vision for the IEA. Those countries were also parties to the OECD Council Decision of 15 November 1974, which positioned them in the Agreement adoption process. The Council Decision alongside the IEP Agreement defined the entire group of 'Signatories' and did not provide for subsequent signatures. It only included a provision for further enlargement of the Agency through accession. The Signatories were obliged to provisionally apply the Agreement before it went into force. To conclude the process, each country was required to deposit respective consent to be obligated under the IEP Agreement or apply the alternative procedure. It allowed declaring the consent by an internal procedure, namely by submitting a written notice to the Governing Board and to the Government of Belgium stating the adoption of the Programme by the Governing Board is binding for the country. It also reflected on the Board's power to make legally binding decisions. The alternative procedure was used only by Japan as all countries presented separate consents.[96]

61. France rejected the project to establish the IEA, thus did not participate as one of the 'Signatories'. Lack of support originated in the nature of the Agency as a counterweight to OPEC power bringing together oil-importing countries.[97] France had a preference in maintaining good relations with Arab oil producers and envisaged itself to serve as an interlocutor between consumers and producers.[98] The

95. Scott, *supra* n. 44 at 105-106.
96. *Ibid.* at 99.
97. Sybille Röhrkasten, *Global Governance on Renewable Energy. Contrasting the Ideas of the German and the Brazilian Governments,* 77 (Springer Fachmedien Wiesbaden, 2015).
98. de Graaf and Lesage, *supra* n. 34 at 298.

French also raised concerns that the US-initiated Agency would use the energy domain to exercise extra powers in European affairs.[99]

B. Accession

62. The provisions of the IEP Agreement stated the openness for accession of OECD member countries that are able and willing to meet the requirements of the Programme. The accession process involves a number of consultations and negotiations between the Agency and candidate country, collection of information and assessments of country's abilities to meet the commitments under the IEA framework. Each prospective country is also obliged to thoroughly get acquainted with the materials and policies produced by the IEA, accommodate its national legal and institutional frameworks to IEA standards and Governing Board decisions. It is the power of the Governing Board to decide on accession requests.

63. There is a procedural accession pattern to follow described in a publication dedicated to the work of the Agency published by the IEA.[100]

(i) *Initiation* – After informal discussions, the prospective country submits an official expression of interest addressed to IEA Executive Director and its Deputy. Following the established practice at the OECD, it is usually done through the Permanent Delegation to the OECD. Additionally, parties hold informal meetings on the next steps to agree on the accession procedures.
(ii) *Collection of documentation* – The IEA Secretariat collects and provides the Governing Board (and other engaged Groups and Committees within the Agency) with relevant documents.
(iii) *Commitment Paper* – The IEA Legal Counsel presents the letter listing commitments under the IEA membership to ensure the prospective country is duly informed about its legal obligations (optional).
(iv) *Official Letter* – The IEA Executive Director receives an official letter stating the interest in entering the IEA and initiates formal discussions.
(v) *Governing Board Action on the Initial Letter* – The Governing Board is asked to grant authorization for the Executive Director to enter into formal discussions. A decision is made in informal session.
(vi) *Information and Negotiation* – This core exercise focuses on information and documentation exchange. The prospective country provides all necessary information in support of its membership. This assessment phase aims to verify country's ability to fulfil the obligations under the IEA membership. It includes its legal and material ability to participate in the emergency response scheme; energy data collection, reporting systems, and energy stakeholders landscape in the country to ensure oil companies are willing to engage with the IEA and the prospective country in oil emergency matters. The candidate

99. *Ibid.*
100. Scott, *supra* n. 44 at 100-104.

country is expected to accept all obligations under the IEA membership; minor adjustment, e.g., on a timeline might be included.

(vii) *Formal Request* – Upon agreement on terms of the membership, the prospective country submits a formal accession request to the IEA Executive Director.

(viii) *Report to the Governing Board* – The IEA Executive Director reports in writing to the Governing Board on negotiations and the fulfilment of membership criteria by the candidate country. It includes a proposal to extend an official invitation to the prospective new member country to become the party to the IEP Agreement. The report is accompanied with a note to the Heads of IEA Delegations elaborating on member's votes weight to present an expected change in membership.

(ix) *Governing Board Invitation* – Based on the report from the IEA Executive Director, the Governing Board adopts a decision. This action includes various elements such as: acknowledgement of factual information and proposal provided by the IEA Executive Director; extension of the invitation to accede the IEP Agreements and a timeline to conclude the procedure; informational note on the Governing Board powers in relation to the accession; amendment of the IEP voting rules; additional questions.

(x) *Participation in Governing Board Meetings* – The new prospective country is invited to participate in the Governing Board meetings as an observer.

(xi) *Provisional Accession* – The new prospective country provides a provisional consent to be bound with the IEP Agreement. It activates an immediate and full participation in the Agency's activities. This instrument facilitates the membership in light of lengthy national procedures to conclude the instrument of accession.

(xii) *Deposit of the Instrument of Accession* – This is the definitive action taken by the country to become a member country. The consent is deposited to the Government of Belgium upon completion of all legislative and other national procedures. The Agreement enters into force ten days after and depository is obliged to inform all members and the IEA Executive Director.

(xiii) *Governing Board Action on Accession* – At the first meeting of the Governing Board following the deposit of the Instrument of Accession, the Board marks the date when the IEP Agreement entered into force for the new member country and agrees on an official date of membership (for purposes related to the new member country contributions).

(xiv) *Scale of Contributions Amendment* – The Governing Board adopts a new scale of contributions and determines the new member's contributions percentage; adjusts the scale for all members for the current financial period; and makes arrangements for increased resources.

(xv) *Accession to the OECD Council Decision* – In addition to the accession to the IEP Agreement, the new country becomes a party to the OECD Council Decision of 15 November 1974.

III. IEA Member Countries

64. Currently, the IEA has thirty member countries representing four continents – Asia, Australia and Oceania, Europe and North America (*see* Table 1). The current landscape of the Agency does not include representatives from Africa and South America. There are two accession countries, Chile and Lithuania.

Table 1 OECD and IEA Member Countries

Country	*OECD Membership*	*IEA Membership*
Australia	X	X
Austria*	X	X
Belgium*	X	X
Canada*	X	X
Chile	X	
Colombia	X	
The Czech Republic	X	X
Denmark*	X	X
Estonia	X	X
Finland	X	X
France	X	X
Germany*	X	X
Greece	X	X
Hungary	X	X
Iceland	X	
Ireland*	X	X
Israel	X	
Italy*	X	X
Japan*	X	X
Korea	X	X
Latvia	X	
Lithuania	X	
Luxembourg*	X	X
Mexico	X	X
The Netherlands*	X	X
New Zealand	X	X
Norway (special status)	X	X
Poland	X	X

Country	*OECD Membership*	*IEA Membership*
Portugal	X	X
The Slovak Republic	X	X
Slovenia	X	
Spain*	X	X
Sweden*	X	X
Switzerland*	X	X
Turkey*	X	X
United Kingdom*	X	X
United States*	X	X

Note: Countries marked with * are founding members of the IEA.

Own source based on https://www.oecd.org/about/members-and-partners/; https://www.iea.org/about/membership.

IV. External Relations

65. From the very beginning, the IEA's focus extended the internal activities. The IEP Agreement provided the Agency with an authority to carry out external relations with non-member countries, international organizations and other relevant energy actors. A wide range of outreach tools and activities was granted to the IEA in autonomy from the OECD.[101] This mandate guided the outreach policy of the Agency and led to the enhanced collaboration with global actors outside the organization. The relations with emerging economies are of a particular importance. Already in the mid-1990s, the Agency took the initiative to engage with China and India to integrate them into global energy governance.[102] It resulted in a status of partner countries in 2009 and a joint statement with a detailed plan for collaborations in various energy-related fields. The IEA concluded special cooperation policy agreements with China, India, and Russia. It also signed a number of IAs focusing on specific domains pending interest from actors outside the organization. Along with the development of the energy sector and the enhancing of global governance frameworks, the IEA focused its efforts on enhancing the collaboration with non-member countries and institutionalize the external policies.

101. de Graaf and Lesage, *supra* n. 34 at 299.
102. Fuzuo Wu, *Energy and Climate Policies in China and India: A Two-Level Comparative Study*, 292 (Cambridge University Press, 2018).

A. Association Countries

66. In 2013, the IEA with its six partner countries (i.e. Brazil, China, India, Indonesia, Russia and South Africa) initiated a new form of partnership through a Joint Declaration.[103] It represented the first expression of interest to pursue a stronger and enhanced cooperation based on a mutual understanding of global challenges and opportunities in a wide range of energy-related areas. An 'Association' provided for a multilateral cooperation with non-member countries in addition to their well-established bilateral work programmes. This new initiative was strongly supported by the US and received an acknowledgement from G20 leaders.[104] The Association had been being consulted between the IEA and (potential) association countries for two years to comprehensively shape the scope of the new partnership that includes both benefits and responsibilities to all the parties. The Association status of the first three countries – China, Indonesia and Thailand – has been activated in November 2015 with the *Joint Ministerial Declaration.*[105] Meanwhile, Brazil, India and South Africa decided to continue the review of the initiative, and Morocco confirmed its interest in joining the process.[106] Eventually, the group of the Association countries has been further extended to eight countries – i.e. Brazil (2017), India (2017), Morocco (2016), Singapore (2016) and South Africa (2018). In addition to multilateral activities, the IEA also concludes joint work programmes with its Association countries.[107] For instance, the Association initiated discussions to establish the IEA-China Cooperation Centre.[108]

67. The activation of the Association marked an important milestone for the global engagement of the IEA and enhanced the collaboration with non-member countries. It aims to build a progressive relationship of an evolving character that will pave the way for higher levels of cooperation in the future.[109] The Association lays out a number of areas of engagement between the IEA and the Association countries. Its framework introduces three initial areas of enhanced collaboration – energy security, energy data and statistics, and energy policy analysis.

---

103. IEA, *Joint Declaration by the IEA and Brazil, China, India, Indonesia, Russia and South Africa on the occasion of the 2013 IEA Ministerial Meeting Expressing Mutual Interest in Pursuing an Association*, https://www.iea.org/media/news/2013/jointdeclaration.pdf (accessed 5 November 2019).
104. Christian Downie, *Global Energy Governance in the G-20: States, Coalitions, and Crises,* 21(3) Global Governance 475, 480 (2015).
105. IEA, *Joint Ministerial Declaration on the Occasion of the 2015 IEA Ministerial Meeting Expressing the Activation of Associatio*n, https://www.iea.org/media/news/2015/press/IEA_Association.pdf (accessed 5 November 2019).
106. IEA, *supra* n. 82.
107. OECD, *Secretary-General's Report to Ministers 2019* (Organisation for Economic Co-operation and Development, 2019).
108. Energy Research Institute National Development and Reform Commission/Grantham Institute Imperial College London, *Global Energy Governance Reform and China's Participation, Final Report*, https://www.imperial.ac.uk/media/imperial-college/grantham-institute/public/publications/collaborative-publications/Global-Energy-Governance-Report-final.pdf (accessed 5 November 201 9).
109. OECD, *Secretary-General's Report to Ministers 2016* (Organisation for Economic Co-operation and Development, 2016).

68. First, the Association explores various dimensions of energy security by outlining key shared priorities and responsibilities. The Association countries reaffirmed the importance of taking common effective measures to meet oil supply emergencies by developing emergency response system. They also intend to build and maintain emergency reserves and coordinate their use with the IEA in case of emergencies. The Energy Security component also provides to examine the level of preparedness of the Association countries to supply disruptions through the IEA Emergency Response Exercises (EREs), Emergency Response Assessments or other relevant means. Before the Association came into force, the IEA had carried out similar EREs with Thailand in 2011,[110] India in 2012 and China in 2015.[111] All presented measures take into consideration the domestic circumstances of the Association countries.

69. Second, the commitments under the Association framework consider the improvement of the consistency, coherency and timeliness of energy data at the national level. The role of the IEA in global energy data and statistics has been acknowledged and provides for further support to the Association countries in this area.

70. The third area of enhanced collaboration focuses on energy policy analysis and benefits of sharing best practices and challenges. The Association countries expressed interest to strengthen and conduct such analysis on selected energy-related topics under mutual agreements.

71. The Association framework also unlocks a number of possibilities for the Association countries to actively participate in the activities of the Agency. Countries are eligible to participate in the meetings of the IEA standing groups, committees and working groups. The Joint Ministerial Declaration specifically lists all relevant organizational units, which are:

- Standing Group on Emergency Questions;
- Standing Group on the Oil Market;
- Standing Group on Long-Term Co-operation and Energy Efficiency Working Party under this Group;
- Standing Group on Global Energy Dialogue;
- Committee on Energy Research and Technology and Working Party on Energy End-Use Technologies, Working Party on Fossil Fuels, Working Party on Renewable Energy Technologies and Fusion Power Co-ordinating Committee under this Group.[112]

---

110. Thijs Van de Graaf, *The IEA, the New Energy Order and the Future of Global Energy Governance*, in Rising Powers and Multilateral Institutions, International Political Economy Series, 79-95 (Dries Lesage and Thijs Van de Graaf eds, Palgrave Macmillan 2015).
111. Wu, *supra* n. 102 at 293.
112. IEA, *supra* n. 105.

72. Moreover, the Association countries are given priority to access training and capacity building activities provided by the IEA across a range of energy topics, including energy efficiency, energy technology, renewable energy, electricity security, grid integration among others, pending collective interest. The training programmes are offered to central government officials and other key national stakeholders (e.g., executive agencies, private sector players), as well as experts in specific energy domains, managers and policymakers.[113] It aims to facilitate working relations, policy dialogue, information exchange and build capacity. This tier of cooperation falls under the Energy Efficiency in Emerging Economies (E4) Programme, IEA Technology Collaboration Programmes (TCP) among others. One of its key activities is the IEA E4 Training Weeks targeted at junior policymakers to build knowledge and skills in planning, implementing and evaluating energy efficiency policies in emerging economies.[114] The E4 Training Weeks have also been expanded geographically. For instance, Singapore takes advantage of this framework to promote regional energy policy capacity building. In 2017, the IEA jointly with Singapore's Energy Market Authority organized the Energy Efficiency Training Week for Asia-Pacific inaugurating the IEA-Singapore Training Hub.[115] It was followed by next editions in 2018[116] and 2019,[117] and other topic-specific training. The E4 Weeks have been also bilaterally organized for Brazil[118] and India.[119] Most recently this format has been introduced for sub-Saharan Africa and hosted in South Africa.[120]

73. The Association countries also benefit from employment opportunities, i.e. secondment positions at the IEA Secretariat.[121] Given official positions at the organization are restricted for the IEA member countries, it embraces gaining experience in international environment, skills enhancement, know-how sharing and network building.

---

113. IEA, *Training, Establishing Ongoing Working Relationships with Participating Countries for Continual Capacity Building,* https://www.iea.org/training/ (accessed 5 November 2019).
114. IEA, *Energy Efficiency, The First Fuel of a Sustainable Global Energy System,* https://www.iea.org/topics/energyefficiency/e4/trainingweeks/ (accessed 5 November 2019).
115. IEA, *IEA Holds Energy Efficiency Training Week in Singapore*, Newsroom, https://www.iea.org/newsroom/news/2017/july/iea-holds-energy-efficiency-training-week-in-singapore.html (accessed 5 November 2019).
116. IEA, *Energy Efficiency Training Week for Southeast Asia 2018,* https://www.iea.org/events/energy-efficiency-training-week-for-southeast-asia-2018 (accessed 5 November 2019).
117. IEA, *IEA Energy Efficiency Training Week for Southeast Asia 2019,* https://www.iea.org/training/calendar/iea-energy-efficiency-training-week-for-southeast-asia-april-2019.html (accessed 10 December 2019).
118. IEA, *2017: Energy Efficiency Training Week for Brazil,* https://www.iea.org/training/calendar/archive/2017/energy-efficiency-training-week-for-brazil-november-2017.html (accessed 5 November 2019).
119. IEA, *Events: Energy Efficiency Training Week for India,* https://www.iea.org/events/energy-efficiency-training-week-for-india-2018 (accessed 5 November 2019).
120. IEA, *Energy Efficiency Training Week for Sub-Saharan Africa 2019,* https://www.iea.org/training/calendar/energy-efficiency-training-week-for-sub-saharan-africa-october-2019.html (accessed 5 November 2019).
121. IEA, *supra* n. 105.

B. Relations with the European Union

74. The IEA and the EU act as partners in global energy governance. The European Commission (initially named European Communities) has been involved in the process of the development of the IEA and continues to actively participate in the Agency's work, including attending meetings of IEA bodies (also the Governing Board) and developing programmes.[122] One of the aspects of the collaboration focuses on energy R&D carried out through the IEA TCP for which the EU provides financial contributions. The IEA and EU (Eurostat) work also together under the *Joint Organisations Data Initiative (JODI)* that collects accurate and transparent oil and gas statistics.[123] The IEA not only reviews the energy policies of EU countries on a regular basis but also conducted such exercise for the EU as a whole in 2008, 2014, and 2020.[124] The IEA provided expert advice to the European Commission on strategies in the energy sector (i.e., EU strategy for Liquefied Natural Gas (LNG); Electricity Market Design).[125] The enhanced cooperation between the IEA and EU has been also a matter of priority in one of the resolutions of the European Parliament[126] and high-level meeting between the IEA Executive Director and European Commissioner for Climate Action and Energy in 2015.[127]

75. There is also consideration given to the possible accession of the EU to the IEP Agreement as explicitly stated in the OECD Council Decision and the Agreement itself. The legal provision does not confirm equal membership criteria which raises a number of institutional questions on the format of EU accession. It considers the scope and nature of EU obligations under the IEA membership and abilities to satisfy such requirements (i.e. oil reserves, demand restraint, allocation, information and other long-term commitments).[128] It is also not clear how the voting structure could be updated whether by assigning additional votes to the EU or allowing the EU to vote in the name of its member countries or its own.[129] Another question highlights the financial arrangements and prospective budgetary contribution of the EU that currently applies only to member countries.[130] As such, the EU accession to the IEA would require major adjustments to the IEP Agreement, its institutional framework and impose a number of Governing Board follow-up actions to facilitate the process.

---

122. Scott, *supra* n. 44 at 151.
123. European Commission, *International Energy Agency,* https://ec.europa.eu/energy/en/topics/international-cooperation/international-organisations/international-energy-agency (accessed 10 December 2019).
124. European Parliamentary Research Service, *supra* n. 42 at 14; IEA, European Union 2020; Energy Policy Review (Country Report – June 2020), https://www.iea.org/reports/european-union-2020 (accessed 7 November 2020).
125. *Ibid.* at 15.
126. European Parliament resolution of 12 June 2012 on Engaging in energy policy cooperation with partners beyond our borders: A strategic approach to secure, sustainable and competitive energy supply (2012/2029(INI)).
127. European Parliamentary Research Service, *supra* n. 42 at 15.
128. Scott, *supra* n. 44 at 77-78.
129. *Ibid.*
130. *Ibid.*

C. Relations with G7, G8 and G20

76. The IEA regularly supports the work of G7 and G20 with its expertise and participates in annual summits. It has been assigned by G7 initiatives[131] with a special mandate to provide analyses and recommendations on gas supply security, energy efficiency and sustainable energy technology.[132] This mandate brought relevant IEA publications, such as: *Energy Technology Perspectives: Scenarios and Strategies to 2050* that has appeared every two years since 2006.[133] The IEA's activity during the G8 summits in 2006, 2007 and 2008 highlighted the *IEA 25 energy efficiency policy recommendations* covering twenty-five fields in seven priority areas: cross-sectoral activity, buildings, appliances, lighting, transport, industry and energy utilities.[134] The G8 Summit in 2008 indeed pledged to maximize their implementation.[135] The IEA presented several reports on G8 countries' developments and performance, such as: *Carbon Capture and Storage 2010*, and *Progress with Implementing Energy Efficiency Policies in the G8*. The IEA also contributed to the 2016 Kitakyushu Initiative on Energy Security for Global Growth under the Japanese presidency in the G7.[136] The G20 framework does not significantly overlap with the IEA mandate and is found more suitable for the broader energy dialogue as it gathers powers that operate outside the IEA membership.[137] The IEA has activated its strong collaboration with G20 in 2009 and provides extensive contributions, including those on energy security, energy data, market transparency, renewable energy, energy access, energy efficiency and the phase-out of fossil fuel subsidies.[138] Only in 2019, the IEA, on G20 Presidency request, presented major inputs to support the G20 programming, such as:

- Landmark report '*The Future of Hydrogen*' that analyses the current state of play and identifies future avenues for development.
- Report '*Technology Innovation to Accelerate Energy Transitions*' that identifies technology and innovation gaps in addressing energy industry challenges across all technology areas.
- Report '*Securing Investments in Low-Carbon Power Generation Sources*' that sets out key priority actions to accelerate energy transition and decarbonization.

---

131. By the 2014 Rome G7 Energy Initiative for Energy Security and the 2015 Hamburg G7 Initiative for Sustainable Energy Security.
132. IEA, *G7, An Informal Group of Seven Industrialised Economies,* https://www.iea.org/areas-of-work/international-collaborations/g7 (accessed 10 December 2019).
133. Florini, *supra* n. 26 at 43.
134. Sara Bryan Pasquier and Aurelien Saussay, *Progress Implementing the IEA 25 Energy Efficiency Policy Recommendations: 2011 Evaluation*, 9 IEA Energy Papers 6 (Organisation for Economic Co-operation and Development, International Energy Agency, 2012).
135. Thijs Van de Graaf, *The G8 and G20 as Global Steering Committees for Energy: Opportunities and Constraints,* 2 Global Policy Special Issue 19, 23 (2011).
136. G7, *G7 Kitakyushu Energy Ministerial Meeting, Kitakyushu Initiative on Energy Security for Global Growth, Joint Statement* http://www.g7.utoronto.ca/energy/160502-statement.html (accessed 10 December 2019).
137. European Parliamentary Research Service, *supra* n. 42 at 13.
138. IEA, *G20, A Global Forum of Major Economies,* https://www.iea.org/areas-of-work/international-collaborations/g20 (accessed 10 December 2019).

– Analysis on the efficiencies of certain sectors of large industry, transport and cooling among G20 countries, including through data sharing.

V. Future of the IEA Membership

77. Since the creation of the IEA in 1974, the global energy market has undergone a considerable development. Among the various challenges the IEA is facing to fulfil its mission, one can mention the rise of new major energy powers; climate change; concentration of gas and oil reserves; and emerging new energy sources.[139] The first of listed challenges considers the fact that the rising economies are shifting eastwards the global energy demand jeopardizing the relevance, authority and effectiveness of the Agency. In the beginning, the stocktaking obligations of the IEA member countries accounted for around 40% of ninety days of global oil demand; this share decreased to 26% in 2016, and, according to the IEA New Policies Scenario (NPS), will shrink to about 12% by 2040 providing for eleven days of global demand.[140] This new global context urged consideration on expanding the circle and reviewing the IEA membership criteria to better reflect economic weight and changing realities.[141] This is found of a particular relevance in case of China and India that have become major energy consumers operating outside the IEA global energy governance framework.[142] There are however certain legal and political impediments for a formal enlargement of the IEA.

78. First, the IEA is nested within the OECD and only its members are eligible to formally enter the Agency. It implicates the requirement for countries interested in the IEA membership to first obtain the OECD membership. This is a very complex process to satisfy membership criteria and procedure as outlined in the OECD Framework for the Consideration of Prospective Members.[143144] As a first step, the initial considerations to open accession talks start at the initiative of the OECD Council or through a written request submitted by a prospective member country. Upon receipt of the formal request, the OECD Secretary General presents it to the Council with comprehensive information on a potential candidate (including on state of readiness; country's commitment to OECD values and membership obligations, institutional framework; key economic indicators; relations with the OECD).

139. de Graaf, *supra* n. 33 at 88.
140. IEA, *World Energy Outlook 2017* (Organisation for Economic Co-operation and Development, International Energy Agency, 2017).
141. Henry Kissinger, *Speech by Henry Kissinger at the IEA Ministerial, 14 October 2009,* https://csis-prod.s3.amazonaws.com/s3fs-public/legacy_files/files/publication/Kissinger%20IEA%20Speech_20091014.pdf (accessed 5 November 2019).
142. Jeff Colgan, *The International Energy Agency: Challenges for the 21st Century*, 6 GPPi Policy Paper Series (2009).
143. OECD, *Report of the Chair of the Working Group on the Future Size and Membership of the Organisation to Council, Framework for the Consideration of Prospective Members*, https://www.oecd.org/mcm-2018/documents/C-MIN-2017-13-EN.pdf (accessed 5 November 2019).
144. OECD, *OECD and Enlargement,* https://www.oecd.org/about/document/enlargement.htm (accessed 5 November 2019).

This serves as a basis for the Council to decide whether or not open accession process, or conclude the engagement through other available OECD global relations tools and means. Upon positive decision with regards to the accession discussion, the Secretary General provides an individual Accession Roadmap defining the terms, conditions and processes and an assessment framework for country reviews in respective OECD Committees in a range of policy areas. Based on the results of technical reviews, each Committee provides a 'formal opinion' to the Council assessing country's alignment to OECD instruments, best policies and practices in specific policy fields. The final decision is taken by the Council and upon a signature of an Accession Agreement, a candidate country is required to conclude domestic ratification procedures and deposit an instrument of accession to the OECD Convention with the depositary, which is the French government.

79. The length of the accession process varies between countries and depends on their level of engagement and cooperation in providing requested information to Committees and addressing recommendations for legislative and policy changes. For instance, Lithuania was invited to open the OECD formal accession discussion in April 2015 and became a member in July 2018. The same year, the OECD began the accession talks with Costa Rica but until now the country has not fully satisfied membership criteria.

80. It demonstrates the complexity of the OECD accession process that may be of a significant burden to potential IEA member countries. Especially, some of the OECD membership values related to open-economy or human rights might be found challenging for countries such as Russia or China.[145] The emerging economies are unlikely to open accession discussions in the short future. None of the Association countries, which are seen as close partners to the IEA, enjoys the status of a candidate country to the OECD. Their engagement with the OECD is carried under Key Partners framework (Brazil, China, India, Indonesia, South Africa);[146] Country Programmes (Morocco,[147] Thailand[148]); and through specific policy initiatives (Singapore).[149] Nonetheless, Key Partners are seen as strategic countries for a possible membership.[150]

81. The coupling of the OECD and IEA memberships is being challenged in the international community. Some of the IEA member countries, led by the US, argue that there is a need to redefine the membership requirement, especially in view of eventual accession of China and India. The US publicly expressed the support for

145. Lesage and de Graaf, *supra* n. 110.
146. OECD, *Our Global Reach*, https://www.oecd.org/about/members-and-partners/ (accessed 5 November 2019).
147. OECD, *OECD Strengthens Co-Operation with Morocco – Renews Morocco Country Programme Agreement*, https://www.oecd.org/newsroom/oecd-strengthens-co-operation-with-moroccorenews-morocco-country-programme-agreement.htm (accessed 5 November 2019).
148. OECD, *A Solid Partnership Between Thailand and the OECD*, http://www.oecd.org/southeast-asia/countries/thailand/ (accessed 5 November 2019).
149. OECD, *Singapore*, https://www.oecd.org/countries/singapore/ (accessed 5 November 2019).
150. OECD, *supra* n. 143 & 144.

China and India to join the IEA with succeeding administrations of George W. Bush and Barack Obama.[151] One of the initiators of the IEA – former Secretary of State in the US – Henry Kissinger also strongly advocated for allowing new market actors to fully benefit from the IEA membership.[152] This argument has been also put forward by the former IEA Executive Director, Nobuo Tanaka, who declared interest and need to accommodate enhanced participation of China and India in the IEA structures with an ultimate goal to offer a full membership. The second group of countries opposing to drop the prior accession to the OECD raises concerns about loosening up ties with the OECD, its homogeneity, interest and values.[153] Any attempts to relax the membership rules and foster institutional flexibility to accommodate the membership of new emerging energy players have not succeeded. Notably, there are precedents of other organizations within the OECD orbit such as the International Transport Forum and the Nuclear Energy Agency (NEA) that offer a broader membership than its parent body. This discussion also reflects on the G20 Principles on Energy Cooperation from 2014 that calls for inclusive and representative international energy governance, including emerging and developing economies.[154]

82. Another legal hurdle considers the IEA-specific membership criterion related to emergency oil stocks equivalent to ninety days of net imports. The collective stock level of ninety days has been normally satisfied and exceeded by the IEA member countries.[155] Countries that are net oil exporters are exempt from the stockholding requirement. Consequently, three IEA member countries operate outside the stockholding obligation, i.e. Canada, Denmark and Norway.[156] Building the emergency oil stock is a costly process. This obligation froze the accession process of Chile that in light of other economic challenges was not able to meet this criterion. Among potential IEA candidates, there are both countries that could easily satisfy the requirement (Russia, Brazil) and those who would be significantly hindered by this membership criterion (China, India).[157] Indeed latter countries started creating their oil reserves but have not reached the level required by the IEA. Potentially, this criterion could be adjourned and extended in time what could facilitate the way for emerging economies to enter the IEA and fulfil stockholding condition already as members.[158]

83. Potentially, the extended membership could be also forced by a legal split of the IEA and the OECD which demonstrates a further complexity. The foundation of

---

151. Andrew B. Kennedy, *China's Search for Oil Security: A Critique* in *The New Politics of Strategic Resources: Energy and Food Security Challenges in the 21st Century,* 34 (David Steven, Emily O'Brien and Bruce Jones eds, Brookings Institution Press, 2015).
152. Kissinger, *supra* n. 141.
153. European Parliamentary Research Service, *supra* n. 42 at 13.
154. G20, *G20 Principles on Energy Collaboration*, https://www.mofa.go.jp/files/000059860.pdf (accessed 5 November 2019).
155. Lesage and de Graaf, *supra* n. 110.
156. *Ibid.*
157. *Ibid.*
158. *Ibid.*

the IEA within the OECD served specific objectives related to the oil crisis of 1973. Thanks to the range of arrangements offered by the OECD (i.e., expertise, staff, administrative facilities, legal status), the IEA immediately became operational to fulfil its mission at the time. However, since the 1970s, the energy markets have been fundamentally reconstructed, and the current setting does not fully correspond to those changes. The link between the OECD and the IEA led to a number of clashes and disagreements, especially related to administration, financial audits and cooperation with China.[159] The separation could indeed unlock certain features but would require extensive discussions on the new IEA framework and structure outside the OECD, including with the French government as a host country. Alternative voices suggest the creation of a new energy-oriented organization with a broad membership framework.[160]

84. Ultimately, extending full IEA membership to non-OECD countries would require a major revision of the IEP Agreement to amend the legal foundations of the Agency if not its circumventing. As far as this could provide an opportunity to rethink the future path for the IEA to sustain its leading position in the global energy governance, there are also difficulties and uncertainty to carry out such extensive reform. Opening up a discussion on legal and institutional framework of the IEA could go beyond the membership criteria and lead to lengthy negotiations over other pressing issues, such as voting system, budget, emergency system and relation with the OECD.[161]

85. From a political perspective, it is to reflect on incentives for emerging economies to join the IEA. Besides reputational benefits, there is a limited membership offer. Several potential member countries have already the opportunity to freeride on the efforts of the IEA membership, including access to expertise, energy supply shock scheme,[162] data and statistics among others. Some features are also available under the Association framework. The IEA membership imposes a number of responsibilities that involve significant costs of financial and sovereignty nature.[163] The stockholding requirement involves costly collection of the required amount of emergency oil stock and maintaining of this reserve. The membership also involves some political and legal restrictions. Countries are obliged to follow directives of the IEA which may limit their policy choices and restrict internal sovereignty. For instance, decisions of the Governing Board are legally binding for all members. Another issue is related to decision-making powers in the Agency. The current voting system and weight of votes allocated to each country in the Governing Board is

159. Bate Felix & Barbara Lewis, *OECD and IEA Ponder Divorce After Years of Friction: Document*, https://www.reuters.com/article/us-iea-oecd-split/oecd-and-iea-ponder-divorce-after-years-of-friction-document-idUSKCN0Y20O1 (accessed 5 November 2019).

160. Jonathan Elkind, *Modernizing the International Energy Agency: A Task Worthy of US Leadership*, Colombia SIPA Center on Global Energy Policy https://energypolicy.columbia.edu/sites/default/files/Modernizing%20the%20International%20Energy%20Agency_CGEP_Elkind.pdf (accessed 5 November 2019).

161. de Graaf and Lesage, *supra* n. 34 at 313.

162. Colgan, *supra* n. 142 at 10.

163. *Ibid.* at 11.

partly based on the level of oil consumption in 1973 (*see* more in Governing Board section below). Despite changes in the IEA countries, the distribution of votes remains unaffected which disadvantages newcomers. It brings into consideration the position of new member countries, as it is not clear whether the system would be revised. The IEA opening for new countries would require reconsidering the framework of rights and responsibilities of its member countries to reflect on the current realities and position of new powers.

§2. Structure of the IEA

I. Organs

A. *Governing Board*

1. Functions and Competences of the Governing Board

86. The Governing Board[164] is the main decision-making and supreme institutional organ in the IEA 'from which all acts of the Agency derive'. It is composed of one or more ministers or their delegates from each member country (and Norway under its special status to the Agency). Upon invitation, meetings of the Governing Board are open for participation of observers. The EU has been one of the most prominent observers that enjoys special rights to receive documents and speak.[165] The Board holds three to four meetings per year at a senior level (Director General or equivalent) to discuss global developments in the energy sector and the current work of the Agency.

87. The Governing Board concentrates the core functions and makes final decisions on matters in regard to the IEA policies and operations, commitments of the member countries under the Agency's membership, accession processes and external relations.[166] It holds a number of responsibilities in administrative and financial issues, such as: adoption of the Agency's Programme of Work and the Budget, authorization of audits, acceptance of voluntary contributions, and consideration of other budget-related questions.[167] It has also the competence to establish new organs and procedures to support the implementation of the IEP and functioning of the Agency. The Board also appoints the Executive Director and other officers and members of the Standing Groups and Committees. Decisions of the Governing Board are binding for all member countries.

164. Mandate: Decision of the Council Establishing an International Energy Agency of the Organisation [C(74)203(Final)]; Arts 49 to 52 of the Agreement on an International Energy Program signed in Paris on 18 November 1974 [C(74)203(Final) Annex II]; Decision on an International Energy Program adopted by the Governing Board at its 1st Meeting on 18-19 November 1974 [IEA/GB(74)9(1st Revision); IEA/GB/DOC.74/5, Annex].
165. Gawdat Bahgat, *Energy Security: An Interdisciplinary Approach* (John Wiley & Sons, 2011).
166. Scott, *supra* n. 44 at 157.
167. Bahgat, *supra* n. 165.

88. The Governing Board facilitates dialogue on energy policies between member countries with the aim to enhance collaboration, develop joint activities and projects, guide the global energy governance and forge formal international commitments.[168] It serves as an 'ultimate authority' for the IEA programming as well as its organs and stakeholders engaged in the Agency's work.[169]

2. Voting System

89. The Governing Board operates on the basis of consensus – functions and decision are usually carried out and taken without severe objections or reservations. An established practice among member countries provides for abstention rather than vote against.[170] This supports a culture of collaboration and reduces polarization or isolation.[171] In recent years, the formal voting has been only used to make decisions in personnel matters, such as election of the Executive Director and the Chair of the Governing Board.

90. The complex voting system in the IEA combines two types of votes. One 'general voting weight' is equal for each member country and accounts to three votes. There is also 'oil consumption voting weight' allocated according to net oil imports of each country in 1973. The latter allocation of votes has not been revised since although the IEP Agreement foresees annual updates of the voting weights based on changes in countries' oil consumption (several attempts have failed).[172]

91. The IEP Agreement sets two types of majority – a general and a special one. The general majority is defined as 60% of the total combined voting weights and 50% of the general voting weights. The special majority is required in the most severe cases, such as blocking activation of the oil emergency scheme or closing an operational emergency programme.[173,174] Unanimity is prescribed only for certain particular decision related to revisions of the IEP Agreement, new functions for the Agency or changes in member countries' obligations and responsibilities (e.g., financial contributions, voting weights).[175]

92. The current distribution of votes in the IEA raises questions and provokes discussion on prospects for a reform. There have been significant changes in countries' energy consumption since 1973 that are not reflected in today's voting structure. It was a problematic issue in the negotiations around the accession of South

168. Scott, *supra* n. 44 at 157.
169. *Ibid.*
170. Robert O. Keohane, *The International Energy Agency. State Influence and Transgovernmental Politics,* 32 (4) International Organization 935 (1978).
171. Bahgat, *supra* n. 165.
172. Colgan, *supra* n. 142 at 8.
173. European Parliamentary Research Service, *supra* n. 42 at 9.
174. The special majority requires 60% of the combined voting weights and depending on the action outlined in Chapter 5 of the IEP Agreement: 63 or 75 general voting rights.
175. European Parliamentary Research Service, *supra* n. 42 at 9.

Korea in 2002 as the voting system did not consider its current economic weight and growth.[176] Eventually, a special clause has been included in the Accession Treaty allowing Korea to raise this issue in future IEA meetings. Currently, Korea is granted with three general voting weights and one oil consumption based. The IEA could update the reference year for the voting weights, but it faces a considerable opposition from some countries. It would reposition the distribution of the voting weights in favour of Japan, Korea, the Netherlands and Spain and bring less votes for the US, the United Kingdom and Canada.[177] The voting system of the IEA is also found obsolete because of the notion of building it entirely on oil imports while many countries have become significant oil exporters or leaders in other energy sources such as: gas or renewable energy solutions.[178] The voting structure is a question of a particular relevance to the expansion of the IEA membership and incentives for new countries to join the Agency.

B. Standing Groups and Committees

93. The work of the IEA Governing Board is supported by several Standing Groups and Committees dedicated to elaborate on specific energy-related areas at the expert level. Meetings are taking place several times a year bringing together governmental representatives. The Standing Committees have been explicitly defined (with the exception of the Standing Group on Global Energy Dialogue that was established in 2006) in the IEP Agreement what guarantees a 'treaty status' and provides a broad mandate, including decision-making and presenting recommendations.[179] In practice, those functions are mainly exercised by the Governing Board while the Standing Groups are responsible for preparing reports and proposals for the Board's consideration. Mandates of the Standing Groups cannot be reformulated or abolished without amending the IEP Agreement.

94. The Committees of the IEA have been established by the Governing Board applying its functions to create additional organs necessary for the implementation of the Programme. The Governing Board has power to decide on the scope of a mandate of each Committee and freely modify it as well as dissolve the Committee. Their functions are similar to those carried out by the Standing Groups, and include examining, studying and reporting on determined energy-related areas. The operational differences between the Standing Groups and Committees are without practical significance.[180]

176. de Graaf and Lesage, *supra* n. 34 at 306.
177. Colgan, *supra* n. 142 at 8; de Graaf and Lesage, *supra* n. 34 at 306.
178. European Parliamentary Research Service, *supra* n. 42 at 9.
179. Scott, *supra* n. 44 at 230.
180. *Ibid.* at 237.

1. Standing Group on Emergency Questions

95. The Standing Group on Emergency Questions[181] plays a crucial role in developing security policies and procedures, including the emergency response scheme. It is held responsible for the IEA Emergency Oil Sharing System as well as the IEA Dispute Settlement Centre for supply emergencies.[182] It reviews on a standby basis the effectiveness of measures applied by the member countries to satisfy the emergency stockholding commitment. It also reviews and assesses their demand restraint programmes and measures; an allocation of oil measures as well as examines computation elements such as 'base period'. The Committee has also assigned a role under the Special Section of the Information System that obliged member countries to make available all information necessary to ensure the efficient operation of emergency measures. It prepares reports identifying precise data required under the Special Section and elaborates on procedures for collecting such data on a regular basis as well as in time of emergency. Such report is consulted with oil companies to confirm the compatibility of the Information System with industry operations. It aims to establish standards for the harmonization of required information/data, ensure its comparability and provide procedures for its confidentiality. The Standing Group on Emergency Questions submits reports for review of the Governing Board that may formulate recommendations to the member countries. This Standing Group collaborates closely with the Standing Group on the Oil Market to exchange data and jointly produce plans to respond to oil supply disruptions.[183]

2. Standing Group on the Oil Market

96. The Standing Group on the Oil Market[184] is held responsible for the oil market information system of the IEA. It monitors international oil market, analyses developments and presents respective assessments to the IEA member countries. The data is collected through consultation with oil companies to ensure that the information system reflects on industry operations.[185] It includes information related to the average cost of crude oils to member countries by major crude streams by

181. Mandate: Art. 55 of the Agreement on an International Energy Program, signed in Paris on 18th November 1974, deposited with the Government of Belgium; Decision on an International Energy Program, adopted by the Governing Board at its 1st Meeting on 18th-19th November 1974 [IEA/GB(74)9(1st Revision); IEA/GB/DOC.74/5, Annex].
182. US Department of Energy, *Secretary's Annual Report to Congress* (1984).
183. James Sperling, *Handbook of Governance and Security* 369 (Edward Elgar Publishing, 2014).
184. Mandate: Art. 56 of the Agreement on an International Energy Program, signed in Paris on 18 November 1974; Decision on an International Energy Program adopted by the Governing Board at its 1st Meeting on 18-19 November 1974 [IEA/GB(74)9(1st Revision); IEA/GB/DOC.74/5, Annex].
185. Richard Scott, *Innovation in International Organization: The International Energy Agency,* 1(1) Hastings International and Comparative Law Review 1, 43 (1977).

month; the average prices of crude oil and oil products to member countries by month; and on a monthly basis, current and expected oil production, net oil imports and oil stocks.[186]

3. Standing Group on Long-Term Cooperation

97. The Standing Group on Long-Term Co-operation[187] has a broad mandate to examine and report on cooperative action in long-term cooperation in the energy field. It serves to meet one of the objectives of the IEA to reduce long-term dependence on imported oil among member countries. It elaborates and promotes collective energy security, efficient use of energy, production and use of alternative sources of energy and environmental protection in a delivery of energy services.[188] This Standing Group extended its mandate and established the Working Party on Energy Efficiency. It provides advice to the Standing Group and other IEA bodies on the means to achieve highly cost-effective energy efficiency policy development, implementation and evaluation in the IEA member and non-member countries; presents good examples of implementation and evaluation; reports on trends, policies and priorities.

4. Standing Group on Global Energy Dialogue

98. The Standing Group on Global Energy Dialogue[189] focuses on maintaining relations and strengthening cooperation with countries and regions outside of the IEA membership. It builds on regional and sectorial expertise and involves joint projects with other divisions of the IEA. Initially, this competence was assigned to the Standing Group on Relations with Producer and other Consumer Countries as outlined in the IEP Agreement. In the meantime, this function fell under an informal Ad Hoc Group on International Energy Relations and Committee of Non-Member Countries that got renamed for the Standing Group on Global Energy Dialogue in 2006.

---

186. US Department of Energy, *supra* n. 182.
187. Mandate: Art. 57 of the Agreement on an International Energy Program, signed in Paris on 18th November 1974, deposited with the Government of Belgium; Decision on an International Energy Program adopted by the Governing Board at its 1st Meeting on 18th-19th November 1974 [IEA/GB(74)9(1st Revision); IEA/GB/DOC.74/5, Annex].
188. US Department of Energy, *supra* n. 182; IEA, *Structure, The IEA is an autonomous intergovernmental organisation within the OECD framework, headed by its Executive Director*, https://www.iea.org/about/structure (accessed 10 December 2019).
189. Mandate: Conclusions of the 30th Meeting of the Governing Board on 27-28 June 1977 [IEA/GB(77)33]; Conclusions of the 124th Meeting of the Governing Board on 11 May 1992 [IEA/GB(92)25]; Conclusions of the 203rd Meeting of the Governing Board on 18-19 October 2006 [IEA/GB/C(2006)3/REV1].

5. Committee on Energy Research and Technology

99. The Committee on Energy Research and Technology[190] explores energy technology policy development to address challenges in the energy sector. It presents to the Governing Board a strategy for energy R&D and oversees its implementation. The work of the Committee also includes regular consultation and collaboration with the Standing Group on Long-Term Co-operation to ensure a close coordination between the strategy and relevant issues of the Programme for Long-Term Co-operation of the IEA. The strategy is also supported by periodic reviews of national programmes of energy R&D which further contributes to identify and promote opportunities for collaboration between member countries. The Committee contributes to key publications of the IEA, *Energy Technology Perspectives (ETP)*, as well as *Roadmaps on Energy Technology*.[191] The multidisciplinary character of its mandate involves engaging a wide range of stakeholders including specialists, academia and business/private sector.[192] The Committee is reporting to the Governing Board on an annual basis. Many initiatives are carried out under the IEA TCP and include a wide range of activities: research, design of pilot plots, demonstration projects and measures to facilitate implementation.[193]

100. To meet its objectives, the Committee on Energy Research and Technology has identified key issues and assigned them to three Working Parties – on Energy End-Use Technologies, on Fossil Fuels, and on Renewable Energy Technologies and one Co-ordinating Committee on Fusion Power. They are responsible for providing advice and recommendations to the Committee and other IEA bodies on energy technology trends, policies and strategies.

6. Committee on Budget and Expenditure

101. The Committee on Budget and Expenditure[194] advises the Governing Board on resource management and financial administration of the IEA. It includes providing an opinion on the annual and other budget proposals. It also discusses other issues such as: audits,[195] procedures for voluntary contributions and grants, budgetary relations with the OECD, transparency and information accuracy of the

---

190. Mandate: Conclusions of the 16th Meeting of the Governing Board on 20-21 November 1975 [IEA/GB(75)94].
191. European Parliamentary Research Service, *supra* n. 42 at 7.
192. OSCE, *IEA Role in International Cooperation on Clean Energy* https://www.osce.org/secretariat/104885?download=true (accessed 10 December 2019).
193. UNFCCC Technology Executive Committee, *Enhancing Financing for the Research, Development and Demonstration of Climate Technologies*, https://unfccc.int/ttclear/docs/TEC_RDD%20finance_FINAL.pdf (accessed 5 November 2019).
194. Mandate: Revision of the Mandate of the Committee on Budget and Expenditure, approved by the Governing Board at its 221st Meeting [IEA/GB(2010)20 and IEA/GB/C(2010)2]; Conclusions of the first meeting of the Governing Board on 18-19 November 1974 [IEA/GB(74)9(1st Revision)].
195. The IEA operates within the financial framework of the OECD where the OECD Council appoints a Supreme Audit Institution of a member country, which carries out an independent external auditing of the IEA.

IEA Budget, personnel of the Secretariat, documentation and use of languages, extension of membership among others.[196] Meetings of the Committee normally take place twice a year – mid-year to discuss pending budgetary issues, the closing of accounts for the previous year, and estimated spending under the current budget; and in November to prepare an opinion of the draft budget of the IEA.[197]

C. Secretariat and Executive Director

102. The Secretariat of the IEA assists the organs of the Agency by carrying out a number of internally oriented tasks under the guidance of the Executive Director. The Executive Director of the IEA Secretariat leads and sets directions of energy policy, IEA activities and other institutional developments and operations.[198] As such, there are no specific provisions defining functions of the Executive Director in the IEA founding documents – the OECD Council Decision and the IEP Agreement. The Executive Director is assigned with a broad and general mandate with some specific terms driven from the IEP Agreement and the position of the Secretariat is conferred by the Governing Board. It encompasses administrative, operational and political duties and powers. The Executive Director provides programme leadership by formulating detailed activities of the IEA, its organs and bodies, as well as budgetary provisions in accordance with policy objectives. It is outlined in the biennial Programme of Work and the Budget. He/she also maintains relations with governments and relevant ministers from IEA member and non-member countries, the Governing Board, Permanent Delegations to the OECD in Paris and other high-level officials. This diplomatic aspect of the Director's work involves building relations with other energy industry stakeholders. The Executive Director also represents the IEA associating a range of public relations functions including presentations of the IEA work outside, participation in interviews, conferences and other relevant events, international visits. His/her internal responsibilities consider personnel of the Secretariat, organization of IEA meeting and conferences, assistance to countries' delegations, coordination and inputs for the Standing Groups and Committees and other relevant units of the Secretariat.

103. The Executive Director is appointed by the Governing Board on the proposal or with the concurrence of the OECD Secretary General for the usual term of four years.[199] The decision is taken through a majority vote in an affirmative manner – of at least half of the member countries' voting reaching at least 60% of the 'combined voting weights'. Such procedure derives from the specific provisions related to the Secretariat, stating that the Governing Board acts by majority to take

196. Scott, *supra* n. 44 at 294.
197. *Ibid.*
198. *Ibid.* at 255-256.
199. The IEP Agreement nor the OECD Council Decision defines the duration of the appointment. In practice, it remains within the discretion of the Governing Board – it is an usual term of four years; IEA, *Leadership, The IEA Secretariat is headed by Executive Director Dr Fatih Birol*, https://www.iea.org/about/leadership (accessed 10 December 2019).

all necessary decisions for the establishment and functioning of the Secretariat.[200] Alternatively, the appointment procedure can be considered under 'management' responsibilities of the Governing Board as outlined in the IEP Agreement.[201] In practice, the appointment of the Executive Director can be also taken by consensus. The Governing Board has also decided on the creation of the function of the Deputy Executive Director.

D. Ministerial Meeting

104. On a biennial basis, ministers from member countries assemble for the IEA Ministerial Meeting. This high-level event aims to define strategic objectives for the Agency by highlighting specific topics and areas or setting desired directions for the Agency's development. The meeting collects a range of ideas for the existing or new work programmes to elaborate and discuss in detail on expert and technical levels in various Standing Groups and Committees. The results are submitted to the Governing Board for approval.

105. The most recent IEA Ministerial Meeting took place in December 2019 and highlighted the importance of energy security, energy transitions and expanding the global reach of the Agency.[202] It has set key global challenges related to climate change, resource efficiency, sustainable consumption, production and energy access. The ministers discussed the IEA modernization strategy focusing on opening doors for emerging economies, expending IEA's security mandate to natural gas and electricity and rearranging the Agency into a global hub for clean energy technologies and energy efficiency. The IEA Ministerial has also approved the mandate to enhance global outreach activities and strategic partnerships, especially with the Association countries to develop and shape global energy governance.

II. Affiliated Groups

106. The IEA work benefits from a wealth of partnerships with various stakeholders across all sectors. These affiliated groups actively contribute and provide valuable inputs into the programme and work of the Agency.

A. IEA Technology Collaboration Programme

107. The TCP operates under the framework of the IEA to support independent and international group of experts (from governments and business) to carry out

200. Scott, *supra* n. 44 at 262.
201. *Ibid.*
202. IEA, *Communiqué of the 2019 Meeting of the IEA Governing Board at Ministerial Level*, https://www.iea.org/news/communique-of-the-2019-meeting-of-the-iea-governing-board-at-ministerial-level (accessed 10 December 2019).

programmes and projects focusing on a wide range of energy technologies and other related topics. The activities under the TCP include energy research, analysis, development and popularization of energy technologies and capacity building. The collaborations bring together over six thousand experts from both public and private organizations located in over fifty countries (what goes beyond the IEA membership) to implement activities across various technology and sector fields: energy efficiency, end-use technologies (buildings, transport, industry and electricity), renewable energy and hydrogen, fossil fuels, fusion power, and cross-cutting issues.[203] The TCP serves meeting the IEA Shared Goals related to global engagement on energy security, environmental protection and economic growth and supports global transition to a cleaner energy future.

B. Energy Business Council

108. The EBC is a major overarching body through which the IEA engages with the world's largest energy companies involved in energy exploration, production and consumption (i.e., oil, natural gas and coal, automobile and appliance manufacturers, wind and solar producers and financial institutions) to examine the state of the global energy system.[204] It serves as a platform to promote dialogue among diverse stakeholders on a number of interconnected energy-related issues with an impact on the global energy landscape. Ultimately it contributes to the long-term policy network to foster investment in sustainable energy infrastructure. The membership to the EBC is dynamic and determined by the priority agenda of the Agency and on invitation only.

109. The EBC discusses current and urgent issues in global energy markets and reflects on short-term and long-term strategies. It provides feedback on the IEA's activities with a particular attention given to its strategic publications including *WEO* among others.[205] The IEA-EBC exchanges not only inform the IEA analysis to reflect on real-world solutions but also provide support to business and industry for informed decision-making. Meetings of the EBC focus on open and structured dialogue to ensure the views from the private sector are considered at the international level. They are held a few times a year in various formats such as: closed meetings with the IEA senior management; joint sessions with the Governing

203. IEA, *3rd Universal Meeting of IEA Technology Collaboration Programmes*, https://www.iea.org/events/3rd-universal-meeting-of-iea-technology-collaboration-programmes (accessed 10 December 2019).
204. IEA, *Energy Business Council, Dialogue among the IEA, the Business Community and Policymakers,* https://www.iea.org/areas-of-work/industry-engagement/energy-business-council (accessed 10 December 2019).
205. IEA, *IEA Celebrates the 10th Anniversary of the Energy Business Council with its Largest Gathering ever in Paris*, https://www.iea.org/news/iea-celebrates-the-10th-anniversary-of-the-energy-business-council-with-its-largest-gathering-ever-in-paris (accessed 10 December 2019); IEA, *IEA Holds Meeting with Energy Business Council,* https://www.iea.org/news/iea-holds-meeting-with-energy-business-council (accessed 10 December 2019).

Board; high-level sessions of the energy industry chief executives with ministers from IEA member, associate and partner countries (usually as part of the IEA Ministerial Meeting); and videoconference.

C. *International Low-Carbon Energy Technology Platform*

110. The International Low-Carbon Energy Technology Platform[206] established by the G8 and IEA Ministers in 2010 serves as a tool for multilateral engagement on low-carbon energy technologies. It brings together IEA member and non-member countries, business communities and other international organizations to facilitate action for the deployments and dissemination of low-carbon energy strategies and policies at various levels. The Technology Platform aims to promote and exchange best practices, build expertise and capacity and introduce technology transition. It envisages to systematically review progress on low-carbon technology to identify gaps and challenges in policies and international cooperation and formulate relevant support through various platforms and fora. The Platform offers a wide range of activities, such as: country-led workshops; development and implementation of roadmaps; strengthening international collaborative efforts; information and data collection and policy advice. For instance, the Platform presented the 'How2Guides' project that aims to guide the development of national energy technology roadmaps.[207]

D. *Renewable Industry Advisory Board*

111. The Renewable Industry Advisory Board (RIAB)[208] gathers selected group of leading private sector entities from OECD member countries and aims to foster relations between the industry and the IEA and its Working Party on Renewable Energy Technologies. The RIAB supports the IEA by providing market-relevant information, industry advice and data. The Advisory Board holds its meetings two or three times a year.

E. *Coal Industry Advisory Board*

112. The Coal Industry Advisory Board (CIAB),[209] created in 1979, brings together high-level executives from coal-related enterprises to provide advice and

206. IEA, *International Low-Carbon Energy Technology Platform, Frequently Asked Questions*, https://www.osti.gov/etdeweb/servlets/purl/21467289 (accessed 10 December 2019).
207. OSCE, *supra* n. 192.
208. IEA, *supra* n. 188.
209. Mandate: Conclusions of the 44th Meeting of the Governing Board held on 11 July 1979 [IEA/GB(79)49] as amended on 3 April 2003 [IEA/GB/C(2003)3] and 7-8 March 2007 [IEA/GB/C(2007)1].

suggestion to the IEA on matters related to coal production, transport, trade and utilization. It also reports on developments and trends in the industry to the Governing Board. The CIAB is composed of individuals from the IEA member and non-member countries approved by the Governing Board upon the recommendation of the Executive Director.

§3. IEA'S MISSION

I. Energy Security

113. Energy security exists when the access to energy supplies is guaranteed for everybody, uninterruptedly and at an affordable price. In order to ensure its realization, both long-term and short-term goals need to be taken into consideration. In the long-term, 'energy security' can be seen as the balance between domestic production and domestic demand. To allow energy supply to keep up with population growth and economic development, periodic investments are required. In the short-term, 'energy security' means that governments are capable of reacting promptly and in an appropriate manner to emergencies and natural/geopolitical energy disruptions[210]

114. Actually, 'energy security' is an evolving concept, which poses increasingly complex challenges.[211] At the time of IEA's foundation, the term referred primarily to the oil supply. After all, oil was the main source of energy available on the market and the sector had just gone through a deep crisis (the 1973 'oil shock'). Since then, the energy system has become much more heterogeneous, as shown in Figure 1. Focusing only on the oil sector is no longer sufficient for ensuring energy security, because an entire new set of vulnerabilities has to be taken into account. For these reasons, today the Agency's work on energy security embraces a wider range of sectors, including electricity and natural gas. A deep focus is also directed towards developing and improving emergency policies and responses, as well as increasing countries' resilience. In the following section, we will further explore each of these areas.

---

210. Evan Hillebrand, *What is Energy Security? Definition and Scenarios*, https://judithcurry.com/2016/03/03/what-is-energy-security-definitions-and-scenarios/ (accessed 30 November 2019).
211. International Energy Agency, *What is Energy Security?*, https://www.iea.org/topics/energysecurity/whatisenergysecurity/ (accessed 30 November 2019).

A. Oil Security

115. Despite the increasing diffusion of other sources of energy, oil still plays a leading role (especially for the transportation sector). As such, the IEA keeps monitoring and analysing the oil market as well as revising and updating its emergency strategies.[212]

116. Today as yesterday, the oil market is subject to several risks, ranging from natural disasters to technical failures and geopolitical tensions. In order to promote oil security and prevent the repetition of crisis such as the 1973 one, developing a certain degree of emergency self-sufficiency is key.

212. International Energy Agency, *Oil Security*, https://www.iea.org/topics/energysecurity/oilsecurity/ (accessed 30 November 2019).

Figure 1 Total Primary Energy Supply by the Fuel of IEA Member Countries

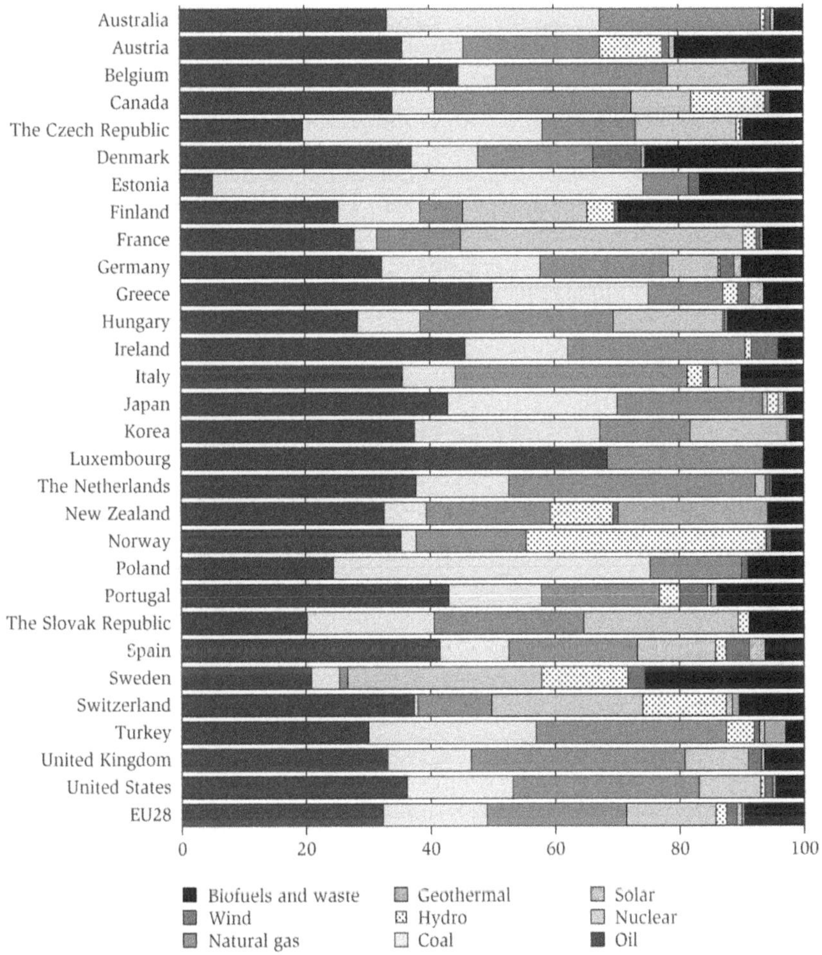

Source: iea.org.

117. In this regard, the IEP Agreement through which the IEA was established indicates that every Member State has the obligation to hold emergency oil reserves sufficient to sustain consumption for at least ninety days without net imports.[213] The stocks can be held both by the government (directly or through its specialized agencies) and by the industries, and the stockholding structure of each state is evaluated every five years by IEA's experts through a peer-to-peer review process. In case of

213. Agreement on an International Energy Program, *supra* n. 181 at Art. 2.

oil shortages, the IEA can activate its collective response system and release the emergency stocks to the market, in order to increase the supply. Moreover, Article 5 of the IEP Agreement urges the governments of each Member State to prepare a programme of oil demand restraint measures and be ready to implement it at all times.[214] The IEA periodically reviews and assesses the effectiveness of the programme and can ask governments to execute it in the framework of a collective response with the purpose of reducing the final consumption of oil and, consequently, the demand. Examples of demand restraint measures include the imposition of driving restrictions, the conduction of public information campaigns to promote voluntary actions, the rationing of fuels and the switch to natural gas.[215]

Figure 2 Emergency Response Measures: IEA Oil Security

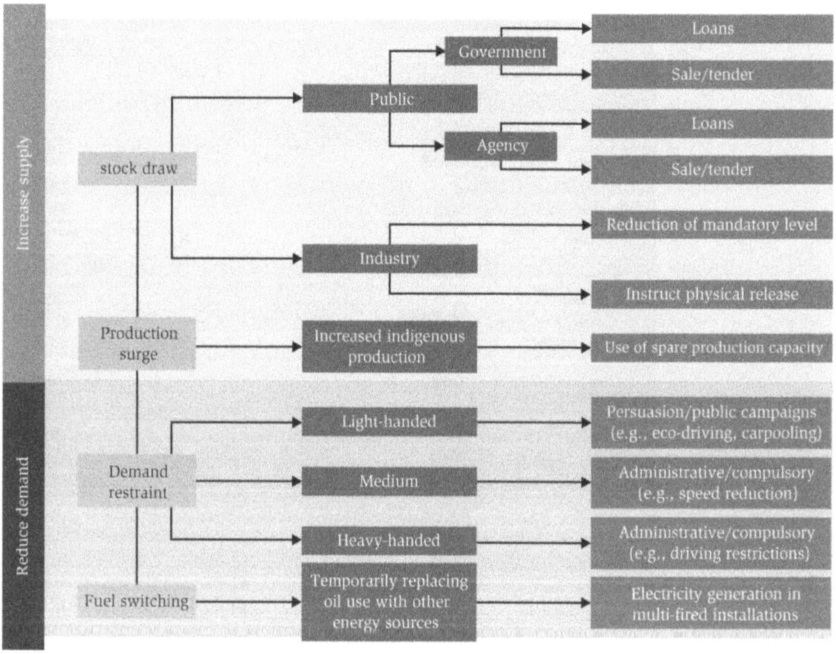

Source: iea.org.

214. *Ibid.* at, Art. 5.
215. International Energy Agency, *supra* n. 212.

B. The Initial Contingency Response Plan

118. In order to guarantee a rapid and effective response to supply disruptions, the IEA developed the ICRP.[216] Under the ICRP, whenever oil security is threatened, the IEA Secretariat must immediately assess the situation, analyse the market conditions and estimate the potential impact of the disruption. Where appropriate, the collective response is activated within 24/48 hours and member countries receive an initial assessment issued by the IEA Executive Director containing a response plan for releasing a specific volume of oil in the first thirty days of the crisis. If there are no objections to the plan, the Executive Director issues a Notice of Activation: within fifteen days, Member States must start implementing the planned emergency measures (*see* Figure 2). Every state's contribution to the action is proportionate to its share of total oil consumption among IEA member countries. The Agency carefully evaluates every progress and, when opportune, interrupts the action. At the same time, it proposes a schedule to replenish the emergency stocks.

119. To date, only three collective responses were activated: the first one during the Gulf War in 1991, the second one after major oil infrastructures were damaged by Hurricanes Katrina and Rita in the Gulf of Mexico (2005) and the third one during the Libyan Civil War in 2011.

1. Long-Term Actions

120. Being prepared to react to crisis is a good strategy to ensure oil security in the short-term. However, long-term security should not be neglected, and states shall focus their efforts on decreasing oil imports, diversifying the energy supply and developing alternative technologies.

C. Natural Gas Security

121. Natural gas markets started as regional markets.[217] Natural gas was either extracted in areas rich of reserves and then delivered to demand regions through dedicated pipelines or converted into LNG and sold into the market in compliance with specific destination clauses. Today the situation is changing, and markets are becoming increasingly interdependent. The main drivers of this transformation are the Chinese market, whose growth is accompanied by a rising demand for LNG, and

---

216. International Energy Agency, *How does the IEA Respond to Major Disruptions in Oil Supply?*, https://www.iea.org/newsroom/news/2011/march/how-does-the-iea-respond-to-major--disruptions-in-the-supply-of-oil-2011-03-10-.html (accessed 30 November 2019).
217. International Energy Agency, *Natural Gas Security*, https://www.iea.org/topics/energysecurity/naturalgassecurity/ (accessed 30 November 2019).

the US, whose production and exports are both expanding.[218] The globalization process brings new security-related challenges since also local natural and geopolitical events can have serious consequences worldwide.

122. For these reasons, even if the market is currently well supplied, the IEA knows that natural gas security cannot be taken for granted. Ensuring production flexibility and shipping fleet availability is considered key, as well as enhancing contractual flexibility. In this context, the Agency expects traditional long-term LNG contracts characterized by destination clauses to be rapidly replaced by less rigid and shorter contracts with flexible destination.[219]

D. *Electricity Security*

123. Highlighting the importance of electricity security in modern days and societies is almost useless. Factories, public offices, infrastructures, private houses and communication networks all depend on electricity and, as such, its supply has to be reliable, affordable and efficient. Recently, the transition to renewable electricity sources raised new challenges, as many of them (e.g., Photovoltaic (PV) and wind energies) are intermittent by nature. Following a request of the Energy Ministers at the G7 in 2015, IEA's experts extensively analysed all possible solutions to better integrate these renewables into the existing electricity grids and concurrently maximize the system flexibility to counterbalance the intermittency. Today the IEA actively assists policymakers and operators in the process, ensuring that the proper adaptations are implemented taking into account technical, economic and institutional factors and that progressively larger shares of low-carb energies are incorporated into the system. In addition, in view of the increasing interrelation among markets, another agency's priority is to guarantee electricity security across borders by interconnecting the national power systems.[220]

E. *Building Resilience*

124. Resilience is defined as the capability to readily react to shocks and neutralize or deeply mitigate their potential negative impacts. To improve their resilience and appropriately adapt to the ever-changing conditions of the market, countries have to strengthen their ability to identify existing and emerging risks. Besides, they have to answer with adequate policies.

---

218. International Energy Agency, *IEA Sees Global Gas Demand Rising to 2022 as US Drives Market Transformation*, https://www.iea.org/newsroom/news/2017/july/iea-sees-global-gas-demand-rising-to-2022-as-us-drives-market-transformation.html (accessed 30 November 2019).

219. International Energy Agency, *Market Flexibility is Improving Thanks to LNG and Markets Currently Well Supplied but Gas Security Remains a Concern,* https://www.iea.org/newsroom/news/2017/october/market-flexibility-is-improving-thanks-to-lng-and-markets-currently-well-supplied.html (accessed 30 November 2019).

220. International Energy Agency, *Electricity Security*, https://www.iea.org/topics/electricity/electricitysecurity/ (accessed 30 November 2019).

125. Possible threats to energy security include earthquakes, weather-related disasters, climate change, armed conflicts and geopolitical tensions. Climate change is leading to a rise in extreme weather events such as hurricanes, cold waves, heatwaves, floods and droughts. These events can disrupt the energy sector in various ways, by damaging power plants and infrastructures, causing sudden blackouts, compromising energy transport and/or decreasing water availability.[221] Recently, the interdependency of energy and water is gaining greater relevance. Water is indispensable for energy production as well as energy is essential for water treatments and distribution. As such, water security and energy security are interrelated, and water scarcity can seriously challenge the reliability of the energy supply.[222] For these reasons, the current priorities of the IEA are to enhance countries' resilience to climate change and reach a deeper understanding of the water-energy nexus, which is considered essential both to guarantee energy security and to achieve a sustainable management of resources.

126. A completely new threat for the energy sector emerged after its extensive digitalization.[223] The system is becoming more and more interconnected and, every day, a greater amount of data is exchanged and/or stored on servers. This process brings a wide range of new opportunities but also new risks, as proven by the increased frequency of cyberattacks affecting market's security and costumer's privacy. Since technologies are expected to play an evergrowing role in the future, strengthening digital resilience is becoming an integral part of the Agency's work.

F. Getting Ready for the Emergency

1. Periodic Evaluations

127. The IEA periodically reviews its Member States' energy security situation by evaluating how they tackle existing and emerging challenges, how they keep their emergency policies up-to-date and they proactively exchange best practices to coordinate and support each other's. The examination's goal is to make sure that each state is sufficiently prepared to deal with emergency and to assess in which extent they can contribute to potential collective actions promoted by the Agency in case of a major crisis. Upon request, the evaluation can be extended to Association and partner countries.[224]

---

221. Caroline Lee, *Commentary: The Energy Sector is Feeling the Heat* https://www.iea.org/newsroom/news/2018/august/commentary-the-energy-sector-is-feeling-the-heat.html (accessed 30 November 2019).
222. International Energy Agency, *Water-Energy Nexus*, https://www.iea.org/weo/water/ (accessed 30 November 2019).
223. International Energy Agency, *Digitalization and Energy 2017*, https://www.iea.org/digital/ (accessed 30 November 2019).
224. International Energy Agency, *Member and Key Partner Country Emergency Policies*, https://www.iea.org/topics/energysecurity/memberandkeypartneremergencypolicies/#d.en.164951 (accessed 30 November 2019).

2. Emergency Response Training

128. Since 2002, the IEA Secretariat organizes biannual EREs with the purpose of training delegates from member and partner countries to better coordinate an emergency response in case of severe oil disruptions.[225] During the training, the Agency's experts recreate hypothetical disruption scenarios to foster a deeper understanding of security-related risk factors and to help participants to familiarize with the emergency response system. Representatives from the IEA Industry Advisory Board and the European Commission as well as other industry stakeholders and the IEA Secretariat staff are also invited to join.

129. Typically, an ERE consists of two exercises: the Exercise in Capitals (EXCAP) and the Main Exercise (EXMAIN). EXCAP is designed to test communication efficiency and data collection capabilities during a crisis, and it is entirely conducted via e-mail. EXMAIN, on the other hand, is specifically designed to guide participants through the ICRP and stimulate discussions about the actions to be taken in the event of a major oil crisis.[226] As such, EXMAIN requires delegates' physical presence in Paris. Recently, the IEA extended its training sessions to non-Member States, holding joint EREs with countries like Thailand (2009), India (2012) and China (2015). It also participates in the Oil and Gas Security Exercise, which is organized annually by the Asia-Pacific Economic Cooperation (APEC), and other similar events.[227]

130. In the future, probably, new training exercises will be hosted to improve the emergency response in other fields, such as natural gas and electricity security.

II. Energy Poverty

131. Energy poverty is defined as the lack of access to modern energy services, like electricity and clean-cooking facilities.[228] As reported by UN, in 2016, 13% of the global population still lacked access to modern electricity and approximately 3 billion people had no clean-cooking solutions available.[229] Since energy is crucial for everyday life as well as for economic development, making sure that everybody can access it in a continuous and affordable way is an absolute priority. Not surprisingly, 'ensuring access to affordable, reliable, sustainable and modern energy for all' is one of the Sustainable Development Goals (SDGs) adopted by the UN General

225. International Energy Agency, *Emergency Response Training and Outreach*, https://www.iea.org/topics/energysecurity/emergencyresponse/ (accessed 30 November 2019).
226. International Energy Agency, *Broadest Ever Participation in IEA Emergency Response Exercise*, https://www.iea.org/newsroom/news/2018/february/broadest-ever-participation-in-iea-emergency-response-exercise.html (accessed 30 November 2019).
227. International Energy Agency, *supra* n. 225.
228. International Energy Agency, *Glossary*, https://www.iea.org/about/glossary/e/ (accessed 30 November 2019).
229. International Energy Agency, *Ensure Access to Affordable, Reliable, Sustainable and Modern Energy*, https://www.un.org/sustainabledevelopment/energy/ (accessed 30 November 2019).

Assembly in 2015, whose purpose is to build a better world for people and for the planet by 2030.[230] Specifically, we are talking about SDG No. 7.

132. The IEA considers universal energy access as an attainable goal, whose achievement will bring many benefits for minimal expenditure.[231] In this context, technological improvements and digitalization are playing a major role by making clean energy solutions cheaper and more efficient. Despite the growing number of options available to satisfy people's needs, however, progress still needs to be made (especially in clean-cooking field).

A. *Electricity Access*

133. Electricity access is realized when a household receives enough electricity to power a set of basic facilities, such as several lightbulbs, a flashlight, phone charging and a radio (as a minimum). Besides, the level of the services has to grow over time to reach the regional average.[232]

Figure 3 The Evolution of Electricity Access

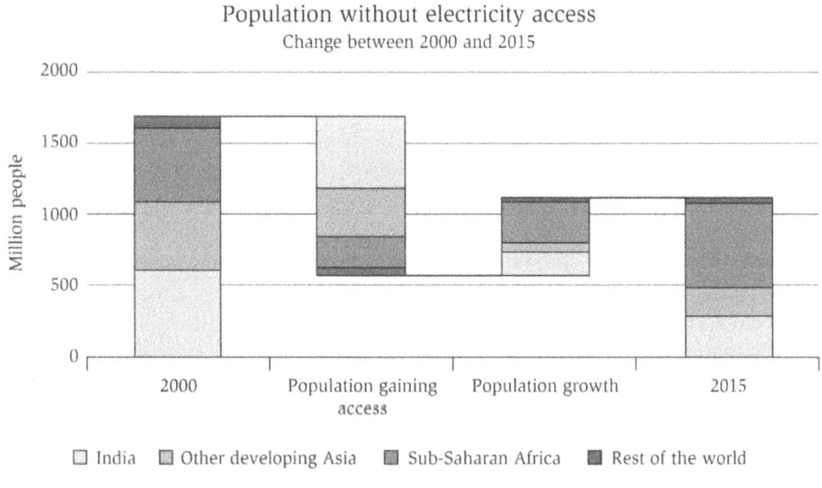

Source: iea.org.

230. International Energy Agency, *Sustainable Development Goals*, https://sustainabledevelopment.un.org/sdgs (accessed 30 November 2019).
231. International Energy Agency, *Energy Access*, https://www.iea.org/energyaccess/ (accessed 30 November 2019).
232. International Energy Agency, *Methodology – Defining Energy Access*, https://www.iea.org/energyaccess/methodology/ (accessed 30 November 2019).

134. The IEA assessed that the number of people without electricity is currently decreasing in all regions of the world, showing that the efforts made are giving good and evergrowing results.[233] In the fifteen years between 2000 and 2015, approximately 1.2 billion people worldwide gained access to electricity, with the biggest improvements recorded in developing Asia (870 million) and, particularly, in India (500 million). Recently, progress has been made also in sub-Saharan Africa, but not enough to keep the pace with the population growth.

135. Nearly the totality of the people gained access to electricity by connecting to the main grid and, in 70% of cases, the energy was generated from fossil fuels. Things, however, are changing. Renewables are becoming more convenient, and in the period 2012-2015, hydropower and geothermal have supplied more than one-third of all new connections. Moreover, innovative business models such as autonomous mini-grid and off-grid systems are gaining greater popularity, progressively shifting the way through which people get electricity access (*see* Figure 3). Thanks to constant efforts, in 2017 the number of people lacking access to electricity fell – for the first time ever – below one billion, which is an encouraging milestone.[234]

B. Clean-Cooking Access

136. When it comes to clean-cooking facilities, the situation is less optimistic. Clean-cooking access is realized when the main source of energy for cooking comes from modern clean fuels such as LNG, natural gas, electricity and biogas.[235] Unfortunately, 2.5 billion people in the world still rely on biomass, 120 million on kerosene and 170 million on coal.[236] These traditional fuels are not only less efficient but also harmful for people's health and for the planet. Their combustion releases much more emissions in the atmosphere and generates indoor pollution, causing the premature death of approximately 2.8 million people per year. Additionally, gathering firewood and cooking with inefficient stoves is highly time-consuming. It requires several hours per day and prevents women from acquiring new knowledge and skills that would allow them to improve their social and economic conditions.

137. Between 2000 and 2015, the number of people with clean cooking access in developing countries has grown by 60% and the use of coal and kerosene has dropped by more than 50%. However, in sub-Saharan Africa the situation remains very serious and the number of people lacking clean-cooking access increased by 40%. In addition, the number of people relying on biomass rose by four hundred million. For the moment, progress cannot keep pace with the population growth.

233. International Energy Agency, *Energy Access Outlook 2017*, https://www.iea.org/access2017/ (accessed 30 November 2019).
234. Laura Cozzi, Olivia Chen, Hannah Daly, Aaron Koh, *Commentary: Population Without Access to Electricity Falls Below 1 Billion*, https://www.iea.org/newsroom/news/2018/october/population-without-access-to-electricity-falls-below-1-billion.html (accessed 30 November 2019).
235. International Energy Agency, *supra* n. 232.
236. International Energy Agency, *supra* n. 233.

C. Towards 2030

138. In the NPS,[237] the IEA shows that ensuring electricity access for all by 2030 is feasible, at least in some regions.[238] The Agency expects the number of people without electricity access to drop from approximately 1 billion to 674 million and electrification rates to reach 99% both in developing Asia and South America. The projections show a positive trend also regarding sub-Saharan Africa, but the electrification rate in the region will not exceed 60%. Therefore, in 2030, 90% of the population without electricity access will be living in sub-Saharan countries (for an overview *see* Figure 4).

139. The IEA expects the majority of new access to be gained through connections to the main grid in case of urban areas and decentralized off-grid and mini-grid systems in rural contexts. Furthermore, 60% of new access will be powered by renewables.

140. Following NPS projections, the number of people without clean-cooking access will drop to 2.3 billion in 2030. The main progress is expected to be made by Southeast Asian countries and, particularly, by China, India and Indonesia, with urbanization, increased availability of clean fuels and vigorous policies against household air pollution playing a major role in the process. Improvements, however, will not be homogeneous. In fact, while in urban areas biomass use will decrease by over 40%, rural settings will witness only a minor reduction, with 60% of the population that will continue to rely on it.

237. The New Policies Scenario, as other scenarios that will be mentioned in the following sections, consists in a comprehensive set of medium and long-term projections developed by the IEA using the World Energy Model (WEM), a large-scale simulation model designed to replicate how energy markets function. Specifically, the NPS takes into consideration energy-related policies already adopted and/or announced by governments around the world. The purpose is to better understand the consequences of these measures and their long-term impact on the energy sector. For further information *see* International Energy Agency, *WEO Scenarios*, https://www.iea.org/weo/weomodel/ (accessed 30 November 2019).

238. International Energy Agency, *supra* n. 233.

Figure 4 Electricity Access in the NPS

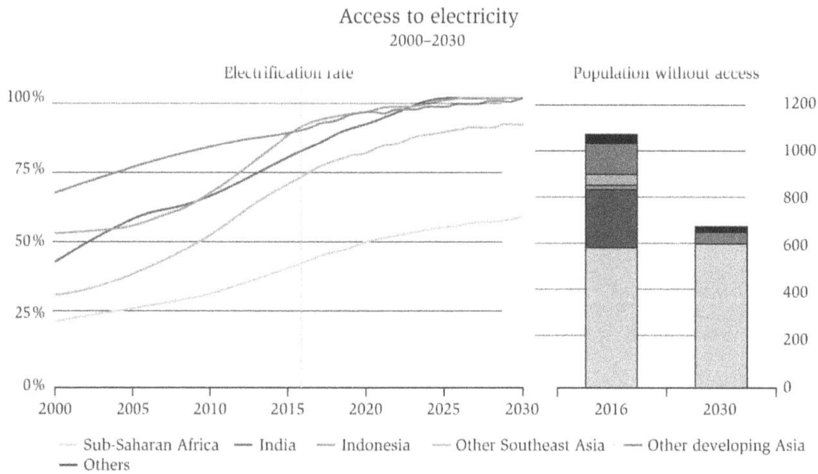

Source: iea.org.

141. In sub-Saharan Africa, once again, the rapid population growth will neutralize any positive result, and the number of people without clean-cooking facilities is expected to slightly increase (for an overview *see* Figure 5).

142. Hopefully, by 2030 the number of annual premature deaths due to cooking-related household pollution will drop by 1 million, and clean-cooking access will allow women to redirect their time towards more productive activities.

D. Universal Energy Access and Sustainability

143. One might expect that expanding energy access will increase the global demand for energy to an environmentally unsustainable level. On the contrary, according to the Agency's calculations, the impact will be extremely limited (0.2%). Moreover, the small rise in CO_2 emissions will be more than offset by the reduction in biomass use, which is associated with the release into the atmosphere of gases with an even higher global potential, such as methane and nitrous oxide. The final result will be a net reduction in GHG emissions, with around 165 Mt of CO_2 equivalent that is expected to be saved by 2030.

1. Investments in Energy Access

144. According to the IEA, in 2013, the investments aimed at reducing energy poverty amounted at approximately USD 13.1 billion.[239] Specifically, 97% of these capitals were used to create new electricity access by boosting power generation capacity and creating new connections in the distribution network, while only 3% was dedicated to improving clean-cooking access.

Figure 5 Clean-Cooking Access in the NPS

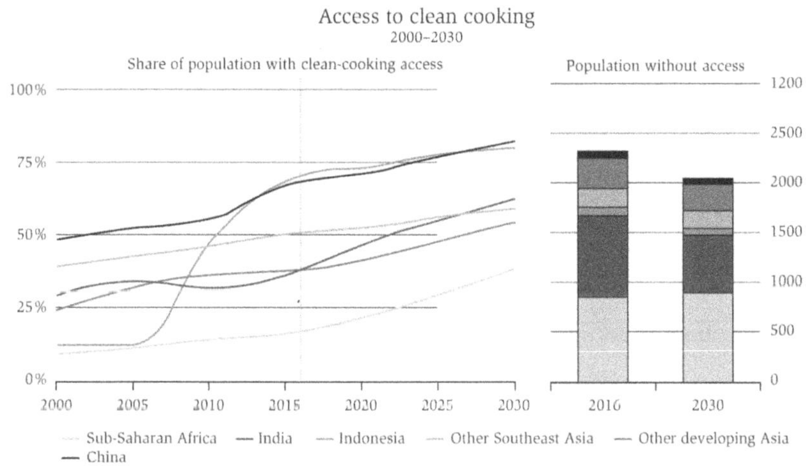

Source: iea.org.

145. The available data are limited, but the Agency's estimates show that 45% of funding for electricity access came from development aid, 37% from developing countries' national budget and 18% from the private sector (*see* Figure 6). Recently, many countries opened up their energy market to private investors, benefitting not only from their money but also from their knowledge and expertise. In the future, public-private partnerships are expected to play a growing role.

146. As for clean-cooking access, its larger contributor is the Global Alliance for Clean Cookstoves, a non-profit organization established in 2010 which collects grants and investments from governments, companies, foundations and individuals to facilitate the worldwide deployment of clean fuels and cookstoves.[240]

239. International Energy Agency, *Financing Energy Access*, https://www.iea.org/energyaccess/financingenergyaccess/ (accessed 30 November 2019).
240. Clean Cooking Alliance, How We Are Funded, https://www.cleancookingalliance.org/about/how-we-are-funded/ (accessed 30 November 2019).

Figure 6 World Energy Access by Type and Source

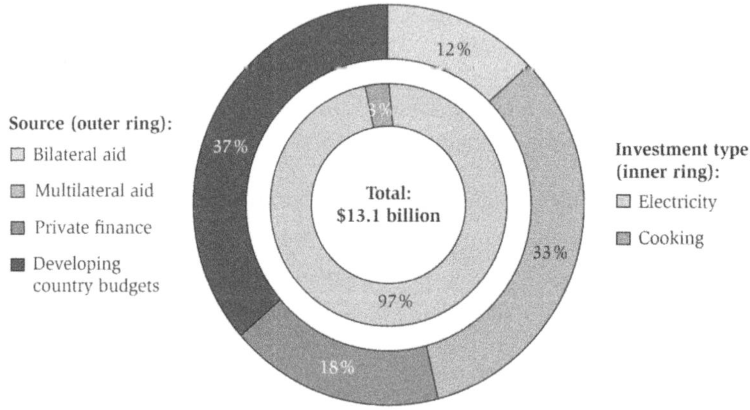

Source: iea.org.

III. Environmental Awareness

147. The energy sector is the number one driver of climate change, accounting for two-thirds of total GHG emissions and 80% of CO_2 emissions.[241] As such, to meet SDG13 of combating climate change and respecting the Paris Agreement on global warming mitigation, a drastic change in the energy system is indispensable. In this context, the Agency envisioned a 'Sustainable Development Scenario' (SDS),[242] outlining the deep transformations required in both energy production and consumption to reach climate goals while ensuring universal energy access. Following the SDS, to limit the temperature increase to well below 2°C, energy-related carbon emissions shall peak as soon as possible (hopefully in 2020) and then rapidly decline, halving by 2040 and reaching 'net-zero' by 2070. To make this scenario a reality, a reassessment of currently adopted and announced policies is

241. International Energy Agency, *Climate Change,* https://www.iea.org/topics/climatechange/ (accessed 30 November 2019).

242. The Sustainable Development Scenario was developed by the IEA in accordance with the energy-related UN SDGs, namely the SDG 3 aiming at reducing the negative health impact of air pollution, the SDG 7 on universal energy access and the SDG 13 on climate change mitigation. Its purposes are to determine what needs to be done to reach the above-mentioned goals in the most cost-effective way and to outline the deep transformations required in both energy production and consumption. For more information *see* International Energy Agency, *Sustainable Development Scenario,* https://www.iea.org/weo/weomodel/sds/ (accessed 30 November 2019).

urgently needed. In fact, the NPS shows that – if nothing changes – the rise of energy-related CO_2 emissions is not going to be stopped before 2040[243] (*see* Figure 7).

Figure 7 NPS Versus SDS

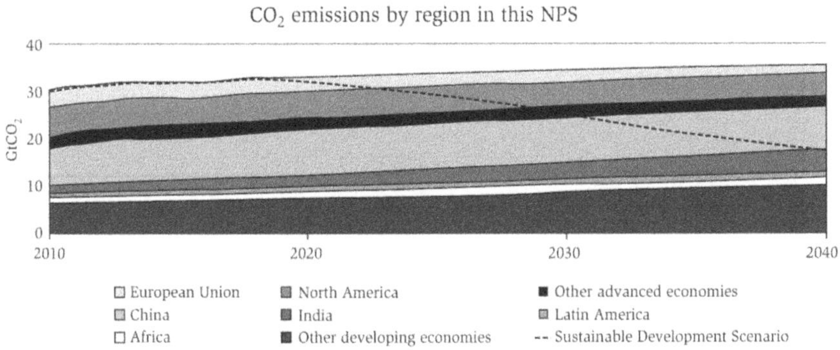

Source: iea.org.

148. By conducting rigorous analysis and drawing up future energy scenarios, the IEA acquires essential tools to better support governments during the clean energy transition. In this context, the Agency's work focuses on three key aspects: energy efficiency, innovation and decarbonization.

A. *Energy Efficiency*

149. Energy efficiency means that either more services are delivered for the same energy input or the same services are delivered for less energy input.[244] Since it can contribute to both economic growth and energy security while simultaneously supporting the goals of global warming mitigation and universal energy access, the Agency strongly welcomes every advancement in the field. Following the Executive Director Fatih Birol, in fact, '*the right efficiency policies could enable the world to achieve more than 40% of emissions cuts needed to reach its climate goals without new technology*'.[245]

150. Every year, the IEA releases an 'Energy Efficiency Market Report', in which all energy efficiency progress made worldwide are collected and analysed. Recent reports indicate that improvements are being made, but their impact on

243. International Energy Agency, *IEA @ COP24*, https://www.iea.org/cop24/ (accessed 30 November 2019).
244. International Energy Agency, *supra* n. 228.
245. International Energy Agency, *Energy Efficiency 2018*, https://www.iea.org/efficiency2018/ (accessed 30 November 2019).

energy consumption is largely outpaced by the overwhelming growth in energy-intense economic activities registered, in particular, in developing countries. As shown by Figure 8, between 2000 and 2017, energy use actually increased.

Figure 8 Impact of Different Factors on Energy Use Increase Between 2000 and 2017

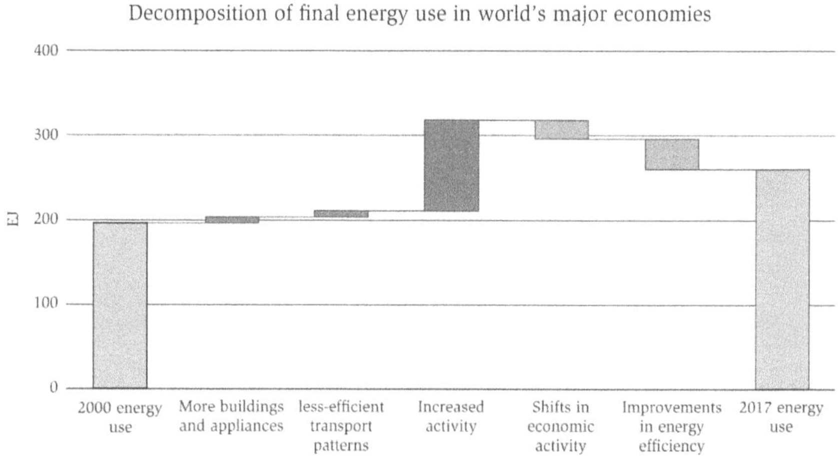

Source: iea.org.

151. To understand what would happen if all governments, by 2040, adopted the most cost-effective and technologically advanced measures to maximize energy efficiency, the Agency elaborated the *Efficient World Scenario (EWS).*[246] In the EWS, the population increases by 20% and the Gross Domestic Product (GDP) doubles. Despite this, the increase in global energy demand is marginal. As in the SDS, the GHG emissions peak before 2020 and then fall. Besides, almost one million people per year are saved from premature death, because cooking becomes more efficient and indoor air pollution decreases. Of course, realizing this scenario requires substantial investments, but the just-mentioned economic, environmental and social benefits are definitely worth the price.

152. Following the IEA, policies to implement include:

- the promotion of more efficient transport choices;
- the creation of bonuses for building energy retrofits and high-efficiency appliances purchase;
- the adoption of increasing standards of performance for industrial equipment.

246. The Efficient World Scenario depicts a world in which all the economically viable investments are realized and all the barriers to energy efficiency still present in the market are eliminated through adequate policies.

153. To facilitate policymakers' job, in 1999 the IEA created the *Energy Efficiency Policies and Measures*, a big database collecting all the measures adopted in the field by over two hundred states.[247] Consulting the database can provide good examples to follow and ensure a deep understanding of the topic. To further facilitate the exchange of knowledge, the IEA organizes periodic workshops and training sessions. Additionally, it promotes energy efficiency through the collaboration with international organizations and the participation in important global forums, such as G7 and G20.

B. Innovation

154. The clean energy transition cannot prescind from innovation.[248] Thanks to research, investments and collaborations, big steps forward are being made in a wide range of energy fields. As a consequence, costs are declining and efficiency is improving, making clean technologies more and more convenient.

155. IEA's data show that investments in innovation are slightly increasing, but much more can be done. Every year the Agency publishes a report called 'Tracking Clean Energy Progress', in which a full range of technologies and sectors considered essential for the clean energy transition are accurately assessed in order to understand if they are on track with the SDS or not. Recent reports show that, out of thirty-eight clean energy technologies, only four are improving at the right pace: solar PVs, Electric Vehicles (EV), lighting and data centres. With regard to the others, twenty-three need improvements and eleven are completely off track, partially due to the fact that the world still too heavily relies on fossil fuels.[249]

C. Decarbonization

156. As the previously mentioned IEA Executive Director Fatih Birol says, '*the world doesn't have an energy problem but an emissions problem, and this is where we should focus our efforts*'.[250] The decarbonization process shall involve multiple

---

247. International Energy Agency, *Energy Efficiency Policies and Measures Database*, https://www.iea.org/topics/energyefficiency/policies/ (accessed 30 November 2019).
248. International Energy Agency, *Innovation*, https://www.iea.org/topics/innovation/ (accessed 30 November 2019).
249. International Energy Agency, *Tracking Clean Energy Progress*, https://www.iea.org/tcep/ (accessed 30 November 2019).
250. International Energy Agency, *Only 4 Out of 38 Clean-Energy Technologies are on Track to Meet Long-Term Climate Goals*, https://www.iea.org/newsroom/news/2018/may/iea-releases-new-and-updated-online-resource-to-assess-global-clean-energy-transi.html (accessed 30 November 2019).

areas of interventions, starting from the already discussed development of clean energy technologies and the energetic requalification of high-emissions infrastructures.[251]

1. Emissions Trading Systems

157. To incentivize the transition, the Agency promotes the implementation of Emissions Trading Systems (ETS), which aim at reducing carbon emissions by leveraging market mechanisms. In ETS, central authorities (generally governments) allocate on the market a limited amount of 'carbon credits', which allow buyers (either countries or companies) to cover the extra emissions they generated. When a participant to the system releases in the environment more CO_2 than it can follow international agreements, it can buy 'permit unit' to avoid penalties. At the same time, participants who keep emissions under the target can sell the corresponding 'carbon credits' and gain money. The first ETS was launched in 2005 by the EU, and similar tools are currently present in other states such as Switzerland, New Zealand, Australia, California and South Korea.[252] Given their positive impact, the Agency keeps promoting ETS through annual workshops, held in collaboration with the International Emissions Trading Association (IETA) and the Electric Power Research Institute (EPRI).

2. Carbon Capture Utilization and Storage

158. In the near future, a growing role in the decarbonization process will be played by Carbon Capture Utilization and Storage (CCUS) technologies, which can mitigate the greenhouse effect by both cutting the volume of new emissions and removing CO_2 from the atmosphere.[253] Essentially, a CCUS technology can capture the CO_2 generated by industrial activities and fuel combustion and transport it to a safe place, via either ship or pipeline. The CO_2 can then be recycled and converted into valuable products, such as neutral fuels and biodegradable materials. Alternatively, it can be geologically stored (Figure 9).

159. An interesting type of CCUS technology is the Bio-Energy with Carbon Capture and Storage (BECCS), which removes CO_2 from the atmosphere by burning plant biomass. Specifically, BECCS exploits the capability of trees and crops to extract and incorporate CO_2 during their growth; once this biomass is burnt in

251. International Energy Agency, *Climate-Energy Policies for Low-Carbon Transitions*, https://www.iea.org/topics/climatechange/climate-energypoliciesforlow-carbontransitions/ (accessed 30 November 2019).
252. Anita Talberg & Kai Swoboda, *Emissions Trading Schemes Around the World*, Parliament of Australia Department of Parliamentary Services (2013).
253. International Energy Agency, *Carbon Capture, Utilization and Storage*, https://www.iea.org/topics/carbon-capture-and-storage/ (accessed 30 November 2019).

power factories and other industries or converted into chemical products (e.g., ethanol), the resulting CO_2 can be captured and injected into deep underground reservoirs, thus producing 'negative emissions' (*see* Figure 10).

160. BECCS was implemented for the first time on a large scale in 2011, in a corn-ethanol plant in Illinois, US. As the Intergovernmental Panel on Climate Change (IPCC)'s calculations show that 400 gigatons of negative emissions could be required by the end of the century to keep the temperature increase well below 1.5°C, the deployment of these technologies is considered indispensable. Nevertheless, unfortunately, investments in the field are still largely insufficient.

Figure 9 CO_2 Capture, Transport and Storage

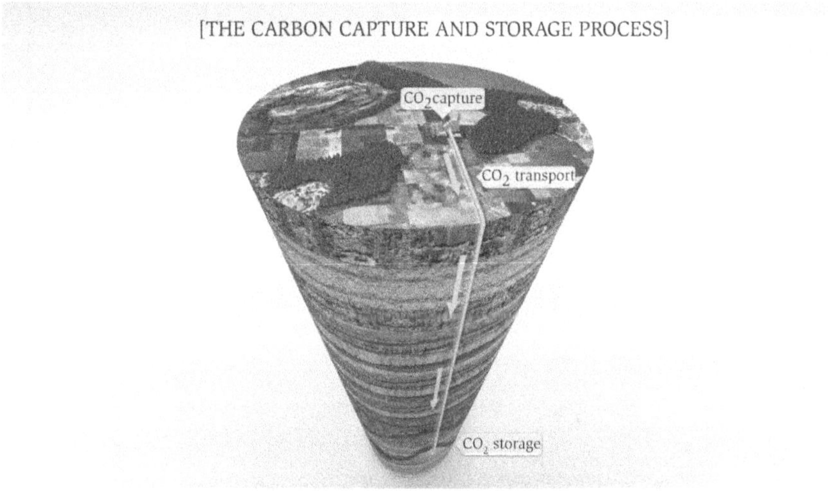

Source: Global CCS Institute.

Figure 10 BECCS Technologies for Negative Emissions

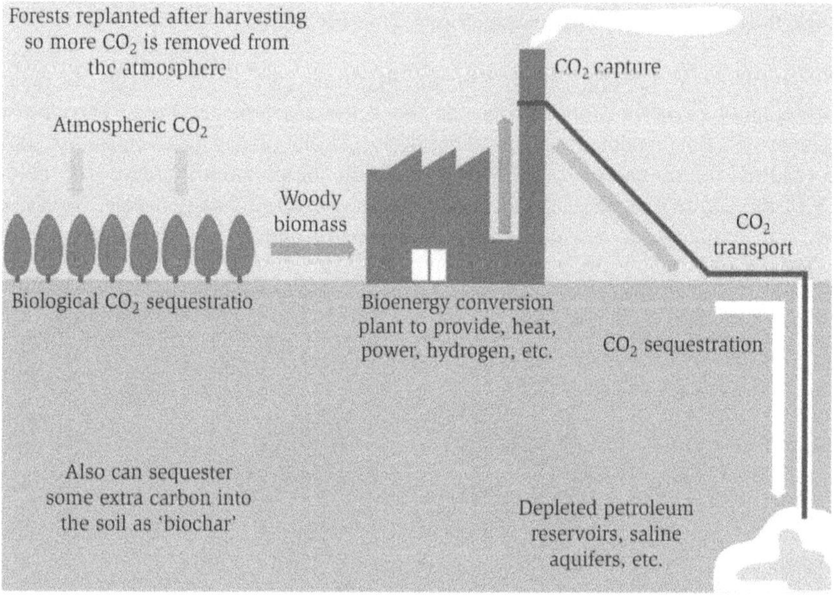

Source: R. Sims et al., *Transition to a Low Carbon Economy for New Zealand: Full Report*, Wellington, New Zealand: Royal Society of New Zealand, 83 (2016).

D. The Importance of Real-World Policies

161. To be effective, the changes required during the clean energy transition must be well integrated and adequate to the local context. As different realities can require different approaches, political, social, environmental and economic factors need to be accurately evaluated. The Agency's role is to assist governments during the selection of the most adapt real-world policies, analysing the potential impact of different clean energy and climate measures on that particular context and verifying their compatibility to make sure they do not interfere with each other's.

IV. Global Engagement

162. Since its inceptions, the IEA engages with regional and international organizations with the purpose of sharing knowledge and identifying ever-better solutions for a wide range of energy-related issues, from energy security to environmental protection.[254] Besides, it also participates at important global forums, providing analyses and recommendations on a variety of topics.

A. *International Cooperation*

1. Technology Collaboration Programmes (TCPs)

163. Since 1975, the IEA promotes international cooperation in energy technology R&D through its TCPs, strategic partnerships established by two or more member countries under the auspices of IEA IAs.[255] IAs are legal contracts designed to simplify collaborations. In fact, as outlined by *The IEA Framework for International Energy Technology Cooperation* adopted in 2003 by the IEA Governing Board, they share a common set of basic provisions, including rules on participation, admission, withdrawal, duration, copyright and general functioning. IAs can see the participation, as contracting parties, of governments, European Communities, international organizations in which governments participate and national public or private entities specifically designated by either governments or the European Communities. In addition, not designated national entities and International Non-Governmental Organizations (INGO) can take part as sponsors. Under the TCPs, independent groups of experts can plan specific research studies, carry out international experiments, share information on national policies and scientific/ technological developments and exchange scientists, technicians and other experts. The IEA Secretariat provide them with guidance, advice and support and the knowledge acquired is shared through hundreds of events.

164. To date, TCPs have involved over six thousand participants, representing about three hundred governments, academic institutions and industries from nearly sixty countries in the world.[256] Experts have worked on around two thousand energy-related topics, giving decisive boost to technological innovation and accelerating the global transition to a cleaner energy system.

2. The Joint Organizations Data Initiative

165. In 2001, the IEA launched the 'Joint Organizations Data Initiative' (JODI) in collaboration with other five international organizations, namely the Statistical Office of the European Communities (EUROSTAT), the Gas Exporting Countries Forum (GECF), the Latin American Energy Organization (OLADE), the United Nations Statistics Division (UNSD), the Organization of the Petroleum Exporting Countries (OPEC) and the IEF. The main purpose of JODI was to raise awareness

254. International Energy Agency, *Our Mission*, https://www.iea.org/about/ourmission/ (accessed 30 November 2019).
255. International Energy Agency, *Technology Collaboration Programme*, https://www.iea.org/tcp/ (accessed 30 November 2019).
256. *Ibid.*

among oil stakeholders about the need of more transparency in the oil market data since precisely the lack of transparency was considered the leading cause of oil price volatility, a phenomenon many policymakers of the time were concerned about.[257] As a first step, the Agency and its partners started collecting Monthly Oil Statistics (MOS) from each of their member countries to assess the oil data situation. The Initiative was a big success and, within one year, seventy countries representing 90% of the global oil market were actively collaborating by sharing their data. As a consequence, in 2008, the IEF Energy Ministers decided to extend the initiative to the natural gas sector. Both JODI's databases are freely consultable by the public at jodidata.org.

3. IEA-IEF-OPEC Symposium on Energy Outlooks

166. Since 2011, the IEA organizes, in collaboration with OPEC and IEF, an annual *Symposium on Energy Outlooks*. OPEC is an intergovernmental organization created in 1960 to coordinate and unify the petroleum policies of the petroleum exporting countries in order to stabilize the market.[258] IEF was established in 1991 with the goal of facilitating the dialogue between energy consumers and producers about globally relevant issues; it sees the participation of both IEA's and OPEC's members countries, but also of other transit states and key energy players such as Argentina, China, India, Russia and South Africa.[259] During the Symposium, analysts and delegates from banks and oil companies discuss the IEA *WEO* and the OPEC *World Oil Outlook*, with the purposes of reaching a greater convergence of data and developing adequate strategies to improve energy security and, simultaneously, environmental and economic sustainability.

4. IEA & IRENA

167. Another international organization with which the IEA closely collaborates is the International Renewable Energy Agency (IRENA), founded in 2009 with the mission of supporting the adoption and sustainable use of all forms of renewable energies throughout the world.[260] In 2012, the two agencies signed a partnership agreement, strengthening their cooperation and launching new initiatives, such as the joint Global Renewable Energy Policies and Measures Database (PAMS).[261]

257. Joint Organisations Data Initiative, *History*, https://www.jodidata.org/about-jodi/history.aspx (accessed 30 November 2019).
258. Organization of the Petroleum Exporting Countries, *Brief History*, https://www.opec.org/opec_web/en/about_us/24.htm (accessed 30 November 2019).
259. International Energy Forum, *Twenty Years of Producer-Costumer Dialogue*, https://www.ief.org/about-ief/history.aspx (accessed 30 November 2019).
260. International Renewable Energy Agency, *About IRENA*, https://www.irena.org/aboutirena (accessed 30 November 2019).
261. International Energy Agency, *New IEA-IRENA Partnership Will Heighten Co-Operation and Policy Collaboration*, https://www.iea.org/newsroom/news/2012/january/new-iea-irena-partnership-will-heighten-co-operation-and-policy-collaboration.html (accessed 30 November 2019).

Moreover, since 2013, the IEA actively supports IRENA's *Renewable Energy Roadmap* (REmap 2030), which aims at doubling the share of renewables in final energy consumption by 2030 (compared with 2010).[262]

B. Cooperation with Regional Organizations

1. IEA & the Asian Development Bank (ABD)

168. The collaboration between the IEA and the ADB, whose mission is to promote economic and social growth in the Asian countries, started in 2012 with the organization of four joint workshops on low-carb energy. During the workshops, which were held at the ADB headquarters in Manila, more than fifty participants from fifteen countries discussed renewable energy-related issues, with a particular focus on wind energy, smart grids,[263] CCUS technologies and other innovations in the power generation field.[264] In addition, on that occasion, the two organizations launched the *How2Guides Related Initiatives* in Asia, with the purposes of collecting best policies on technological development and guiding governments through the innovation of their national energy systems. In 2017, by signing a memorandum of understanding, the IEA and the ABD expanded their cooperation to other fields, starting to collaborate on topics like energy statistics, energy efficiency, data modelling, renewables deployment and energy security analysis.[265]

2. IEA & the Association of Southeast Asian Nations

169. The Association of Southeast Asian Nations (ASEAN) is an organization founded in 1967 by several Southeast Asian countries in order to promote active cooperation and mutual assistance among its members, support economic, social and cultural development and stabilize the region.[266] The partnership between the Agency and ASEAN officially began in 2011, with the signature of a memorandum of understanding through which they decided to work closely on a wide range of topics, such as energy efficiency, climate change, clean energies, energy security,

262. International Renewable Energy Agency, *REmap 2030: A Renewable Energy Roadmap* (IRENA 2014).
263. Smart grids are innovative systems capable of monitoring and managing electricity flow and usage in order to better balance demand and supply.
264. International Energy Agency, *Asian Development Bank and IEA Hold Joint Workshops on Low-Carbon Energy*, https://www.iea.org/newsroom/news/2012/october/asian-development-bank-and-iea-hold-joint-workshops-on-low-carbon-energy.html (accessed 30 November 2019).
265. International Energy Agency, *IEA and Asian Development Bank Commit to Step Up Co-Operation*, https://www.iea.org/newsroom/news/2017/march/iea-and-asian-development-bank-commit-to-step-up-co-operation.html (accessed 30 November 2019).
266. Association of Southeast Asian Nations, *Overview*, https://asean.org/asean/about-asean/overview/ (accessed 30 November 2019).

power sector development and market integration.[267] Moreover, the IEA became an official Dialogue Partner of ASEAN and, as such, it annually takes part in the annual meeting of its Energy Ministers. Considering the evergrowing role Southeast Asian countries are destined to play in the energy market, the alliance is considered highly strategic.

3. IEA & the Asia Pacific Economic Cooperation (APEC)

170. APEC is an economic forum created in 1989 with the purpose of promoting economic growth and cooperation in the Pacific area. The IEA actively participates in its summits, organizes training with its member economies and supports its efforts to promote sustainable growth by sharing knowledge on topics like energy efficiency and innovation. With the sign of a letter of intent in 2015, the cooperation was further extended to other areas, such as energy security, energy market analysis and resilience.

4. IEA & the African Union

171. In 2018, the IEA established a strategic partnership with the African Union (AU), which was established in 2002 with the goals of promoting the socio-economic development of the continent and addressing globalization-derived challenges. The purpose of the partnership is to accelerate the eradication of energy poverty, by ensuring electricity and clean-cooking access to all in an economically and environmentally viable way.

C. Participation at Global Forums

1. IEA & United Nations Framework Convention on Climate Change

172. The United Nations Framework Convention on Climate Change (UNFCCC) is an international environmental treaty adopted in 1992 during the Rio de Janeiro *United Nations Conference on Environment and Development (UNCED)*, informally known as 'Earth Summit'.[268] The IEA strongly supports the UNFCCC, attending its annual Conferences of Parties (COPs) and providing analysis, expertise and policy advice. During COPs, the Agency organizes numerous side

267. International Energy Agency, IEA, *Association of Southeast Asian Nations (ASEAN) Agree to Strengthen Co-Operation*, https://www.iea.org/newsroom/news/2011/september/iea-association-of-southeast-asian-nations-asean-agree-to-strengthen.html (accessed 30 November 2019).
268. International Energy Agency, *IEA and the UNFCCC*, https://www.iea.org/topics/climatechange/ieaandtheunfccc/ (accessed 30 November 2019).

events to share its research and inform countries about the strategies and tools available to tackle climate change and better facilitate the clean energy transition. Moreover, it assists the UNFCCC during negotiations and directly collaborates with its Secretariat (e.g., by reviewing developed countries' annual GHG inventories).

173. Two times per year, the IEA hosts, together with the OECD, the Climate Change Expert Group (CCXG) Global Forum, which provides an occasion for governments, private sector and civil society representatives to continue the dialogue started during the COP about climate-related issues and policies.

2. The Clean Energy Ministerial

174. The CEM is a global forum created in 2010 with the purpose of accelerating the clean energy transition.[269] It sees the participation of energy ministers and other high-level delegates from the member countries, which represent together about 75% of total GHG emissions and 90% of clean energy investments. In 2017, the CEM Secretariat was moved from the US Department of Energy in San Francisco to the IEA headquarters in Paris, providing the Agency with the opportunity to enhance its collaboration with non-member countries such as Brazil, China, India, Indonesia, Mexico, Russia, Saudi Arabia, South Africa and United Arab Emirates.[270] Additionally, the IEA actively supports many CEM Initiatives, including the Electric Vehicles Initiative (EVI) and the Multilateral Solar and Wind Working Group.

3. G7 and G20

175. The IEA consistently contributes to the G7 and the G20, international forums during which major economies discuss questions of global relevance in many fields, including energy.[271] More specifically, the Agency takes part in the meetings, shares data and knowledge on topics like energy security, renewables, innovation, energy efficiency and cybersecurity and provides viable solutions and policy advice.

---

269. Clean Energy Ministerial, *About the Clean Energy Ministerial*, http://www.cleanenergyministerial.org/about-clean-energy-ministerial (accessed 30 November 2019).
270. International Energy Agency, *Clean Energy Ministerial Secretariat Finds New Home at the IEA*, https://www.iea.org/newsroom/news/2016/june/clean-energy-ministerial-secretariat-finds-new-home-at-the-iea.html (accessed 30 November 2019).
271. International Energy Agency, *Global Engagement*, https://www.iea.org/countries/cooperation/ (accessed 30 November 2019).

Chapter 4. Activities of the International Energy Agency

176. As discussed in the previous chapters, the IEA is a multifunctional autonomous intergovernmental organization constantly contributing to the fostering of global energy development. It can be referred to as the global energy authority providing data, analysis and solutions on all fuels and all technologies.[272] Its activities involve multiple areas, but currently all evolving around a basic goal – securing reliable and affordable clean energy worldwide. The importance of energy transition does not have to be particularly emphasized in light of the current climate change adaptation and mitigation efforts, and the SDGs set by the UN.

177. This main point of orientation did not always correspond with the current SDGs and providing energy, which is clean and affordable. There has been a significant shift from the original purpose of creating the IEA as a reaction to the oil crises of the previous century. Stocking oil, as the main energy source by Member States of the IEA and implementing a crisis mechanism in case of a shortage due to global turbulence on the energy market slowly got into the background.[273]

178. Currently, the main activities of IEA can be classified based on different criteria – on the basis of the particular activity type, the fuel type related to an activity, while some of these criteria still stem in energy, but also climate change-related SDGs. This does not mean that the original goal focusing on fossil fuels has been completely abolished, and that the transition towards fostering clean energy transition has been ultimate. Within this chapter, we will try to analyse each of these categories establishing overlaps between different activities, but at the same time trying to cover all the efforts of the IEA, proceeding from the basic levels towards more complex functions. From a structural point of view, the chapter will be divided according to activity aims, within which all related activities will be organized around different energy sources, while dealing with the methodology and realization of the activity types throughout the final sections.

179. The core activity types of the IEA include: policymaking (advising), monitoring, data analysis (statistics), advising on investments, R&D and building partnerships between governments and organizations. Policy monitoring, statistical data collection and analysis, reporting and preparing future projections in the field of energy being the most robust areas, therefore the chapter will try to devote distinguished attention to these fields of activities. The energy sources do not require a deeper explanation – the activities of the IEA always have a particular energy source (renewable/ non-renewable) at their basis, through which the results commit to solving a global sustainability issue of tremendous proportions.

180. Finally, when it comes to these SDGs, it is rather hard to isolate a handful of these goals claiming that the IEA's work products do not contribute to some of

272. International energy Agency, *Official Website* https://www.iea.org (accessed 9 August 2019).
273. For further information, *see* Chapter 2 of the monograph on the Genesis and Historical Development of IEA.

them at all. Energy-related activities have an impact on all of these goals since they are all interconnected in a very narrow way. On the other hand, we can underline three of them, which have specific attention of the IEA: SDG No. 7 (*Affordable and Clean Energy*), 9 (*Industry Innovation and Infrastructure*) and 13 (*Climate Action*)[274] as the top of the priority list, where the most significant contributions are made. According to these main goals, we can categorize the activities of IEA being oriented on:

- Energy Security
- Energy Access
- Energy Transition
- Mitigating and Adapting to Climate Change
- Technological Development

274. *See:* United Nations, *Sustainable Development Goals* https://sustainabledevelopment.un.org (accessed 9 August 2019).

Table 2: Illustrative Heatmap of Overlaps Between Activity Types, Their Aim and Energy Sources

within AIM | within TYPE | within both

ACTIVITY AIMS - > / *Energy Sources*	*Energy Security*	*Energy Access*	*Energy Transition*	*Mitigation/ Adaptation*	*Tech. Develop.*
Coal	Coal Industry Advisory Board (CIAB)			CIAB Plenary Meetings	Technology Collaboration Programme (TCP)
Electricity	Electricity Security	Electricity Market Design/ Future Scenarios	Nuclear Power (electricity generation)		Electricity Technology Collaboration Programme
Natural Gas	Global Gas Security	Gas Market Report/Key Trends	Natural Gas Statistics	IEA Unconventional Gas forum	TCP on Gas & Oil Technologies
Nuclear		Costs of electricity generation/ Future Scenarios	Nuclear Statistics	Nuclear Energy Agency	Technology Roadmap/ Nuclear Fusion Technology
Oil	Oil Security (oil stock reserves)	Oil Market Report/ Future Scenarios	Monthly Oil Data Service (MODS)		
Renewables	Policies and Measures Database (PAMS)*	Renewable Report/ Future Scenarios	System Integration of Renewables/ Renewables Statistics	IEA Partners	
CCUS					Enhanced Oil Recovery
ACTIVITY TYPES - >	Policymaking	Projections & Monitoring	Statistics & Statistical Analysis	Investment-Related Activities	RD & D

Own source based on www.iea.org.

* Please note that the website of the IEA had undergone some substantial changes at the end of 2019, and from 2020 the Policy and Measures Database (PAMS) can be found referred to as Policies Database reachable at the following link: https://www.iea.org/policies. Notwithstanding it contains the same online service collating the widest range of global/regional/national/municipal/urban energy-related policies and measures taken.

§1. ACTIVITY TYPES AND AIMS (WHAT? & WHY?)

I. Activity Types: WHAT Does the IEA Do?

181. Similarly, to the activity aims, or objectives, the particular activity types of the IEA can be also categorized around five main groups:

(1) Policymaking.
(2) Projections & Monitoring.
(3) Statistics & Statistical Analysis.
(4) Investment-Related Activities.
(5) Research & Development.

A. *Policy-Related Activities*

182. Policymaking being part of governance in general has already outgrown the borders of countries and national governments. Energy is being one of the goods regarding which intergovernmental organizations, exactly like the IEA, have taken initiative. This is due to the fact that energy generation and utilization are goods general enough to have an international character, while the natural resources, from which energy is produced, as well as the process itself is connected to potential negative effects – such as environmental impact and other externalities, which can be handled more efficiently on a larger global scale involving a wider range of public and private stakeholders.[275]

183. The reference to policymaking at the beginning of this section might be slightly misleading, since the IEA's activities regarding policy include multiple layers related mainly to energy, but spread out among various industrial sectors:

1. Policymaking
2. Policy advising.
3. Policy database.

184. The OECD member countries have multiple common policy goals fostering sustainability, climate change mitigation and adaptation, while multiple policy tools have been worked out in order to shift to a more sustainable and clean energy system. These are made throughout policy cycles (*see* Table 2), each of them being applied and evaluated during the implementation. The consensus between the members makes it easier and more efficient to work on achieving these goals. It allows identifying policy weaknesses and beginning the remediation process in the form of

---

275. Ann Florini & Benjamin K. Sovacool, *Who Governs Energy? The Challenges Facing Global Energy Governance*, 37 Energy Policy 5239, 5240 (2009).

a post evaluation from cycle to cycle.[276] Naturally, there have been several inconsistencies in the past due to poorly developed international policies, or incorrect approaches exacerbating their negative effects compared to the scenario without any policy at all.[277]

185. The role of the IEA in the process of creating suitable energy-related policies is to provide the necessary expertise and collect data mainly from the members themselves. In this sense policymaking, advising and maintaining a policy database are interconnected into an organic whole.

186. The available policy tools vary from regulatory and economic instruments, through fiscal/ financial incentives, codes and standards, information and education, strategic planning, grants & subsidies, energy performance standards all the way to R&D deployment, and even voluntary approaches by stakeholders. Some of these instruments can be carried out on a national level via hard law implementation; some of them remain on an international scale in the form of soft law recommendations and guidelines. This practically is the simplified and logical delineation between policymaking and policy advising *stricto sensu* based on the following. We can talk about policymaking activities of the IEA when a wide-scale international policy is being drafted with the involvement and cooperation of both national governments and private entities (undertakings and other stakeholders). This can result in globally, multilaterally, or at least bilaterally applicable[278] soft law provisions, e.g. strategic planning, voluntary approaches, minimum standards or informative and educative programmes. Policy advising from the IEA's perspective on the other hand usually means expert aid to shaping national policies of particular member/ association countries[279] (or their smaller region or other territorial/administrative unit) assessing an already existing policy aim and the tools at disposal to successfully achieve it. These policies with a national scope can take a slightly harder character – e.g. regulatory/economic instruments, fiscal instruments, subsidization, etc., in order to bring tangible results and contribute to the long-term wider endeavours. Of course, this brief comparison does not intend to suggest a strict distinction between policymaking and advising, since dogmatically it is not possible. The intention was just to shed light on the process of creating a consensus under the aegis of

276. Andrew Chapman, Benjamin McLellan, Tetsuo Tezuka, *Strengthening the Energy Policy Making Process and Sustainability Outcomes in the OECD through Policy Design*, 6(9) Administrative Sciences 1, 2 (2016).

277. The requirement of policy consistency on a national and international level has been underlined by multiple scholars, especially in relation to renewable energy. *cf.* William White, Andres Lunnan, Erlend Nybakk, Biljana Kulisic, *The Role of Governments in Renewable Energy: The Importance of Policy Consistency*, Biomass and Bioenergy, 1-9 (2013).

278. In this sense a multilaterally implementable policy can be in reference to a particular region (Europe – throughout the European Union, North America, the Middle East, etc.), while bilaterally implementable policies indicate a policy goal most efficiently achievable by two (neighbouring) countries.

279. For more details on differences between the IEA members and Association countries *see* Chapter 3.§1.IV.A.

the IEA regarding the fulfilment of energy – and indirectly also environmental, ecological and sustainability goals set out. Furthermore, in the light of the above-mentioned consistency, it is important to emphasize that wider energy policies created by/with the help of the IEA need to serve a basis for deduction of more narrow ones – regardless whether from a territorial or functional perspective.

187. The IEA also maintains a database of policies applicable since the 1950s, currently with a total number of 5,510 measures mainly of energy-related fields supporting the reduction of GHG emissions, improving energy efficiency and supporting renewable energy development. The database, called initially PAMS and originally launched in 1999, has been later (in 2003) extended by two other policy information websites titled: *Dealing with Climate Change* and *Renewable Energy Policies and Measures in IEA Countries*. The former featured 'data on energy-related policies and measures taken or planned by the IEAs 26 members, to reduce greenhouse gas emissions'.[280] The latter contained references mainly to 'legislation designed to encourage the development and market uptake of renewable energy sources'.[281] These websites evolved gradually into its present form, currently being referred to as Policies Database on the IEA's Official Website. The policies available via this service of the IEA are periodically (twice a year) reviewed by delegates from members.

280. IEA, *IEA Launches Climate Change and Renewable Energy Websites* https://www.iea.org/news/iea-launches-climate-change-and-renewable-energy-websites (accessed 28 December 2019).
281. *Ibid.*

Figure 11 The Simplified Circle of Policy Creation and Various Activities of the IEA Providing Input or Creating Output

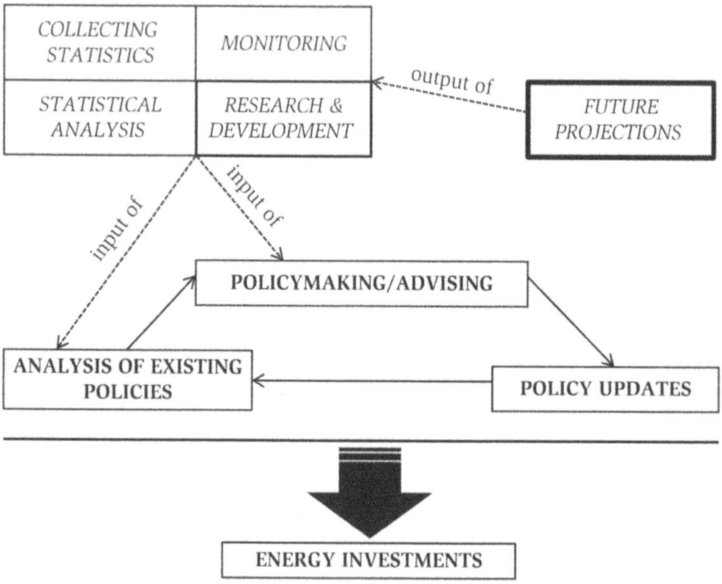

Own source based on www.iea.org.[282]

188. The types of policies and measures are spreading across multiple sectors from buildings (including residential), electricity, transport (including road transport), heating and cooling, to energy generation and industry-related ones with some of them overlapping. The database collates policy information gathered either directly from governments (also of non-IEA members), extended by the policy analyses carried out by the IEA.[283] Some of these policies have already been carried out (currently in total 1,117 already have the 'Ended' status), the latest currently being listed from 2019,[284] but the vast majority is still in force (total of 4,351), and some of them are in the phase of planning (currently 42 available). All of these policy descriptions are very concise, focusing only on their core mission, providing comprehensive information about the contents, the expected results and the stage of their implementation (together with their potential extension or

282. Chapman, *supra* n. 276.
283. Clean Energy Solutions Center, *IEA Policies and Measures Database* https://cleanenergysolutions.org/resource/pams (accessed 28 December 2019).
284. The city policy of Amsterdam in the Netherlands to subsidize the purchase of electric commercial vehicles ended on the 1st of October 2019. The Dutch government also considered to launch the next scheme starting from the 1st of December 2019. IEA, *Amsterdam City Subsidies for Electric Commercial Vehicles,* https://www.iea.org/policies/7222-amsterdam-city-subsidies-for-electric-commercial-vehicles?status=Ended (accessed 28 November 2019).

achieved results). The main idea is not presenting highly scientific data, which needs to be further interpreted and undoubtedly would cause difficulties to laypersons being overall contra-productive.

189. The policy database of the IEA serves one main purpose – disseminating information on past, present and future endeavours towards its activity aims and objectives previously listed. The simple access guarantees reaching wide ranges of the public, keeping them up-to-date about the latest developments of satisfying global energy needs parallelly moving towards sustainability and environmental protection. This is one of the key types of activities the IEA is putting a large emphasis on. However, it is very important to emphasize that these brief policy descriptions can under no circumstances be considered as official acts of governments. As stated above, they are complementing the policy analysis carried out by the IEA (see also: policy advising, as previously indicated).

B. Monitoring

190. Another equally important activity type is *monitoring*. This includes not only the monitoring of energy markets worldwide – which is of course the key area of this activity type – but also monitoring of policy development, implementation of various measures related to clean energy transition, climate change adaptation and mitigation, etc. This is the section, where policymaking and monitoring as activity types are closely interconnected. Especially the policy database previously mentioned is using mainly the results of these monitoring activities not only for collecting the relevant energy-related measures and policies but also keeping the database up-to-date. Monitoring activities help assessing the efficiency of existing policies and draw important conclusions for the future development of energy security, efficiency, transition to cleaner technologies, etc.

191. In relation to monitoring development on the energy front, indicators play a key role. These energy indicators are not just mere statistics, but they go beyond raw numerical data and provide a deeper understanding of causal relationships in the energy-environment-economics nexus highlighting linkages, which might not be obvious just from simple statistics.[285] The IEA needs to update these energy indicators based on the latest available datasets it collects. This is crucial for correct interpretation of monitoring results. In 2018, the IEA highlighted the importance of up-to-date resources by updating its Energy Efficiency Database with annual data from 2000 to 2016, expanded geographical coverage and interactive visualization tools, which makes monitoring, e.g., of final energy consumption of countries more

285. Ivan Vera & Lucille Langlois, *Energy Indicators for Sustainable Development*, 32 Energy 875, 876 (2007).

accurate.[286] The energy indicators used by the IEA since 2018 include energy generation – electricity from various clean/fossil sources, production (mining) of natural resources and Total Primary Energy Supply (TPES). Besides these explicitly mentioned ones, one can list also Total Final Consumption (TFC). Naturally, these indicators vary, depending on the particular aspect of energy monitoring aims. Different indicators are determined in relation to energy efficiency, energy security, clean energy transition, energy poverty, etc.[287] The importance of different indicators for sustainable energy development varies even from country to country, depending on particular characteristics of the country, national energy priorities and the selected sustainability and development criteria and the objectives of the particular monitoring.[288] Objective-based criteria are used by the IEA too, but unlike the states, the IEA needs to use and assess a much wider range of indicators due to the fact of collecting data from countries with different policy backgrounds, in order to secure the permeability of the monitoring results and their appropriate interpretation by the public depending on their context. Some studies even go as far as suggesting overlapping and combined indicators between various sustainability goals (e.g. food, water related) and energy (in relation to the SDGs previously mentioned). Notwithstanding the indicators used by the IEA during monitoring activities can be considered common for energy, which is also proved throughout various research articles using similar, or the same ones.[289]

C. Projections

192. In relation to monitoring activities of the IEA, at this point it is important to mention also *future projections* based on them. Although they use information from all the activities serving as inputs for policy creation and updates, projections are closely related mainly to monitoring, since neither raw statistical data, which is analysed during monitoring, nor pure R&D activities can solely be extrapolated to predict future development of energy.

193. In relation to projections, it is necessary to distinguish between the various results of these IEA activities. The WEO is one of the most important outputs of the IEA making future energy projections based on monitoring results and statistical

286. IEA, *Update to the IEA Energy Efficiency Indicators Database* https://www.iea.org/news/update-to-the-iea-energy-efficiency-indicators-database accessed 28 December 2019.

287. For the full list of energy indicators used by the IEA for data collection purposes *see:* 1.1.4.2 Areas of Data Collection.

288. Besides the indicators directly mentioned on the IEA website, the related guidelines and methodology lists further categories of indicators including various economic, social and environmental ones. *See*: International Atomic Energy Agency (IAEA), *Energy Indicators for Sustainable Development: Guidelines and Methodologies (IAEA, UN Department of Economic and Social Affairs, IEA, Eurostat and European Environmental Agency)* https://www-pub.iaea.org/MTCD/publications/PDF/Pub1222_web.pdf (accessed 28 December 2019).

289. E.g. Linked Indicators for Food, Energy and Water Availability (LIFEWAY) including energy use, renewable energy share, access to electricity, etc. *cf.* Mei-Hua Yuan & Shang-Lien Lo, *Developing Indicators for the Monitoring of the Sustainability of Food, Energy and Water,* Renewable and Sustainable Energy Reviews (2019).

data collected from various energy market participants and stakeholders. Published on an annual basis, the WEO provides critical analysis and insights on trends in energy demand and supply, and what they mean for energy security, environmental protection and economic development. The first WEO was published in 1977. The outlook has become a yearly publication only since 1998. Since there is no single interpretation of collected and analysed statistics and monitoring results making only one 'story' about the future of global energy, the WEO uses a scenario-based approach to highlight key choices, consequences and contingencies that lie ahead, and to illustrate how the course of the energy system might be affected by changing some of the key variables within policies adopted by governments around the world. By 2020, the WEO has become the world's most authoritative source of energy market analysis and projections.[290] The annual editions of the WEO are available in the IEA webstore, among other publications.[291]

194. The WEO, besides being a complex report, also has more specific technology and country reports.[292] The technology reports refer to key areas of energy generation applying innovative new industrial processes and improving efficiency and sustainability in general.[293]

195. Country reports, on the other hand, take a narrower region or a particular country as their subject of analysis, usually based on the overall importance of the country/ region and its stage of economic/social/environmental development.[294]

196. The projections of the WEO are made using a large-scale simulation model designed to replicate how energy markets function – the World Energy Model (WEM). The WEM is the principal tool used to generate detailed sector-by-sector and region-by-region projections for the WEO scenarios.[295]

---

290. IEA, *World Energy Outlook (About the WEO)* https://www.iea.org/topics/world-energy-outlook (accessed 28 December 2018).
291. For the summary of these publications also *see* Chapter 6.
292. *See also infra Analysis of Data* for more details on specific reports.
293. One of the recent examples of a WEO Technology Report is the Offshore Wind Outlook 2019, which analyses the offshore wind market on a global scale during the years 2010-2018 formulating key findings, based on which future projections are made on the overall potential of wind energy being an important part of the energy mix. It also provides a geospatial analysis assessing the technical potential of offshore wind development, taking into account also the latest wind projects implemented. *See*: IEA, *Offshore Wind Outlook 2019* https://www.iea.org/reports/offshore-wind-outlook-2019 (accessed on 28 December 2019).
294. A very good example of country reports is the WEO 2017: China. The selection of a country well reflects the potential and recent changes, which took place in China regarding energy. Not only did it skyrocket among the largest energy consumers in the world, but it also become the country with the fastest development of the renewable energy industry, as well as with the application of multiple innovative technologies in the field of energy. IEA, *World Energy Outlook 2017: China* https://www.iea.org/reports/world-energy-outlook-2017-china (accessed 28 December 2019). Further below, we will also mention the African Energy Outlook, as one of the projected energy development scenarios.
295. IEA, *World Energy Model* https://www.iea.org/reports/world-energy-model# (accessed 28 December 2019). The WEM includes several new policy development directions referred to as the *New Policies Scenarios.*

197. The WEM is a very data-intensive model covering the whole global energy system. Much of the data on energy supply, transformation and demand, as well as energy prices is obtained from the IEA's own databases of energy and economic statistics. Additional data from a wide range of external sources is also used. The current version of WEM covers energy developments up to 2040 (2050 for the SDS) in 25 regions. Depending on the specific module of the WEM, individual countries are also modelled: 12 in demand; 101 in oil and gas supply; and 19 in coal supply. The WEM is designed to analyse:

- Global and regional energy prospects: These include trends in demand, supply availability and constraints, international trade and energy balances by sector and by fuel.
- Environmental impact of energy use: CO^2 emissions from fuel combustion are derived from the projections of energy consumption. Other greenhouse gases and local pollutants are also estimated linking WEM with other models.
- Effects of policy actions and technological changes: Alternative scenarios analyse the impact of policy actions and technological developments on energy demand, supply, trade, investments and emissions.
- Investment in the energy sector: The model evaluates investment requirements in the fuel supply chain needed to satisfy projected energy demand. It also evaluates demand-side investment requirements, including energy efficiency, electric vehicles and industrial carbon capture and storage.

198. Modern energy access prospects: These include trends in access to electricity and clean cooking facilities. It also evaluates additional energy demand, investments and CO2 emissions due to increased energy access.[296]

199. These areas of analysis are in overlap with the activity aims of the IEA, which we are going to deal with more in detail in section §1.II and also in section §2 of this chapter. The model itself has a complex structure containing a supply side being interconnected with primary (including transformation), secondary (final) demand of energy itself, but also energy-related services (the various industries using energy for primary production of goods) (see also Figure 12).

296. IEA, *World Energy Model (Abstract)* https://www.iea.org/reports/world-energy-model/documentation#abstract (accessed on 29 December 2019).

Figure 12 World Energy Model Overview

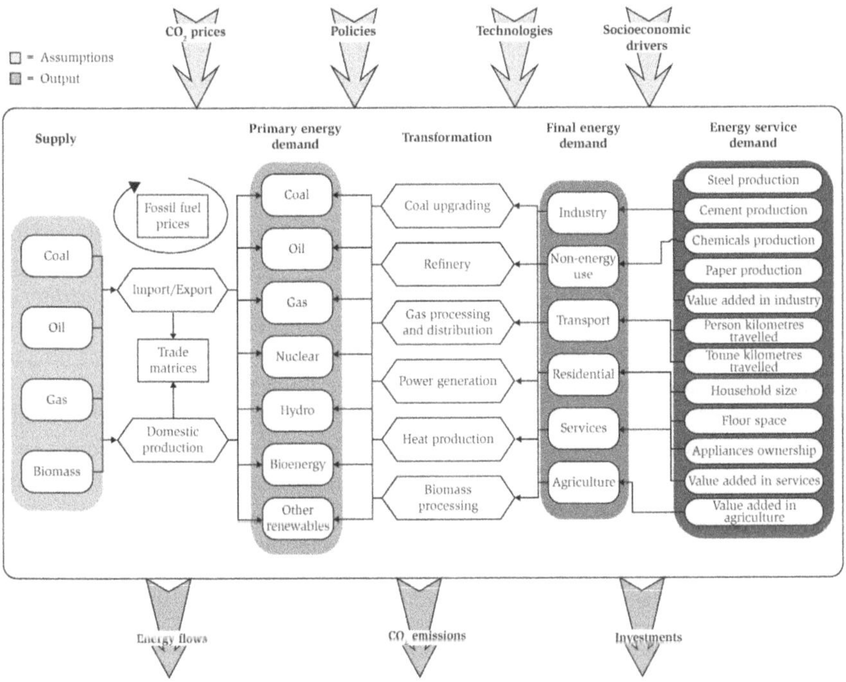

Source: IEA, WEM Documentation 2019.

200. The annual WEO reports contain multiple of these scenarios, always taking into account the related *Current Policy Scenario* (CPS) as a baseline. The CPS operates under the assumption that none of the governments make changes in their existing policies and measures, and the projections are made accordingly.

201. The most recent WEO contains the following scenarios completing CPS and drawing a picture about possible future outcomes if presumed energy development takes a certain direction, in compliance with the most up-to-date targets set by countries, but also by global energy stakeholders.

202. *Stated Policies Scenario* (SPS) – This scenario assumes that the existing policies and recently announced commitments and plans including those yet to be formally adopted are implemented in a cautious manner. Similarly to the CPS, its objective is also providing benchmarks in order to assess the potential achievements (and also limitations) of recent developments in energy and climate policy.[297] Compared to the CPS, which takes into the account already enacted and adopted policies remaining unchanged for the upcoming years, the SPS also considers policies, which have been announced, commitments, which have already been taken and plans, which have been formulated to be implemented in the near future. This can also serve as a benchmark scenario, but with a slightly wider context and differing projection results, than CPS.

203. Sustainable Development Scenario (SDS) – This is an integrated scenario, introduced in WEO 2017, specifying the pathway with multiple aims. These aims include mainly ensuring universal access to affordable, reliable, sustainable and modern energy services by 2030,[298] substantially reducing air pollution[299] and taking effective action to combat climate change.[300] At the introduction of this chapter, we have referred to the UN's SDGs and have underlined their interconnection with the activities of the IEA – the various policy scenarios, as results of the IEAs projection related activities further expand this interconnection. The main objective of the SDS itself is mainly to demonstrate a plausible path to achieve universal energy access, set a path towards meeting the objectives of the Paris Agreement on climate change and significantly reduce air pollution.[301]

204. Besides these key scenarios within WEO 2019, there are further more specific scenarios under the aegis of the IEA, which are also worth mentioning.

205. The Africa Case – This projected scenario evolves from the SPS, but focuses specifically on Africa reflecting also on the Agenda 2063.[302] This scenario is also closely related to the *Africa Energy Outlook* (AEO) 2019 being a comprehensive and detailed work on energy across the African continent, with particular emphasis on sub-Saharan Africa. The AEO includes also energy profiles of eleven

---

297. IEA, *World Energy Model Documentation 2019 Version* https://iea.blob.core.windows.net/assets/6c2b060b-f6b2-48cc-9091-d8129182f0dd/WEM_Documentation_WEO2019.pdf (accessed 29 December 2019).
298. This aim is included in SDG No. 7.
299. This aim is included in SDG target no. 3.9. This target requires substantially reducing the number of deaths and illnesses from hazardous chemicals and air, water and soil pollution and contamination by 2030. UN Department of Economic and Social Affairs (Statistics Division), *SDG Indicators – Metadata Repository of SDG 3* https://unstats.un.org/sdgs/metadata/?Text=&Goal=&Target=3.9 (accessed on 30 December 2019).
300. This aim is included in SDG No. 13.
301. *Ibid.*
302. Agenda 2063 was signed by African head of governments in May 2013, and it contains the ambitious plan of transforming Africa into the global powerhouse of the future during the upcoming fifty years. The agenda includes meeting SGDs and among its goals and priorities one can find the objective of building environmentally sustainable and climate resilient economies and communities, which also includes transition to renewable energy utilization. African Union, *Agenda 2063: The Africa We Want (Overview)* https://au.int/agenda2063/overview (accessed 28 December 2019).

countries including Nigeria, South Africa, Ethiopia, Kenya and Ghana, the economies of which make up three-quarters of the region's GDP and energy demand.[303]

206. The Future is Electric Scenario (FES) – Its title already reveals that this scenario projected by WEO 2018 evolves around electrification. Starting from the NPS, it explores key areas of uncertainty for future electricity demand – mainly the rapidly increasing electricity demand, increasing not only the demand for natural resources being input material for power generation but also requiring increased efficiency measures to be taken.[304]

207. 450 Scenario – This is one of the oldest projected scenarios of the IEA introduced in 2009 in relation to energy transition. The name of the scenario refers to 450 parts per million (ppm), a CO_2 concentration, which in 2009 was seen as consistent with the aim of keeping the average global temperature rise below 2°C.[305] This scenario is slightly outdated and a new one is gradually taking its place, but it can still serve as a basis of comparison monitoring policy developments between 2009 and 2019.

208. The 1.5C Scenario – The newly projected scenario outlined by the IEA in November 2019 would put the global development in line with one of the toughest conditions of the Paris Agreement – holding global warming, i.e. global temperature rise below 1.5°C, compared to the 450 Scenario above. However, the outline published at the end of the year is already facing some criticism from experts, and also some of the member countries might be reluctant to support it due to its very strict requirements – e.g. the US. The basis of the scenario is coming from the original commitment taken on by states in the Paris Agreement, which involved staying under a 2°C rise and stretching towards 1.5°C. This has been considered also when shaping the projected scenario, but it immediately opened up a debate about the IEA's role in setting norms around global energy use.[306] This is due to the fact that the scenario outlines with high accuracy what needs to happen in order for the scenario to become real and global temperatures increments staying around 1.5°C (not even below, because chances are that this would result in the rise being 1.8°C). Oil demand needs to peak during the next few years, universal energy access needs to be achieved by 2030 and energy-related CO_2 emissions need to continuously fall at least by 3.8% p.a. reaching less than 10 gigatons in 2050 and 0 in 2070. These rather strict conditions are nowhere near to, e.g., the CPS and SPS versions, but on the other hand this outline still requires further research and analysis of past data, since it does not evaluate whether deploying a negative emission at scale in the last part

303. IEA, *Africa Energy Outlook 2019* https://www.iea.org/reports/africa-energy-outlook-2019 (accessed on 29 December 2019).
304. World Energy Model, *Part of World Energy Outlook*, Report (October. 2020), https://www.iea.org/reports/world-energy-model (accessed 07 November 2020).
305. *Ibid.*
306. Karl Mathiesen, *IEA Develops Pathway to Ambitious 1.5°C Climate Goal*, Climate Change News https://www.climatechangenews.com/2019/06/11/iea-develops-pathway-ambitious-1-5c-climate-goal/ (accessed on 29 December 2019).

of the century is feasible or sustainable.[307] In spite of the criticism and inconsistencies between the IEAs approach within the latest WEO and the 1.5C Scenario, one has to bear in mind that the projections of the IEA are under no circumstances binding or 'set in stone', but they present scientific results based on available data and multiple assumptions during modelling. The efforts of the stakeholders need to foster achieving the goals of the Paris Agreement, but maintain their balance also with the pace of global economic, social and environmental development, since the energy industry cannot subdue completely to environmental goals set. It is not the aim of sustainable development in general.

209. In general, the IEA's scenarios are occasionally considered conservative on a wider scale, unlike in the case of the needed emission reductions of the 1.5C Scenario. This is due to the fact that the projections of the IEA often count on slower deployment of necessary innovation and technologies, so in this way they are slightly more pessimistic than justified. If we refer back again to the 1.5C Scenario, the opposite is obvious – the IEA's projection counting on a much larger scale of, e.g., CCUS being utilized during energy production, as well as within other industries worldwide, in order to achieve the goals to be feasible.[308] This requires not only technological development but also the rapid reduction of costs related to building facilities. Nevertheless, once again, the terms 'projection' and 'scenario' indicate just an extrapolation of the analysis of collected data along a set of conditions previously defined, followed by a simulation, and it does not require strict follow-up and implementation. Furthermore, the pressure such a projection might create on various technology markets and regarding national policymaking can have a positive and negative impact. Therefore, they can be deemed utmost necessary to foster and speed up investments and complying regulatory policies throughout the areas of sustainable development.

D. Statistics and Statistical Analysis

210. Collecting and processing data is a crucial aspect of IEA's activities. It not only serves as the primary source of policy monitoring and assessment but is also a key input for future projections and reports prepared annually on a global or regional basis. 'Consistent, accurate and timely energy data and statistics are fundamental to developing effective and efficient national energy policies, as well as a key element in longer-term planning for investment in the energy sector. To this end, the IEA Energy Data Centre provides the world's most authoritative and comprehensive source of global energy data.'[309] The IEA is collecting, evaluating and further disseminating energy statistics mainly on supply and demand, which are

307. Chloé Farand, *IEA World Energy Outlook Outlines 1.5C Scenario*, Climate Change News https://www.climatechangenews.com/2019/11/13/iea-world-energy-outlook-outlines-1-5c-scenario/ (accessed 29 December 2019).

308. *cf.* Gerry Carrington, Janet Stephenson, *The Politics of Energy Scenarios: Are International Energy Agency and Other Conservative Projections Hampering the Renewable Energy Transition?*, 46 Energy Research & Social Science 103, 110 (2018).

309. IEA, *Data and Statistics* https://www.iea.org/data-and-statistics (accessed on 29 December 2019).

compiled into balance sheets. Additionally, the Energy Data Centre works with other self-developed energy-related indicators, including prices on energy markets, measures of energy efficiency and measures in development.[310]

211. The focus is on quality, comparability, and alignment with internationally agreed definitions and methodologies, and close collaboration with national offices responsible for energy statistics and other relevant stakeholders. This emphasis on sound data provides a unique platform for modelling work and tracking both short-term shifts and long-term trends in countries having energy transitions, particularly for clean energy. Furthermore, the IEA Energy Data Centre has established close cooperation with national and regional organizations on training and capacity building activities. As well as allowing for expanded coverage, this further ensures the quality of the Centre's data products.[311]

1. Means of Data Collection

212. Data collectors and users submit the data collected and processed by the IEA. This process is supported by various manuals and questionnaires, as well as hands-on training provided not only by the IEA itself. In 2005, the IEA launched its *Energy Statistics Manual* in cooperation with Eurostat, in order to help statisticians to better understand the fundamentals of energy statistics and to aid in the preparation of annual energy questionnaires. The concept of statistics-related manuals proved to be useful; therefore the IEA is constantly improving them in cooperation with other organizations focusing on statistics. In 2009, the IEA also created a questionnaire dedicated specifically to energy efficiency statistics, which has also contributed to higher quality and more consistent statistics being collected, still improving year after year. Based on the wide range of responses from statisticians, the IEA expanded this concept and initiated a more robust global survey in order to collect a large number of best practices on how countries collect statistics and develop indicators. As a result, more than two hundred practices were collected covering surveys, metering/ modelling on residential, services, industry and transport sectors all over the world.[312] These are not only being used by the IEA but have been disseminated to other states, including non-members. Regarding the questionnaires, separate ones are used (including reporting instructions, templates and user manuals related to filling them out) for coal, oil, natural gas, electricity, renewable energy and energy efficiency-related information necessary for the purposes of the IEA.

213. Furthermore, the statistical manuals also include external sources, e.g. the *International Recommendations for Energy Statistics* (IRES) issued in 2018 by the UN Department of Economic and Social Affairs. The main purpose of IRES is to provide harmonization of official statistics worldwide to secure their consistency

310. *Ibid.*
311. *Ibid.*
312. IEA, *Energy Efficiency Indicators: Fundamentals on Statistics*, OECD 2014, p. 14.

and interconnections. This includes recommendations on concepts, definitions, classifications, data sources, compilation methodology, data quality assessment, metadata and dissemination policies.[313]

214. Besides the IRES, external cooperation of the IEA regarding statistics and data collection also involves the JODI. The progress of this initiative dates back to the late 1990s, when the need for available, reliable and transparent data gained momentum, due to price volatilities on the markets – back at the time on the markets with oil. This basically culminated in six international organizations including Eurostat, IEA, OPEC and others, together with some of their member countries joining their efforts and starting to build a global database of oil statistics and other information in 2001. Six months later, there were already seventy participating countries covering 90% of the global oil supply and demand in the early 2000s. Currently, the JODI – Oil World Database and the JODI – Gas World Database exist, together with the appropriated manuals on collecting statistics and using the appropriate indicators, also being disseminated within the statistics-related activities of the IEA.[314]

215. In order to see the full picture regarding data collection means, the arsenal of the IEA also includes the IEA *Guide to Reporting Energy RD&D*[315] Budget/Expenditure Statistics, and the previously briefly indicated *Energy Efficiency Indicators: Essentials for Policy Making*.

2. Areas of Data Collection

216. Collected data is categorized according to different criteria, based on which separate statistical reports are prepared. Simultaneously, the IEA official website contains a data browser and various data tables in reference to key energy indicators (including supply and consumption), as well as to various energy sources.

217. Organization of the data pools, mainly on the website, has various overlaps in order to ensure easy access and to allow searches based on logical filters. However, the main indicators, which need to be emphasized beyond the key ones previously mentioned (*see:* B. Monitoring), are the following ones:

Emissions
- CO_2 emissions per capita;
- CO_2 emissions per unit of GDP (including the basis of purchasing power parity – PPP);

313. UN Economic & Social Affairs – Statistics Division, *International Recommendations for Energy Statistics (IRES)*, Series M No. 93, 2018, par. 1.13.
314. JODI, *Historical Background: JODI and Oil Data* https://www.jodidata.org/about-jodi/history.aspx (accessed on 30 December 2019).
315. Research, Development and Demonstration – for more details on R&D-related activities *see* the R&D part of this chapter.

- CO_2 emissions (by energy source, by sector, by drivers);
- CO_2 emissions from electricity and heat by energy source;
- CO_2 intensity of energy mix (CO_2/TPES);
- CO_2 intensity of power;
- Carbon intensity of industry energy consumption;
- Carbon intensity of road transport energy consumption;
- Final energy carbon intensity

Electricity

- Electricity consumption per capita;
- Electricity final consumption;
- Electricity final consumption by sector;
- Electricity generation by source;
- Electricity generation from biofuels and waste by source;
- Low-carbon electricity generation by source;

Natural Resources

- Coal production by type;
- Coal final consumption (by sector, by type, by capita);
- Natural gas production;
- Natural gas final consumption (by sector);
- Oil production;
- Oil final consumption (by product, by sector);
- Share of biofuels in transport energy consumption;
- Heat generation by source;
- Nuclear heat generation;

Trade & Totals

- Net energy imports;
- Import versus export (coal, crude oil, crude oil/NGL, oil products, electricity, natural gas);
- TPES (by per capita, by GDP, by GDP (PPP), by source);
- TFC (by sector, by source);
- Total CO_2 emissions;

Renewable Energy

- Heat generation from renewables and waste by source;
- Renewable electricity generation by source (non-combustible);
- Hydroelectric electricity generation;
- Solar PV electricity generation;
- Wind electricity generation;

SDGs

- Renewable share in final energy consumption (including modern renewables) (SDG 7.2[316]);

---

316. SDG 7 includes ensuring access to affordable, reliable, sustainable and modern energy for all; its target no. 7.2 requires increasing substantially the share of renewable energy in the global energy mix by 2030. UN Department of Economic and Social Affairs (Statistics Division), *SDG Indicators – Metadata Repository of SDG 7* https://unstats.un.org/sdgs/metadata/?Text=&Goal=&Target=7.2 (accessed on 30 December 2019).

– Energy intensity per unit of GDP (SDG 7.3[317]);
– CO_2 emissions per unit of value added (SDG 9.4[318]).

218. These indicators are used in relation to various charts containing data from 1990 to 2017, while complementary data to these charts organized in tables, also in relation to energy balances, coal, electricity, natural gas, oil, renewables and waste, contain information mainly on the natural resources of generation and generation process, import/export, stock changes, TPES, losses, and consumption – in case of natural resources their consumption regarding energy production, in case of energy regarding its consumption by various industries. [319]

219. The specific statistical reports briefly mentioned are using the same data pool collected by the IEA in the areas and concerning indicators listed above, but they also include explanations, narratives and conclusions. In 2019, these statistical reports included monthly OECD statistics on natural gas, oil and oil prices, electricity; annual statistics regarding CO_2 emissions from fuel combustion, energy technology RD&D budgets, energy statistics and balance sheets with global coverage, annual information on natural gas, oil and electricity.

220. The monthly statistics are updated based on an annual schedule usually published by the IEA at the beginning of each year.[320] They present the charts and tables in a comprehensive way, broken down to countries and regions, together with comparisons of previous time periods underlining the direction of development, and highlighting overall trends. The same is extrapolated regarding the natural resource and electricity-related annual statistical reports (the Natural Gas, Oil and Electricity Information) – the data is similarly organized, just has a wider range and comparisons are made instead of a monthly basis, on a yearly basis.

221. Statistical reports on specific issues, i.e. the CO_2 Emissions From Fuel Combustion 2019, are not published every year, but contain a dataset from all the available data (in this particular case, emissions stemming from energy use since

---

317. SDG target 7.3 requires doubling the global rate of improvement in energy efficiency by 2030. UN Department of Economic and Social Affairs (Statistics Division), *SDG Indicators Metadata Repository of SDG 7* https://unstats.un.org/sdgs/metadata/?Text=&Goal=&Target=7.3 (accessed on 30 December 2019).
318. SDG 9 includes building resilient infrastructure, promoting inclusive and sustainable industrialization and fostering innovation; its target no. 9.4 requires upgrading infrastructure and retrofit industries to make them sustainable, with increased resource-use efficiency and greater adoption of clean and environmentally sound technologies and industrial processes, with all countries taking action in accordance with their respective capabilities by 2030.
UN Department of Economic and Social Affairs (Statistics Division), *SDG Indicators Metadata Repository of SDG 9* https://unstats.un.org/sdgs/metadata/?Text=&Goal=9&Target=9.4 (accessed on 30 December 2019).
319. *See* IEA Website for further details.
320. The 2020 schedule regarding monthly oil, monthly gas and monthly oil price statistics is already available at the IEA website: https://iea.blob.core.windows.net/assets/986d77bf-5aed-441b-a822-d28ab79c8067/Schedule_monthly_gas.pdf (accessed 13 January 2020).

1971 to 2017 for 150 countries). Besides raw data, the report also contains evaluations, comparisons, causal reasoning and conclusions. Similarly, the report titled Energy Technology RD&D Budgets 2019 is highly specific assessing the volumes of investments into Research, Development and Demonstration (RD&D) by the IEA Member States.[321]

3. Analysis of Data

222. The statistical data collected and stored in various data centres[322] either directly by the IEA or using external organizations are thoroughly analysed by the IEA, in order to draw conclusions and make factual connections between partial findings. Of course, analyses of the IEA are not provided simply based on pure numerical statistics and charts, but they are the basic foundation of their outputs. This is the reason why we discuss it under this section.

223. We have previously mentioned multiple reports, as the primary outputs of analyses, as an organic part of reviewing the other activity types of the IEA, but they can be categorized as follows:

a) Flagship Reports;
b) Country Reports;
c) Statistics Reports;
d) Tracking Reports;
e) Technology Reports;
f) Fuel Reports;
g) General Reports.

224. Furthermore, partial analyses can be provided also on a more subjective manner, by experts (from either the IEA or external ones) via articles and commentaries, focusing only on a small segment of reports, or a particular issue, which rose from the result of a more extensive analysis. These articles and commentaries very

321. For more details on investment and R&D-related activities of the IEA *see:* E. Investment-Related Activities and F. Research & Development.

322. These data centres also consume a significant amount of energy, in which case energy efficiency measures and integration policies (meaning mainly the interconnection of global centres ensuring mutual access for collectors and expert analysis) undoubtedly need to be taken into consideration. There are multiple studies, primarily focusing on Europe, assessing the current possibilities of such integration and improving their energy consumption/overall power performance ratio. For these efforts to be successful technical infrastructure and legal frameworks are necessary *Cf.* Carolina Koronen, Max Ahman, Lars J. Nillson, *Data Centres in Future European Energy Systems – Energy Efficiency, Integration and Policy*, Energy Efficiency 1-16 (November 2019). *See also* IEA, *Data Centres & Networks* https://www.iea.org/fuels-and-technologies/data-centres-networks (accessed on 22 December 2019).

often basically just answer one question, but in a very detailed way. The key difference between the articles and commentaries is that commentaries are written by renowned, named experts of the IEA, while articles are often 'spinoffs' from or parts of a wider analysis – i.e., a report.[323]

225. Steering the 'wheel' of this section back to the reports mentioned above, the *flagship reports* (e.g. the *Oil Market Report* (OMR), WEO) are the most extensive and most authoritative sources of energy market-related analyses and also projections. Their importance lies in the quality and quantity of the data processed, the complexity of key findings, and their potential impact on the global energy governance development. Due to their vast scientific robustness, usually these reports are not publicly available in full-text. *Country reports*, which have to be distinguished from the specific country reports of the WEO,[324] can aim at reviewing the existing policies of an IEA member/non-member[325] country regularly updated, providing recommendations based on the conducted research and data collected. Furthermore, the topic of country reports can also revolve around a country-specific energy issue, as is the case regarding the Partner Country Series.[326,327] *Statistics reports*, among them the monthly/ annual analyses, have also been touched upon previously – they are technical raw data concerning a particular energy segment, organized into tables, charts and balances calculated from different indicators and coefficients. Regarding their structure, each of these reports has key trends and other highlights from a particular segment summarized at the beginning, while the tables and charts are partially also based on OECD data, besides IEA. These monthly reports mainly focus on short-term changes and the comparison of results at the beginning and at the end

---

323. An example of the most recent commentary: Dr Fatih Birol, *India's Rise on the Global Energy Scene* https://www.iea.org/commentaries/indias-rise-on-the-global-energy-scene (accessed on 15 January 2020); while the contents of an article could be demonstrated also by a recent one, related to the fuel report: Renewables 2018 – IEA, *Will System Integration of Renewables be a Major Challenge by 2023?* https://www.iea.org/articles/will-system-integration-of-renewables-be-a-major-challenge-by-2023 (accessed on 9 January 2020).

324. These focus on a wider region, than specific reports mentioned in this part. Similarly the WEO has specific technology reports as well, but again, the technology, statistical or fuel reports discussed here have a more limited scope.

325. The series dealing with member country policies is called Energy Policies of IEA Countries, while the non-member country reports are titled: Energy Policies Beyond IEA Countries. *See e.g.:* IEA, *Energy Policies of IEA Countries: United States 2019 Review* https://webstore.iea.org/energy-policies-of-iea-countries-united-states-2019-review (accessed on 30 December 2019); IEA, *Energy Policies beyond IEA Countries: Morocco 2019* https://webstore.iea.org/energy-policies-beyond-iea-countries-morocco-2019 (accessed on 30 December 2019).

326. The Partner Country Series focus on one particular measure or policy within a country – usually a brand new project being introduced for the first time, and the series assesses the potential and long-term implications within. *See e.g.:* IEA, *Partner Country Series – Thailand Renewable Grid Integration Assessment* https://webstore.iea.org/partner-country-series-thailand-renewable-grid-integration-assessment (accessed on 30 December 2019).

327. Due to the original mission of the IEA – handling oil emergencies, i.e. emergencies on the oil markets by stocking up reserves and working out a response system, the country reports use to include the review of related policies within the Oil and Gas Emergency Policy series. The last issue of the series was published in 2012. *See:* IEA, *Oil and Gas Emergency Policy: Turkey 2013 Update* https://webstore.iea.org/oil-and-gas-emergency-policy-turkey-2013-update (accessed on 30 December 2019).

of a particular month.[328] Furthermore, there are specific statistical reports, based on IEA data, focusing more on indicators, which have impact on tackling environmental problems – e.g. energy efficiency, CO_2 emissions, etc.[329] *Tracking reports* are built around a key goal – mainly closely related to an SDG, and they 'track' the progress made in a particular timeframe to reach that goal. Fuel supply can serve as a good example. The related report[330] takes statistical data and results of policy monitoring and make certain long-term projections in order to determine whether achieving the particular goal is 'on track' or not. In case the results show that achieving the relevant goals of fuel supplies are off the track (not on track), the report analyses the reasons, underlining key factors, which influenced the slow pace of the expected development, as well as making suggestions and recommendations for future action, in order to get the endeavours back on track. *Technology reports*, as their title already indicates, analyse an energy-related technology, which is either under development, or its actual trends presuppose a large 'boom' in a particular sector, influencing the energy markets – either the generation segment, energy transport, efficiency, or others. The technology reports can have features of a future projection,[331] or can have a very specific character, focusing on a global non-energy-related issue being tightly interconnected to energy, fostering the achievement of environmental, economic, but also social goals at the same time. The focal point of these reports primarily is not the scientific side of a technology, but usually the human factor being present in a particular achievement.[332] *Fuel reports* are somewhat similar to the tracking reports, being a classic compilation of data and policies focusing on a key fuel type. They are also providing key findings and policy recommendations at the end of each analysis.[333] Last but not least, the IEA *reports*,

---

328. The main market segments, these statistical reports, using OECD data, are focusing on are, e.g., the oil and natural gas market, including their monthly price changes, as well as the electricity markets globally, and in a country-specific way – the availability of OECD data secures the robustness and up-to-date features of these reports. *See*: IEA, *Monthly OECD Electricity Statistics* https://www.iea.org/reports/monthly-oecd-electricity-statistics (accessed on 19 January 2020).

329. For example, the report titled Energy Efficiency Indicators 2019 is designed to help understand what drives final energy use in IEA member countries in order to improve and track national energy efficiency policies. It is a comprehensive selection of data that the IEA has been collecting each year, after its members recognized in 2009 the need to better monitor energy efficiency policies. This year, the report continues to progressively expand its scope to countries beyond IEA. It includes country-specific analysis of end uses across the largest sectors – residential, services, industry and transport. *See*: IEA, *Energy Efficiency Indicators 2019* https://www.iea.org/reports/energy-efficiency-indicators-2019 (accessed on 19 January 2020).

330. Christopher McGlade, Tim Gould, Glenn Sondak, *Tracking Fuel Supply (Tracking Report of the IEA)* https://www.iea.org/reports/tracking-fuel-supply-2019#recommended-actions (accessed 19 January 2020).

331. From the most recent ones *see*: IEA, *supra* n. 293; IEA, *Solar Energy: Mapping the Road Ahead* https://www.iea.org/reports/solar-energy-mapping-the-road-ahead (accessed on 15 January 2020).

332. *See* e.g.: IEA, *Seven Women Entrepreneurs of Solar Energy,* https://www.iea.org/reports/seven-women-entrepreneurs-of-solar-energy (accessed on 17 January 2020).

333. One of the most recent examples is the *Energy Efficiency 2019*, which could also be a tracking or statistical report, but it takes these reports further, by closely focusing on the particular reasons for the 'recent deceleration in efficiency progress and also includes a special focus on the ways in which digitalisation is transforming energy efficiency and increasing its value'. IEA, *Energy Efficiency 2019* https://www.iea.org/reports/energy-efficiency-2019#abstract (accessed on 17 January 2020).

compared to its flagship reports, are processing rather short-term data, focusing on more particular areas and are published on a more regular basis, as, for example, compared to the annual *OMR* or WEO. Their importance is however not lowered by the fact that they contain only parts of the data from the OMRs or WEOs; on the contrary, these robust annual flagship reports are built from these partial short-term reports processing all the data in advance and making short-term conclusions, which can be reflected on within the annual publications.

226. The analyses of the IEA use the classic methodology of data collection and deduction, improving the results with classifications and comparisons before drawing final conclusions. At the end of the most extensive reports (e.g., *Key World Energy Statistics*), there are the selected indicators listed, general conversion and unit abbreviations described and made accurate, as well as definitions of key terms used throughout the monograph. These help to put the data and results into context and indicate the accuracy of the statistics, while making it possible to backtrack the measurement methods for their greater comprehension. The analysis outputs also use results from other IEA activities – mainly monitoring and policy-related ones, which is another good evidence for these activities being a rather closely interconnected whole, the parts of which can be analysed separately, but never exist on their own effectively.

4. Data Services

227. Although the datasets of the IEA are currently one of the most complex, comprehensive and widely available pools of information regarding energy, in spite of this wide availability, some of the reports and other publications are accessible only as a part of complex data services provided by the IEA only for subscribers.

228. The data service includes also a specific feature, i.e. the IEA *Monthly Oil Data Service* (MODS) making available a 'detailed database of historical and projected information used in preparing the monthly IEA's OMR.[334] This service comprises three packages, available separately or combined, as an annual subscription on the Internet. It is updated every month and is available on the same day as the *Monthly Gas Data service* and the OMR. A Beyond 20/20* software package is included, allowing user-friendly access and manipulation of the data tables. Alternatively, data text files are made available to facilitate direct importing of tables into other database software. (Unless otherwise noted, each package includes historical data back to January 1984.)'[335]

334. The Oil Market Report is also a flagship publication of the IEA, containing timely sources of data, forecasts and analysis on the global oil market – including detailed statistics and commentary on oil supply, demand, inventories, prices and refining activity, as well as oil trade for OECD and selected non-OECD countries. IEA, *Oil Market Report* https://www.iea.org/topics/oil-market-report (accessed 29 December 2019).

335. IEA, *Monthly Oil Data Service* https://www.iea.org/monthly-oil-data-service (accessed 29 December 2019).

229. Furthermore, the MODS data service packages include supply, demand, balances and stocks on which separate monthly/ quarterly/ annual data are made available in relation to OECD and non-OECD countries, categorized according to the most characteristics indicators, and using the most common and interchangeable units.[336] Similarly, a data service package is also included for trade and supply containing monthly information on OECD member countries' imports from over ninety origins and exports to over eighty destinations for twenty-one products. Included are: crude oil, NGL, motor gasoline, gas/diesel oil, residual fuel oil and sixteen other products.[337,338]

230. Undoubtedly, the focus on providing oil-related data on a large scale and with precision can be accounted to the expertise the IEA has regarding oil markets and their development since its creation. This is naturally due to the fact that – as mentioned in one of the introductory chapters of this monograph – originally it was created as a reaction on the oil crisis, with its main activity type and aim stemming in maintaining sufficient oil reserves via member countries.[339]

E. Investment-Related Activities: The Possible Impact of the IEA's Activities on Energy Investments

231. Advising regarding investments is a rather narrow slice of activities of the IEA carried out mainly through its affiliated groups in particular industries, e.g. the CIAB and the EBC.[340] It overlaps with other activities, which provide most of their inputs – e.g., policymaking, monitoring, collecting statistical data and conducting statistical analysis, projections based on simulation models (scenarios), as well as results of R&D (*see* Figure 11). Based on these inputs, but mainly from tracking energy investments and assessing the policy frameworks implemented by countries, the IEA is able to evaluate also the pace of energy investing dictated not only by government strategies but also by financial institutions and the sectors of the energy industry.

232. In order to understand the mentioned relationship between energy investments, potential IEA advising and other activities of the IEA, its flagship publication – the *World Energy Investment (WEI)* – might serve as a good example. Its 2019 edition '*looks at trends in investment and financing* in 2018 across all areas of energy supply, efficiency, and research & development, key markets and the sectors driving these trends, from electricity in Asia to fuel supply in North America, as

336. IEA, *MODS – Supply, Demand, Balances and Stocks* https://www.iea.org/monthly-oil-data-service/supply-demand-balances-and-stocks (accessed on 29 December 2019).
337. IEA, *MODS – Trade* https://www.iea.org/monthly-oil-data-service/trade (accessed on 29 December 2019).
338. IEA, *MODS – Field by Field Supply* https://www.iea.org/monthly-oil-data-service/field-by-field-supply (accessed on 29 December 2019).
339. For more details on the origins of the IEA and the gradual transition from its original objectives within global energy governance *see* Chapter 2.
340. *See* Chapter 3.§2.I.

well as the sectors and regions where energy capital flows are constrained. The analysis also *examines how industry is responding to investment risks and opportunities*, including through shorter-cycle oil and gas projects, financial risk management strategies for renewable power, financing models for energy efficiency, and in capital allocation decisions across sectors. And it *looks at the implications of today's trends, such as whether investment is sufficient to satisfy the world's growing demand for energy,* and whether enough capital is going into energy efficiency, renewable energy, and other low-carbon technologies to accelerate the pace of global energy transitions.'[341]

233. The three main ideas underlined in the above passage are as follows:

(1) Examining the trends in investment and financing,
(2) Examining the risks of investing and investment opportunities, as well as
(3) Examining the volumes of investments compared to the constantly growing energy needs all need to stem in other activities.
  - The possibility to review and examine investment trends comes from the wide range of collected data taking into account the appropriate energy indicators (to put in a very simple way: e.g., electricity generation from renewables – their increase presupposes either improved efficiency of existing generation facilities or setting up new ones, both of which require additional investment).
  - Examining the risks related to investments and investment opportunities require constant monitoring of newly introduced national policies and hard law regulations, as well as advising and shaping future policy development trends, which are impossible without projections, and statistical analysis (again, to simplify: e.g., the investment environment of a particular country/region, or a particular industry sector, depends indirectly on policies and regulations, and directly on the situation on a particular market segment – oil, natural gas, electricity, etc. – these segments are all monitored by the IEA within its reports and analyses based on statistical and policy data).[342]
  - Last but not least examining and comparing the volumes of investments also require statistics and analysis, but also projections and monitoring (along the previous simplifications, e.g. in order to be able to determine whether the current pace of investments is going to be able to satisfy the growing energy demand, it is inevitable to simulate and analyse different scenarios

341. IEA, *World Energy Investment 2019* https://www.iea.org/reports/world-energy-investment-2019 (accessed on 30 December 2019).

342. For the sake of complexity, we would like to highlight the extensive amount of existing studies analysing various risk indicators within particular countries and on particular markets, which go way beyond the ones mentioned in this section. From among the most recent ones *see e.g.*: Liu Junxia, *Investments in the Energy Sector of Central Asia: Corruption Risk and Policy Implications*, 133 Energy Policy 1-7 (2019); Ali Shimbar, Seyek Babak Ebrahimi, *Political Risk and Valuation of Renewable Energy Investments in Developing Countries*, 145 Renewable Energy 1325-1333 (2020); Fei Duan, Qiang Ji, Bing-Yue Liu, Ying Fan, *Energy Investment Risk Assessment for Nations Along China's Belt & Road Initiative*, 170 Journal of Cleaner Production 535-547 (2018) and others.

on how the future energy indicators, and investment volumes will evolve based on the most recent trends; only then can the IEA step to comparisons and to formulating the appropriate related conclusions).

234. Investment activities on the energy markets are also widely influenced by R&D activities. These, together with the appropriate amount of investment, spur innovation and know-how development, all in all unavoidable for the fulfilment of SGD goals and also the separate activity aims and objectives of the IEA. The close link between investment-related activities mentioned above, and R&D is underlined also by the fact, that the *WEI Report* has a dedicated section containing statistics on energy-related R&D spending by the biggest and most influential governments, the private sector (including venture capital filled into start-up companies and small-businesses) etc.[343]

235. The impact of the IEA activities on energy investments is already tangible and has a truly global scale. Naturally, the IEA is not the only organization to support such endeavours in the field of energy. Similar investment-related activities are also carried out by other international organizations and non-governmental platforms.[344]

F. Research & Development (R&D/ RD&D)

236. The general notion of R&D has to be narrowed down for the purposes of the IEA activities and also in order to understand technologies used and developed in the field of energy and also climate change mitigation/ adaptation – fulfilling SDGs in general. The concept of RD&D in this regard is best summarized as 'the process through which new, improved and cheaper technologies are developed and their utility demonstrated in a real-world context. *Research* refers to the search for new knowledge and solutions, the starting point for the emergence of new technologies. *Development* refers to the next step where new possibilities emerging from the research phase are translated into concrete technologies. This technology is then refined through testing in the laboratory or simulated field conditions to improve its performance and give it the shape of a usable product. The *demonstration stage* refers to the use of the product in actual field conditions where its performance and feasibility can be demonstrated and evaluated by actual or potential users'[345] (see also Figure 13).

---

343. IEA, *World Energy Investments 2019 – RR&D and New Technologies* https://www.iea.org/reports/world-energy-investment-2019/rd-and-d-and-new-technologies#investment-in-energy-rdd (accessed on 30 December 2019).

344. The International Renewable Energy Agency (IRENA), the World Bank, but partially also the World Energy Council can be mentioned, as examples. *See*: https://www.irena.org/publicationsearch?irena_topic=d9ffd261e70d47779872dabf3f14fb24; https://data.worldbank.org; https://www.worldenergy.org/publications.

345. UNFCCC Technology Executive Committee, *supra* n. 193 at 6.

237. These three stages lead to new and more efficient technologies being used during the utilization of natural resources,[346] energy consumption – improving their efficiency, as well as during generation – reducing the ecological impact of certain processes. Naturally, RD&D is not a linear process, and each step of the innovation system (as visualized in Figure 13) connects to the previous ones via feedbacks provided not only by the users of a certain technology, and not only to researchers themselves. Other stakeholders are included, e.g. consumers, firms, institutions and also the society as a whole.

238. In the light of this, the IEA activities in the field of fostering RD&D activities focus mainly on their monitoring and analysis of key trends – including investments, results and direct impact on industrial technologies. The IEA on the other hand does not do direct technology RD&D. It is not its goal, to replace institutions, academics and other scientific organizations, which include experts on a particular field, having the necessary equipment and accessories in order to create hypotheses, test them, and come up with solutions for a particular problem. Nevertheless, instead based on the analysis, monitoring and projection activities, the IEA tracks RD&D trends, provides developing analyses and recommendations on innovation in the energy sector. Tracking mainly involves investment trends within both the public and private sectors, as key for any RD&D development. Analyses include providing in-depth reviews of the innovative solutions and how they fit into the current technological framework while collecting and organizing RD&D best practices, and policy recommendations are included into future roadmaps, taking into consideration the results of all the previously mentioned activities.[347]

---

346. *See:* Chapter 4.§2.

347. IEA, *Technology Innovation to Accelerate Energy Transitions* https://www.iea.org/reports/technology-innovation-to-accelerate-energy-transitions (accessed on 20 January 2020). This technology report being one of the recent examples, where the IEA melds together results of policy review, analyses, monitoring and investment-related activities, etc. into a comprehensive and robust whole, with high-level policy recommendations for G20 priority action.

Figure 13 Evolution in Thinking of Innovation Process

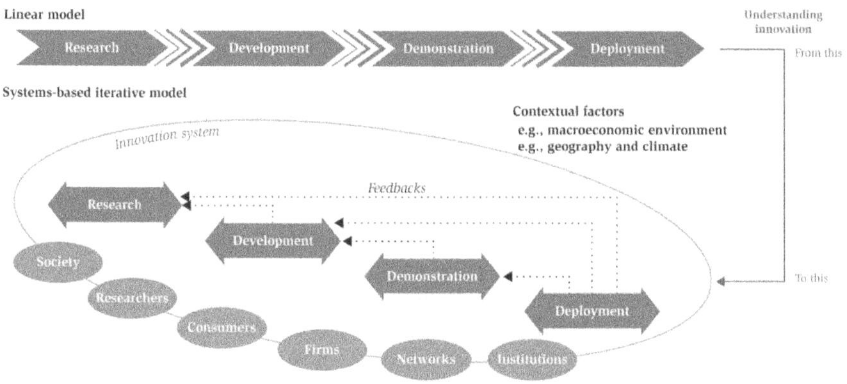

Source: IEA, Energy Innovation Partnerships, June 2019.[348]

239. Notwithstanding the IEA's goal in the field of RD&D is primarily to connect these various research platforms and their research goals, as well as to aid the dissemination of their results. The international cooperation in RD&D plays an important role in identifying priorities, challenges and innovation gaps, as well as sharing best practices to improve performance, reduce costs and deploy the key energy technologies, which have been created. Due to the complexity of energy systems, such collaboration between researchers under the aegis of a global, multi-governmental organization (i.e. the IEA) increases effectiveness, facilitates action and maximizes the impact of innovation efforts.[349]

240. International cooperation in the field of RD&D is enhanced mainly via the partnerships with IEA participation. Recently these partnerships include the IEA TCPs and the so-called Mission Innovation (MI) launched in 2015 as collaboration outside of the IEA, to which the IEA provides full support, mainly when it comes to data collection and analysis.[350] 'Important contributions are also being made regionally, for example, under the EU framework, and through initiatives with a mandate broader than innovation, for example the Clean Energy Ministerial (CEM) [*see* Chapter 3, §3.IV.C *supra*]. However, despite the central role of innovation in global energy transitions and the potential of international collaboration, there is

348. *cf.* Thomas B. Johansson, Anand Pathwardhan, Nebojsa Nakicenovic, Luis Gomez-Echeverri (eds), *Global Energy Assessment: Towards a Sustainable Future*, IIASA, CUP (2012). *cf.* Fionn Rogan, Paul Bolger, Brian Ó Gallachóir, *Climate Technology – Realising the Potential*, Environmental Protection Agency (EPA) Research Report (2012-CCRP-FS-10), EPA Research Programme 2014-2020 (2016), p. 22.
349. IEA, *Energy Technology Innovation Partnerships* https://webstore.iea.org/download/direct/2810 (accessed 14 January 2020).
350. More details on Mission Innovation: http://mission-innovation.net/about-mi/overview/ (accessed on 17 January 2020).

limited information available on the full landscape of multilateral initiatives and how they interact.'[351] This is the main reason why the previously mentioned dissemination and mapping is crucial. Furthermore, the IEA also provides the comparison of collaborative mechanisms (TCP, MI and other, regional ones, e.g. the European Technology and Innovation Platforms) using five criteria: (i) institutional framework, (ii) membership structure, (iii) sector and/or technology focus, (iv) scope and outputs of activities, and (v) cross-mechanism interactions.[352] The institutional framework marks the features of the Agreement creating the partnership (either legally binding or a forum based on a non-binding document); the membership structure underlines the territorial scope of the partnership (global/ regional, and the governmental/ non-governmental composition); the technology focus delineates the particular technology cluster being at the centre of attention (single sector/ cross-cutting); the scope of activities can include policy and market analysis, policy dialogue, network experts, knowledge transfer or project implementation; and finally whether the initiatives interact with one another directly on an institutional, political, technical level, or only occasionally.[353]

241. If we take the above criteria to describe the main partnerships under the aegis of the IEA, they can be briefly characterized by the following. The TCPs (originally called the IAs by the IEA) have been playing a key role from the beginning of the IEAs creation. These programmes are rather flexible mechanisms for the IEA members and other partner countries, as well as industries to foster cooperation, including R&D, proof-of-concept, pilot and demonstration projects, measurements and scientific exchanges. The overall thirty-nine TCPs have been established 'in response to participants' needs, whereby their structure, funding and other aspects of their research projects vary widely. They share costs and tasks, and participation is based on the equitable sharing of obligations, contributions, rights and benefits. The IEA also collects and publishes national energy R&D expenses, making it an authoritative source on public energy R&D expenditure'.[354,355] In sum, the TCPs of the IEA are based on non-binding cooperation, involving a large variety of countries with different areas of expertise (i.e., currently over six thousand experts representing three hundred public and private organizations, located in fifty-five countries around the globe), having vivid interactions through technology transfer, knowledge sharing and covering energy-related areas such as buildings, electricity,

351. IEA, *supra* n. 350.
352. *Ibid.* p. 2, *cf.* Ingrid Barnsley, Sun-Joo Ahn, *Mapping Multilateral Collaboration on Low-Carbon Energy Technologies*, IEA Insight Series, OECD/IEA (2014).
353. Barnsley, *supra* n. 353 at 15.
354. Birte Holst Jørgensen, Katrine Krogh Andersen, Elisabeth J. Wilson (eds), *DTU International Energy Report 2018 Accelerating the Clean Energy Revolution – Perspectives on Innovation Challenges*, Technical University of Denmark (May 2018), p. 11.
355. The public energy RD&D budgets and expenditures throughout various IEA countries are collected within the IEA's statistical reports. The most recent one has been published in October 2019. *See*: IEA, *Energy Technology RD&D Budgets: Overview* https://webstore.iea.org/download/direct/2776 (accessed on 20 January 2020).

industry, transport, renewable energy, fossil fuels, fusion power and cross-cutting.[356] The most innovative areas of TCP coverage are undoubtedly fusion power,[357] and the cross-cutting programmes aiming at activities relevant for multiple sectors and sources including modelling, and women's participation in clean energy.[358]

242. The activity types described in the previous sections are all part of an organic whole not only within the IEA but also within the global network of agencies, institutions and organizations oriented on energy and sustainable development in their widest sense. These activity types in their entirety reflect on particular aims, which have been indicated at the beginning of this chapter, and which will be briefly elaborated on below.

II. Activity Aims: Why All These IEA Activities?

243. As partially already referred to in Chapter 3.§3, the IEA defines its main objectives (missions) at the beginning of all their publications as follows:

- Securing access to reliable and ample supplies of all forms of energy – particularly via maintaining energy reserves for the case of disruptions (*energy access; energy security*).
- Promoting sustainable energy policies fostering economic growth and global environmental protection (*mitigation/ adaptation; energy transition*).
- Supporting cooperation in the field of technological development to secure future energy supplies and to mitigate their environmental impact, focusing primarily on

356. IEA, *Technology Collaboration: Advancing the Research, Development and Commercialisation of Energy Technologies* https://www.iea.org/areas-of-work/technology-collaboration (accessed on 16 January 2020).
357. 'The Fusion process is the same one that powers our sun (you can think of a star as one gigantic fusion reactor): hydrogen atoms forced together under immense heat and pressure break their atomic bonds, fusing into a new heavier element, helium. Some mass is lost in the process, however, and great amounts of energy are released as a result.' An International Thermonuclear Experimental Reactor (ITER) is currently under construction, supported via vast investments and RD&D efforts by multiple countries involved. *See*: Ariel Cohen, *Is Fusion Power Within Our Grasp?*, Forbes (14 January 2019) https://www.forbes.com/sites/arielcohen/2019/01/14/is-fusion-power-within-our-grasp/#29cec059bb4b (accessed on 20 January 2020). The IEA through the ESEFP TCP (Environmental Safety and Economic Aspects of Fusion Power) supports the project by providing a platform for scientists and engineers to exchange information and further enhance the collaboration coordinating international efforts to bridge the scientific and technical gaps between the International Thermonuclear Experimental Reactor (ITER) and DEMO (a proposed nuclear fusion power station that is intended to build upon the ITER experimental nuclear fusion reactor), and supporting governmental policies and raising awareness of fusion energy developments and potential to the general public. *See*: IEA, *Fusion Power* https://www.iea.org/areas-of-work/technology-collaboration/fusion-power (accessed on 20 January 2020).
358. E.g. Clean Energy Education and Empowerment (C3E TCP), Energy Technology Systems Analysis (ETSAP TCP). *See*: IEA, *Cross-cutting* https://www.iea.org/areas-of-work/technology-collaboration/cross-cutting (accessed on 17 January 2020).

energy efficiency and the implementation of low-carbon technologies (*mitigation/ adaptation; technological development*).[359]

244. These general aims have formed gradually and are a reaction to the overall development on both global energy markets and society in general. Sociological trends have a direct impact on all levels of energy utilization from production to consumption via consumer behaviour, technological advance and economic growth. The original aim of the IEA, stemming from oil security included not only the ability to promptly react on fluctuations in its supply and prices but also becoming more independent from a centralized group of hydrocarbon suppliers.[360] The new global energy context forming the above-listed main objectives was the result of emerging countries becoming huge energy consumers, climate change mainly manifesting in global warming, and the so-called 'oil peak', according to which the oil production will reach its maximum and then be on a constant decline – the length of which is difficult to predict (2035, 2040, 2050 – depending mostly on the pace of overall transition towards clean energy).[361] While in the past the remaining hydrocarbon reserves were centralized in the hands of a few countries with political background considered unstable, the current global energy map is in the process of being redrawn.[362] In particular, the US has become a major oil exporter throughout the last decade, thanks to the shale industry rapidly expanding under the Trump administration. The IEA even forecasts the US to become completely self-sufficient in energy during the 2020s.[363]

359. These objectives comply also with the four main areas of the IEA's focus: energy security, economic development, environmental awareness and engagement worldwide. International Energy Agency, *Official Website – Our Mission* https://www.iea.org/about/ourmission/ (accessed 9 August 2019).
360. Mainly from the Organization of the Petroleum Exporting Countries (hereinafter 'OPEC'), which still has a major control over the global supply and prices of crude oil on the energy markets through their decisions. Nevertheless, discovery and exploitation of alternative hydrocarbon deposits from deeper wells, thanks to newer technology reducing related costs, as well as the introduction and rapid development of renewable energy production have all contributed to a somewhat increased decentralization and diversification of energy producers. *See*: Kimberly Amadeo, *OPEC and Its Goals, Members, and History* https://www.thebalance.com/what-is-opec-its-members-and-history-3305872 (accessed 10 July 2019).
361. There is an active debate when this maximum will be reached, but the IEA has already predicted in its 2010 World Energy Outlook that crude oil production will never regain its all-time peak of 70 million barrels per day (mb/d) reached in 2006. However, although the overall oil reserves are finite, according to the same study, it is a misconception that the amount of recoverable oil is fixed, since we only have a vague notion of the amount of oil originally in place (oil that was ever in the ground). IEA, *World Energy Outlook 2010* (Organisation for Economic Co-operation and Development, International Energy Agency, 2010), pp. 48, 125.
362. *cf. Thijs Van de Graaf,* Obsolete or Resurgent? The International Energy Agency in a Changing Global Landscape, 48 Energy Policy. 233, 235 (2012).
363. John C. Hulsman, *The Shale Revolution and Donald Trump*, 4 Aspen Review 30 (2018); IEA, *United States to Lead Global Oil Supply Growth, While no Peak in Oil Demand in Sight* https://www.iea.org/newsroom/news/2019/march/united-states-to-lead-global-oil-supply-growth-while-no-peak-in-oil-demand-in-si.html (accessed 9 August 2019).

245. The current activity's aims reflect well these developments and underline the overall importance of the IEA among the other international institutions with similar missions, mainly the:

a) *International Energy Forum* – with the aim of fostering 'greater mutual understanding and awareness of common energy interests among its members' while being a 'neutral facilitator of informal, open, informed and continuing global energy dialogue' (www.ief.org).
b) *International Energy Charter* – providing a unique multilateral framework for energy cooperation, while being 'declaration of political intention aiming at strengthening energy cooperation between the signatory states and which does not bear any legally binding obligation or financial commitment' (www.energy-charter.org).
c) *Intergovernmental Panel on Climate Change (IPCC)* – created under the aegis of the World Meteorological Organization and the United Nations Environment Programme (UNEP), it provides reports, and regular assessments of the scientific basis of climate change, its impacts and future risks, and options for mitigation and adaptation; therefore unlike the IEA it focuses only on a part of its overall scope, but it does so in a more detailed way, and with similar activity types (more on https://www.ipcc.ch/about/).
d) *United Nations Framework Convention on Climate Change (UNFCCC)* – its Secretariat was established in order to support a global response to the threat of climate change; therefore, similarly to the IPCC, it also has climate change mitigation and adaptation as the main area of focus, but through facilitating negotiations between the member countries, it has also a(n) (rather) indirect impact on policy and technological development in the field of energy (mainly transition, efficiency and SDG related areas) (more on https://unfccc.int/about-us/about-the-secretariat).

246. It is rather easy to find overlaps between IEA and the above institutions; each of them could be compared to the IEA based on the five criteria outlined in section F, related to the collaboration programmes (most of them have a binding legal basis, and work on a global basis, with different, but overlapping scopes of activities, etc.). The key is to underline their interconnections, and in order to understand the IEA's place in this global governance system, we will introduce the abovementioned IEA activity aims more in detail through the lenses of particular energy sources and related technologies, all being an organic part of the IEA portfolio of operations, and stemming in the visualized heatmap in Table 2 at the very beginning of this chapter.

§2. ENERGY SOURCES: FUELS, TECHNOLOGIES AND THE IMPACT OF THE IEA'S ACTIVITIES ON THE GLOBAL ENERGY MIX

I. Coal

Overview of Coal-Related Technologies[364] in the Light of IEA Activity Aims

Related Technologies/ Fuels	*Relevant Activity Aim*
• Carbon Capture, Utilization and Storage (CCUS)	• Mitigation/ adaptation • Technological development (HELE technologies)
• Iron & Steel	• Energy transition (material efficiency) • Energy security (coal supplies) • Technological development
• Cement	• Energy transition (material efficiency) • Energy security (coal supplies)
• Methane Abatement	• Mitigation/ adaptation (reduction of GHG emissions) • Technological development

Own source based on www.iea.org.

247. As previously briefly referred to in Chapter 3.§3, energy security stems in two notions: *uninterrupted availability* and *affordable prices*. Uninterrupted availability evolves from timely investments and considering environmental impacts from a long-term perspective, as well as reactions on sudden shortages from a short-term perspective. Affordable prices on the other hand stem from the classic market mechanisms – primarily from the interaction of energy supply and demand. Although this seems to be a rather simple equation to achieve global energy security, the notion of energy security (or security of supplies) has further aspects beyond mere availability (geological element) and affordability (economic element) – i.e. accessibility (geopolitical element) and acceptability (environmental and societal element).[365]

364. Regarding these related fuels and technologies, there are overlaps between the various energy sources; therefore we are marking each of them only once within the part, where they have the largest impact and most direct connections from the perspective of their utilization.

365. Bert Kruyt, D.P. van Vuuren, H.J.M de Vries, H. Groenenberg, *Indicators for Energy Security*, 37 Energy Policy 2166, 2167 (2009).

248. In order to understand the activities of the IEA in the field of energy security in relation to coal, it is necessary to understand the role of coal in securing uninterrupted energy supply for affordable prices.

249. Coal is still one of the most important components in providing energy supply worldwide. The latest statistics do underline this, whereas the supply of energy from this source has slightly but increased compared to 1973 levels.[366] In spite of the fact that most OECD countries gradually reduced their coal production[367] and switched to more sustainable energy sources, the balance in the overall energy mix is still not tilted towards renewables and clean energy, but more towards natural gas and nuclear energy (naturally it does not mean that energy transition is not an ongoing process). The demand side of the global coal market (considering TFC) is not so different either, with overall decrease in consumption compared to 1973 levels from 13.6% to 10.5% in 2017.[368]

250. Do these statistics mean that the world is not taking the problem of carbon emissions seriously enough, despite the dangers of ecological consequences generated by climate change? Does it mean that the IEA is missing one of its aims to mitigate and adapt to these changes? Absolutely not, since the overall picture of coal production and consumption is not only the result of rapidly increasing energy demand but also the features of coal and the emission-reducing technological development in the field of carbon utilization.

251. The main advantages of coal as an energy source and the reasons why is it still a key part of the global energy mix, especially in case of developing countries, are according to the IEA CIAB[369] the following:

- Lower overall costs of generation compared, e.g., to renewables.
- Flexibility of energy generation from coal due to easy dispatching of plants and easy transport of coal as an energy source.
- Potential positive effect also on environmental impacts, due to the usage of advanced technologies – e.g., High-Efficiency Low-Emission Power plants (HELE plants),[370] Carbon Capture and Storage technologies (CCS),[371] since there is no direct trade-off between the reduction of coal usage and the increase of renewable energy in the energy mix.[372]

---

366. TPES of coal in the overall energy mix – 24.5% (1973), 27.1% (2017). A decrease of coal TPES occurred only within the OECD countries – 22.6% (1973), 15.9% (2018). IEA, *Key World Energy Statistics 2019* (Organisation for Economic Co-operation and Development, International Energy Agency, 2019).
367. While in 1973 OECD countries produced 55.6% of the total amount on a global scale, in 2018 China's coal production takes up 45.6% of the global supply, while the share of OECD countries was reduced to 22%. *Ibid.* at 16.
368. Also in this case the most significant decrease took place within OECD countries (from 10.8% in 1973 to 2.8% in 2017). However, China is the leading country also regarding the total final consumption (TFC) of coal-generated energy (20.6%) on a global scale. *Ibid.* at 35.
369. This organ of the IEA (mainly its structure) is discussed more in detail in Chapter 3.§2.I.
370. 'High-efficiency, low emissions (HELE) technologies in operation already reach a thermal efficiency of 45%, and technologies in development promise even higher values. […]Combined with

252. Due to these characteristics of coal, the global trends already have the tendency to stabilize and coexist with other clean energy sources in order to ensure worldwide energy security. Such tendencies will be crucial in coal intensive industrial segments, such as iron and steel production, and the production of cement.

253. For these purposes, and for keeping track with the development, the IEA is publishing regular statistics (e.g., *World Energy Balances 2019*, *Coal Information 2019*), tracking reports (e.g., *Tracking Clean Energy Progress (TCEP): Iron & Steel/ Cement*), and technical reports (*Material Efficiency in Clean Energy Transitions*), as well as projections (*Technology Roadmap: Low-Carbon Technology for the Indian Cement Industry*) for stakeholders to disseminate the results reached so far. This pushes policymakers and lawmakers towards creating a more and more efficient regulatory framework on a national and multinational level to ensure sustainability of coal-based energy generation.

II. Natural Gas

Table 3 Overview of (Natural)[373] Gas-Related Technologies in the Light of IEA Activity Aims

Related Technologies/Fuels	*Relevant Activity Aim*
• Heating	• Energy security (natural gas supplies) • Mitigation/ adaptation (energy efficiency)
• Chemicals	• Technological development • Energy security (natural gas supplies) • Mitigation/ adaptation (reducing GHG emissions via catalytic processes)

CCS, HELE technologies can cut CO2 emissions from coal-fired power generation plants by as much as 90%, to less than 100 grams per kilowatt-hour. HELE technologies will be an influential factor in the deployment of CCS.' *See*: IEA, *Technology Roadmap – High-Efficiency, Low-Emissions Coal-Fired Power Generation* https://www.iea.org/reports/technology-roadmap-high-efficiency-low-emissions-coal-fired-power-generation (accessed on 6 January 2020).

371. IEA, *supra* n. 253.

372. CIAB, *The Role of Coal for Energy Security in World Regions*, https://thecoalhub.com/wp-content/uploads/attach_168.pdf (accessed 22 November 2019).

373. The reference to gas into this part has to be taken in a broader sense than just natural gas, because also biogas is becoming an energy source to be taken into consideration when it comes to energy transition, naturally with the complementary evolution of GHG emission-reducing technologies. *See*: IEA Energy Technology Network, *Task 37: Energy from Biogas* http://task37.ieabioenergy.com/about-task-37.html (accessed on 20 January 2020).

Own source based on www.iea.org.

254. Compared to other fossil fuels, natural gas is the cleanest burning one currently on the rise, and covering almost one-third of the global energy demand. Its demand is still on the rise; according to the IEA's related fuel report in 2019, it has risen by 4.6% compared to 2018. The two most important issues regarding this are maintaining competitive prices with other energy sources – mainly coal – and the constant efforts of reducing GHG (mainly methane) emissions on the way to clean energy transition.[374]

255. The transition from coal to natural gas, mainly in the electricity generation sector, is a constantly ongoing process, which has already lead to a total reduction of CO_2 released into the atmosphere by almost 700 million tons in the past ten years, mainly due to the transition processes in the US and China. Burning natural gas in general releases less CO_2 than coal – understandably, therefore the trends from switching from one energy source to another cleaner one appear to be a worthy investment, especially from a sustainability point of view contributing also to the fight against climate change.[375] The aim of mitigation and adaptation together with supporting the necessary technological development introducing innovative new processes[376] has the potential lead to an enhanced speed of energy transition securing energy for the constantly increasing coal demand of these industries.

256. However, this transition process does not have equal conditions everywhere. While in Europe and in the US it can be done with relatively low costs, since most of the existing coal firing power plants are more than 40 years old and require significant upgrades in order to comply with the present standards – not only environmental but also regarding efficiency and safety. Therefore, the costs of switching to natural gas do not exceed significantly the costs of the necessary modernization. In comparison, e.g. in China, India and other emerging economies, the investments have been aiming also on the development of the coal sectors. Especially China built multiple plants in the past decade, which did not yet fulfil their expected investment returns, and therefore pumping additional resources into a completely new sector would induce considerably higher costs in general. In spite of this, recent studies particularly in the case of China predict the development of the natural gas

---

374. IEA, *Gas 2019* https://www.iea.org/reports/market-report-series-gas-2019 (accessed on 20 January 2020).

375. IEA, *The Role of Gas in Today's Energy Transitions* https://webstore.iea.org/download/direct/2819?fileName=TheRoleofGas.pdf (accessed on 20 January 2020).

376. In particular catalytic processes in relation to the chemical and petrochemical industries are worth mentioning. These catalyst and related process improvements could reduce energy intensity for these products by 20% to 40% as a whole by 2050 combining all scenarios. *See*: IEA, *Technology Roadmap – Energy and GHG Reductions in the Chemical Industry via Catalytic Processes* https://www.iea.org/reports/technology-roadmap-energy-and-ghg-reductions-in-the-chemical-industry-via-catalytic-processes (accessed on 19 January 2020).

industry and increased consumption of this fuel type.[377] Besides the model predictions, another reason for natural gas to be still considered a 'bridge fuel' during the energy transition process – mainly in the generation of electricity – is natural gas being relatively cheap compared, e.g., to renewables, and less ecologically intensive energy source compared to coal and oil, but sticking to it for too long might result in other cleaner technologies catching up in becoming more cost-effective.[378]

257. In order to monitor these trends in market and technological development – mainly the sufficient supplies of natural gas for increasing global demand and the RD&D activities related to the reduction of GHG emissions – the IEA regularly publishes natural gas-related reports, while keeping track on the process of energy transition (e.g., *Tracking Fuel Supply*, *The Role of Gas in Today's Energy Transitions* and others).[379]

III. Oil

Overview of Oil-Related Technologies in the Light of IEA Activity Aims

Related Technologies/ Fuels	*Relevant Activity Aim*
• Transport (Aviation, Rail, Trucks & Buses)	• Mitigation/ adaptation (reducing GHG emissions) • Energy transition (usage of clean energy) • Energy security (enhanced oil recovery) • Technological development (energy efficiency)
• Petrochemicals	• Technological development (clean solutions) • Energy security (enhanced oil recovery)

Own source based on www.iea.org.

377. 'When using static and dynamic scenario analyses to predict natural gas consumption in China based on the best predictive model, we find that the seasonal effect of natural gas consumption under the 'rapid growth' regime is obvious, and gas consumption may be remain in this regime for a long time to come.' *See*: Ting Liang, Jian Chai, Yue-Jun Zhang, Zhe George Zhan, *Refined Analysis and Prediction of Natural Gas Consumption in China*, 4 Journal of Management Science and Engineering 91, 103 (2019).
378. *Cf.* Kenneth W. Costello, *Why Natural Gas has an Uncertain Future,* 30 The Electricity Journal 18-22 (2017).
379. The full list of the main publications related to natural gas is available at https://www.iea.org/fuels-and-technologies/gas.

258. The oil market is undergoing significant changes recently, which is also a part of the gradual energy transition process and all the efforts being made for reaching the sustainability goals in the upcoming decade(s). This is not only tangible in the shift from the IEAs original activities (responding on emergency throughout the global oil markets, mainly reflecting in its price fluctuations (we have previously analysed these activities of the IEA throughout Chapters 2 and 3.§3.I.A), but also within the shift in increased oil demands from developed to developing countries of emerging economies, as well as from other industries to transportation and petrochemicals (as indicated in Table 3). Aviation, rail transport, trucks and buses are all using oil and oil products, but changes in used fuels are visible also in these segments of the transport sector.

259. In fact, the outlook for oil demand varies dramatically depending on the basis which particular scenario are we applying for our predictions (*see* §1.I.C Projections). 'Under the Stated Policies Scenario, oil use in passenger cars peaks in the late 2020s and during the 2030s demand increases by only 0.1 mb/d on average each year. However there is no definitive peak in oil use overall, as there are continued increases in petrochemicals, trucks and the shipping and aviation sectors. In contrast, in the Sustainable Development Scenario, determined policy interventions lead to a peak in global oil demand within the next few years. Demand falls by more than 50% in advanced economies between 2018 and 2040 and by 10% in developing economies.'[380]

260. On the other hand, staying more in the field of realities and moving away from projections, although oil is on the decline as an energy source, technologies for better utilization are still contributing to energy security to some level. One of these, even if in a very limited range, is Enhanced Oil Recovery (EOR) as part of CCUS, which barely makes any headlines, but is still on the radar of the IEA's scope of activity aims.[381]

261. The IEA through its activity types makes crucial efforts regarding this sector too, shaping raw information into highly relevant factual conclusions and recommendations, reaching far beyond securing sufficient oil supplies for IEA members.[382]

IV. Nuclear

262. Nuclear energy is a rather controversial source of energy since the existence of our postmodern world, but one of the largest contributors to clean energy

380. IEA, *World Energy Outlook 2019 (Oil)* https://www.iea.org/reports/world-energy-outlook-2019/oil#abstract (accessed on 21 January 2020).
381. *See*: Christophe McGlade, Glenn Sondak, Mei Han, *Whatever Happened to Enhanced Oil Recovery?* https://www.iea.org/commentaries/whatever-happened-to-enhanced-oil-recovery (accessed on 20 January 2020).
382. The full list of the main publications related to natural gas is available at https://www.iea.org/fuels-and-technologies/oil.

generation. Although these controversies largely slow the process of its development down, currently there are 452 nuclear reactors in operation worldwide. Their main benefit can be summarized as follows: 'Nuclear power plants contribute to electricity security in multiple ways. Nuclear plants help to keep power grids stable and can be a good complement in decarbonisation strategies since, to a certain extent, they can adjust their operations to follow demand and supply shifts. As the share of variable renewables like wind and solar photovoltaics (PV) rises, the need for such services will increase.'[383] Furthermore, nuclear energy can also play a key role in the energy transition process, and that is why it is worth underlining that the IEA's activities also cover this particular area.

263. Furthermore, although whole publications can be and are made on this topic, and it is not the aim of the current chapter to analyse it more in detail, we would like to emphasize the importance of the NEA,[384] similarly to the IEA operating also under the aegis of the OECD in close mutual cooperation, but with an understandably much more narrow scope. The scope of activities of the NEA covers not only technology and regulation of nuclear power, safety, nuclear waste management, nuclear law but also sustainable development, where its activities mostly overlap with the ones of the IEA. Regarding the types of activities, they are also similar to the ones described above in relation to the IEA – policy recommendation, reporting, monitoring, statistical analyses, etc.[385]

264. Similar activities and cooperation between organizations with various scopes – like in the case of the IEA and NEA – strongly foster, and basically double the efficiency of nuclear power development (e.g., via TCPs, data sharing and knowledge dissemination, or even technology transfer).[386] Consequently, the global energy scene needs to decide whether to enhance its utilization in spite of the risks and dangers, or to look for safer alternatives, like renewables.

383. IEA, *Nuclear* https://www.iea.org/fuels-and-technologies/nuclear (accessed on 20 January 2020). All the related publications (reports, statistics, comments and news) can be found here too.

384. *See also* Chapter 3, §11.

385. *See*: NEA, *Official Website* https://www.oecd-nea.org/general/about/ (accessed on 20 January 202 0).

386. *See also* the heatmap provided as Table 2.

V. Renewables and Electricity Generation

265.

Overview of Renewable and Electricity-Related Technologies in the Light of IEA Activity Aims

• Biofuels	• Mitigation/ adaptation • Technological development • Energy transition
• Energy Storage	• Energy transition • Energy security (energy integration)
• Wind & Solar	• Mitigation/ adaptation • Technological development • Energy transition
• Pulp & Paper	• Mitigation/ adaptation (energy efficiency) • Energy security (electricity supplies)
• Hydrogen	• Mitigation/ adaptation • Energy transition • Energy access • Technological development (water electrolysis deployment)

Own source based on www.iea.org.

266. The two most important resources closely interconnected and playing a crucial role on today's energy markets, influencing everything from RD&D, through investments, all the way to tackling climate change are: renewables and the electricity, which is generated from them.

267. We have decided to analyse these in the light of the IEAs aims, due to the fact that their relation is of energy source and energy itself and while electricity can be generated basically from all the other energy sources (i.e., combustible), the utilization of renewables on the other hand serves mainly serves this purpose (e.g., coal, natural gas and oil can be also utilized as heating materials and inputs for the transport industry among others, while electricity and therefore renewables have a rather narrow scope of use therein).

268. Currently, the global share of renewables in electricity generation is around 26%, which means that renewables have quickly become the most rapidly evolving segment of the energy market, with constantly reducing costs and becoming more and more competitive with the rest of the energy mix components and also have a key role in the energy transition processes.[387]

269. In spite of the fact that there is scepticism regarding the complete transformation of the energy markets being dependent on renewables, arguing against these sources being fluctuant and unstable, therefore rather easier to use as fill-in complementary energy sources, they are still critical in overcoming environmental degradation and securing a sustainable future.[388] The IEA takes on a difficult, but undoubtedly necessary burden to promote these energy sources and constantly provide evidence – based on statistics, development trends and research results – that renewables, in spite of their barriers and limitations, can be the future of electricity generation and society does not have to depend on fossil fuels until their complete depletion.

270. Naturally, these efforts of the IEA are not boundless and are not trying to overly accelerate the process of transition pushing energy markets and RD&D activities into a dead-end of overpromising and under-delivering. Such pressure would create a vacuum in which other industry segments cannot catch up with, e.g. vast investing into building renewable energy-related infrastructure.

271. In sum renewables and electricity have a real chance to become the change the energy world has been looking for in the past fifty years, and the activities of the IEA can make a huge contribution to it hand in hand with all the initiatives paving the way for sustainability and clean energy utilization for the sake of the planet.

---

387. IEA, *Renewables* https://www.iea.org/fuels-and-technologies/renewables (accessed on 21 January 2020). The main publications on the topic are also available here.
388. *cf.* Patrick Moriarty, Damon Honnery, *Can Renewable Energy Power the Future?*, 93 Energy Policy 3-7 (2016).

Chapter 5. Finance

272. The IEA undertakes a wide range of activities,[389,390] which have been enlarged with the passing of years. This organization was initially designed in order to help countries in the field of oil supply, after the crisis of 1973/74.[391] Its founding treaty aimed at drawing emergency measures to react to oil crises. It coordinated the energy policies of its twenty-eight member countries, which derive from the OECD. Such a treaty is defined as the I.E.P. Agreement, which dates back to 1974. This document is a treaty under international law. It made clear the elements of the Agency and its goals. More specifically, the IEA mission dealt with three key commitments for its member countries: first, they had to maintain national oil reserves, set at ninety-day worth of net oil imports; second, a programme of demand restraint measures equal to 7% and 10% of national oil consumption was required; and third the member countries had to participate in an oil allocation system if necessary in a severe emergency. From that original aim, the IEA activities have focused on many other issues linked to energy more in general, such as energy efficiency, renewable technologies, access to energy. The focus has substantially expanded a lot. Consequently, the IEA evolved even more and embraced new fields like the environmental protection and economics, with still exerting a high pressure on those related to energy security. Such a change of the Agency is obviously linked to a change of the geopolitical landscape itself. First of all, it has to be noticed that new energy consumers have emerged (especially China and India). While in 1974, around 63% of global oil consumption was focused on the IEA Member States, it has decreased to about 38%. Second, another change has occurred from 1974: back then the IEA was the only multilateral energy organization, while nowadays the international landscape is enriched by other institutions.[392] Global dialogue with non-IEA countries and international organizations now represents a core activity of the IEA. This is made clear by the fact that an entire article of the IEP Agreement specifically deals with relations with other entities.[393] Third, the electricity sector is experiencing a transformation, especially because of the big issue of climate

389. The structure of the IEA is well described at: https://www.iea.org/about/structure/; the Energy technology RD&D Budgets 2019 is available at: https://webstore.iea.org/energy-technology-rdd-budgets-2019-overview accessed 13 April 2019.

390. These activities derive from the IEA goals defined in its mission at: https://www.iea.org/about/ourmission/ accessed 13 April 2019.

391. As in many other fields, the knowledge of the roots of the Agency is of extreme interest in order to understand the context. *See*: https://www.iea.org/about/history/ accessed 13 April 2019 *See also*: Jacoby KD (2009) Energy Security: Conceptualization of the International Energy Agency (IEA). In: Brauch H.G. et al. (eds) Facing Global Environmental Change. Hexagon Series on Human and Environmental Security and Peace, vol 4. Springer, Berlin, Heidelberg.

392. Florini & Sovacool, *supra* n. 275 at 5239-5248; Ann Florini and Navroz Dubash, *Introduction to the Special Issue: Governing Energy in a Fragmented World,* 2(S1) Global Policy 1-5 (2011); Jeff Colgan, Robert O. Keohane, Thijs Van de Graaf, *Punctuated Equilibrium in the Energy Regime Complex,* 7(2) The Review of International Organizations 117-143 (2012).

393. According to Art. 63 of the Agreement on an International Energy Program, 'In order to achieve the objectives of the Program, the Agency may establish appropriate relations with non-participating countries, international organisations, whether governmental or non-governmental, other entities and individuals.'

change.[394] All these facts considered, the IEA has faced a sort of internal crisis and it had to struggle to uphold its leading position in the global energy governance. It is interesting to know that this crisis was also confirmed in 2009 by the American Secretary of State Henry Kissinger who said '*the IEA now stands at a critical juncture. [The] world has changed considerably since 1973. In order to be effective in this new landscape the IEA must be prepared to evolve with* it'.[395] A rethink of the IEA role was clearly necessary. Moreover, it is worth noting that the extra value of the IEA lies in its flexible nature. The gradual expansion of the institution beyond the original energy security goal represents a key element of the IEA.[396] Furthermore, the variety of issues investigated by the IEA opens up to a potential cooperation with the EU, especially considering that twenty out of thirty IEA countries are also part of the EU.[397]

273. According to the *WEO* 2018, IEA policies will enhance the 'reliability, affordability and sustainability of energy' of its member countries. Four are the main areas of interest: energy security, economic development, environmental awareness and engagement worldwide.[398] More concretely, the IEA nowadays monitors the market of energy sources (such as oil, gas and renewables); it conducts research and provides policy advice and works along with other international bodies, like IRENA, and other institutions.

274. The operability of the IEA is based on the founding treaty (the I.E.P. Agreement), the Programmes of Work, programme decisions made by the Governing Board and the necessary adjustments to meet new developments.[399]

275. The Programmes of Work are of huge importance: all the particular activities planned by the IEA for a period of time are compiled in a Programme of Work. Decisions are taken by the Governing Board, whose financial and personnel decisions are then formally approved by the OECD Council.[400] The Governing Board has not only internal power (concerning the Agency policy and its organization) but also decides over the external influence of the Agency (the member countries' commitments and the admission of new potential members). This important Board is described in Articles 50 and 51 of the I.E.P. Agreement. According to Article 51, it adopts 'decisions and recommendations which are necessary for the proper functioning of the Program'[401] and also 'shall review periodically and take appropriate

394. Anna Collins, *The Climate Change Crisis*, Lucent Press 2019; the importance of Climate Change is proven by the fact that in 2015 the WEO released a Special Report on Energy and Climate Change, and a related Special Briefing for COP21 in October 2015.
395. Kissinger, *supra* n. 141.
396. Graaf and Lesage, *supra* n. 34 at 302.
397. Slovenia, Croatia, Cyprus, Malta, Estonia, Latvia, Romania and Bulgaria are the EU Member States which do not belong to the IEA.
398. The Agency goals are available at: https://www.iea.org/media/about/IEASharedGoals.pdf accessed 13 April 2019.
399. Richard Scott, *The History of the International Energy Agency, 1974-1994 Volume I Origins and Structure* (OECD/IEA 1994), 276.
400. Scott, *supra* n. 185 at 1-56.
401. I.E.P. Agreement, Art. 50.1.

action concerning developments in the international energy situation, including problems relating to the oil supplies of any Participating Country of Countries, and the economic and monetary implications of this development'.[402] The Governing Board also focused on the external dimension, Article 51 follows underlining that it shall take into consideration the competence and activities of international institutions potentially influencing economic and monetary questions. It has the power to make binding decisions[403] but also recommendations.[404]

276. Concerning the structure of the Governing Body, it is composed of the energy ministers of the member countries or their delegates.[405] It usually holds four times per year in order to discuss global energy trends and future activities. Every two years there is the IEA Ministerial: a different configuration of the Governing Body. Duty of this meeting is to set broad strategic priorities. In particular, the Secretariat has to develop new ideas and plans for new work Programmes to be presented to committees and Standing Groups. The method adopted by the Governing Board is usually by consensus or majority. The voting system[406] is quite complex: on the one hand there are general voting weights (every member country has three votes) and on the other hand there are additional voting weights which date back to the net oil imports of 1973.[407] According to the I.E.P. Agreement, a majority is met with 60% of general voting weights of the countries and 50% of the combined voting deriving from both the general ones and the oil-based voting weights. In some cases unanimity is strictly necessary. For example, it is required to change the voting weights, the scale of financial contributions and the revision of the I.E.P. Agreement. In other specific cases, the Governing Board has to achieve special majorities.[408] To practically concretize the planned activities in the Programme of Work, the IEA recourses to a Budget to decide on the appropriation of funds for carrying out these activities. It as well decides on the means of obtaining and collecting these funds. The Programmes of Work and Budget, which is the size of the IEA Budget and the scope of its work, are determined every two years by the IEA member countries. Being established as an autonomous body within the OECD, the IEA works within the financial framework of the OECD. In fact, the OECD Council Decision on the Establishment of the IEA was the first to provide provisions related to the finance and budget. Particularly, Article 10(a) of the said Council Decision provides the following:

> The budget of the Agency shall form part of the Budget of the Organisation and expenditure of the Agency shall be charged against the appropriations

402. I.E.P. Agreement, Art. 50.1.
403. I.E.P. Agreement, Art. 52.1.
404. I.E.P. Agreement Art. 52.2.
405. I.E.P. Agreement, Art. 50.1.
406. Agreement on an International Energy Program (as amended 17 February 2018), Arts 61 and 62.
407. *See Annex for a full list of voting weights.*
408. Depending on the type of action, the special majority required can be either 75/84 general voting weights (i.e., 89% of IEA member countries) or 63/84 of general voting weights and 60% of the combined (total) voting weights.

authorised for it under Part II of the Budget which shall include appropriate Budget estimates and provisions for all expenditure necessary for the operation of the Agency. (…)

277. According to the I.E.P. Agreement, the Governing Board has total powers over the financing of the Agency and its internal financing administration. By analysing Article 64 of the I.E.P., it is clear that the Agency depends on the Member States' contributions. The scale of contribution can be modified only by the Governing Board through unanimity.[409]As described in Article 64.3 of the I.E.P., the Board has the duty to make financial regulations for the Agency, but this rarely happens. The general rule adopted by the Agency is that the OECD refers to the OECD Financial Regulations when making transactions for the IEA. However, the Governing Board has always the power to adopt financial regulations or taking other decisions.

278. To put it briefly, the IEA is funded primarily by its member countries on the basis of their economic weight. In addition, it relies on additional voluntary contributions and grants, as well as ancillary resources through IEA publications and statistics as will be detailed below. The Program, Budget and financing institutional mechanisms are further elaborated in this chapter.

§1. IEA BUDGET AND THE SCOPE

279. The IEA Budget cannot be explained without discussing the Programme of Work whereby the IEA Budget and the Programmes of Work accompany each other.[410] Obviously, since the Budget derives from the decisions taken regarding the activities planned, its draft begins once the Programme of Work is at least defined with basic lines. The Budgets of the IEA are essential for financing and proving operational instruments to effectively implement the Programmes of Work. Consequently, the IEA seeks to prepare and adopt both the Programme of Work and the Budget in a coherent and realistic way. For this reason, there is an extremely strict and evident nexus between the IEA activities, its budget and the fundings at the base of the resources allocation. The IEA structure of the presentation of the Programmes of Work and its financing follows the OECD scheme. Both the Programme of Work and the Budget are under the control of the Governing Board which decides over them and all the financial issues concerning the IEA administration. To get an idea of the *quantum*, consider that the annual budget defined for 2018 is EUR 27,849,686.[411]

280. In order to understand the link between these two activities, an analysis of the Programmes of Work is first necessary. The Programmes of Work define the

409. I.E.P. Agreement, Art. 64.1.
410. Scott, *supra* n. 400 at 285.
411. The IEA 2018 budget is available at: https://www.iea.org/about/structure/ accessed 13 April 2019.

lines of work of the Agency. They have a double nature: on the one side there is a policy approach, while on the other side the perspective adopted is basically pragmatic.

281. Concerning the pragmatic side of the programmes, the activities of the year to come are listed. These activities are described in detail and labelled as 'Core', by which it is meant a key activity, or 'Other'. For each activity, an estimated number of staff per months is attributed. The description is particularly detailed: crossing activities are defined and tabular presentations to give an idea of the necessary effort are included. A fundamental concept concerning this topic needs to be kept in mind: even if this kind of level of description is considered very important, there is always the possibility to change these activities because of a change of circumstances and/or priorities. This happens because the Programmes of Work are flexible tools. They try to better identify the real needs of the following two years and, in case of repenting changes, they have to be ready to be aligned with the current necessity.

282. Furthermore, there can be an influence by the members, which are often invited to meet in 'brainstorming' sessions regarding specific topics. Their contribution can come through both official and unofficial communications to the Secretariat.[412]

283. The Governing Board[413] of the IEA is vested with the legislative powers on financial matters pursuant to the I.E.P. Agreement. In other words, it is the institutional organ of the IEA. It has been defined by the OECD Council Decision on the Establishment of the Agency as 'the body from which all acts of the agency derive'.[414]

284. Article 64 of the I.E.P. Agreement provides that the Governing Board adopts the Budget suggested by the Executive Director, and it shall take all the necessary financial decisions with respect to the financial administration of the IEA.[415] Having said that, it appears that the Governing Body has the autonomous power to decide and regulate the IEA's financial policy and administration and take the decisions necessary for the effective implementation.

285. On the Governing Board's first meeting in November 1974, the first organ to be established was the Committee on Budget and Expenditure (commonly referred to as the 'IEA Budget Committee'), pursuant to Article 10(a) of the OECD Decision, with a primary purpose to 'advise the Governing Board as required on the

412. Scott, *supra* n. 400 at 283.
413. The Governing Board is made up of one or more ministers or their delegates of the Member States of the IEA.
414. Art. 4 of the OECD Council Decision on the Establishment of the Agency.
415. Agreement on an International Energy Program (as amended 17 February 2018), Art. 64.

financial administration of the IEA and to give its opinion on the annual and other budget proposals submitted to the Governing Board'.[416]

286. The IEA Budget Committee is one of the three permanent and plenary Committees of the IEA established by the Governing Board. The establishment of this Budgetary Committee (BC) not independent from the OECD Budget committee was found essential so that this BC would set all its focus on the IEA's financial business and the financial means necessary to reach its objectives along with any problems it might tackle within its operations.[417] This Committee has met twice per year while some informal meetings have been held, at the request of the Executive Director, in order to face particular administrative and financial issues.

287. The role of the Executive Director, head of the IEA Secretariat,[418] is also of particular importance; it assists the Governing Board. It has a considerable influence on the financial life of the IEA. Among his tasks, the Executive Director develops proposals, suggests recommendations and participates in the processes leading up to the adoption of financial decisions and the Budget. As previously underlined, the Budget has an interconnection with the Programme of Work. Actually, it is the financial institution for realizing the Programme of Work and it has clear implications on it. For that reason, the Budget and the Programme of Work are planned together and accompanied together for submission and adoption by the Governing Board. Their preparation shall be coherent, realistic, careful and thorough to ensure balance between them for an effective and economic IEA work execution. Their adoption is necessary to allow the IEA a smooth progress in clear activities with budgetary appropriations in place and identified financing.

288. It has to be noticed that while the size of the IEA and its scope are determined every two years, the IEA refers to the financial framework of the OECD. This means that the OECD Council gives a Supreme Audit Institution of a member country the duty to operate as independent external auditing of the IEA account and financial management. More in general, this means that the IEA has full agency but, in the meanwhile, both the IEA and the OECD contributes to the other.[419] Upon the reasons of why the IEA was established under the OECD is to be provided by an institutional 'home' governed primarily by the I.E.P. Agreement, and benefit from sophisticated and effective logistical support necessary to carry its functions.[420] Notwithstanding the foregoing, the IEA enjoys autonomy. Yet, the IEA has adopted, to

416. Decision of the OECD Council Establishing an International Energy Agency of the Organisation (adopted by the Council at its 373rd Meeting on 15th November 1974. The Delegates for Finland, France and Greece abstained).
417. Scott, *supra* n. 400 at 239.
418. Agreement on an International Energy Program (as amended 17 February 2018), Arts 59 and 60.
419. Craig S. Bamberger, *The History of the International Energy Agency, 1974-1994 The First 30 Years, Supplement to Volumes I, II & III* (OECD/IEA 2004), 129.
420. Scott, *supra* n. 400 at 129.

a large extent, the practices of the OECD with respect to the format and presentation of the financing arrangements in addition to the Programmes of Work.[421]

I. Scope of the Budget and the Programme of Work

289. The IEA needed a widget for determining the span of activities to be applied during each segment of time. Although any IEA action could emanate from the I.E.P. Agreement, this latter is deemed very wide as it only sets the broad programme of the IEA. Some major detailed decisions throughout the mandate of the IEA have been adopted to develop some objectives set out in the I.E.P. Agreement, like the Long-Term Co-operation Program. Still, the domain of the stated programme and decisions remains vast. The IEA could not really find in them a support for carrying out activities and implementing the core fundament of the IEA, i.e. promoting energy security.

290. The above among other things derived the need for the IEA to determine periodically the specific particular activities to be undertaken in order to attain its objectives and implement the broad I.E.P. Agreement along with the ancillary decisions. Therefore, the practice of elaborating an extensive Programme of Work that would itemize every operation the IEA shall conduct has been built. The Programme of Work is not explicitly mentioned in any statutory reference. Though, it could be stemmed from Article 51 of the I.E.P. Agreement. This article, focused on the Governing Board, includes the duty to adopt decisions that are necessary for the proper functioning of the IEA programme. The preparation of the Programme of Work usually commences and takes thirteen months before the relevant financial year. During this preparation period, which is crucial, the Programme of Work is discussed and activities are prioritized, so as to reflect on appropriation decisions, and identifying activities that might be eliminated if certain levels of resources of the Budget, for instance, were unavailable.[422] In the IEA Ministerial Meeting, which is held once every two years, the Programme of Work is discussed between the Secretariat and IEA standing groups and committees. Ultimately, a draft Programme of Work is submitted to the Governing Board for his approval. In the debate on the draft Programme of Work, pillars for modernizing the actions of the IEA are discussed. At this stage, the IEA is most likely to use the innovation IEA policy that is the vehicle employed to bring changes and adaptation to the present circumstances at the time. For instance, and by virtue of such policy, the sustainable economic development into the substantive work of the IEA was introduced. Once the Programme of Work is adopted by the Governing Board, it is transmitted to the OECD for information purposes only. The Programme of Work constitutes an element of authorization for effectuating the IEA activities.

421. The Programme of Work usually sets a, *inter alia*, summary of the main points of work to be undertaken annually and details particular activities. The Programme of Work as well provides the elements of policy and operational context, and any changes with respect to the personnel or the organization, or even the IEA activities each year.

422. Bamberger, *supra* n. 420 at 101.

291. Every draft Budget contains extremely specific details (from appropriations for staff, operating expenditures, documents) and defines the financial analysis, underlining the Secretariat's requests. They are formally presented in the same document and include a comparison with the Budget of the previous year. The report of the Budget Committee is attached (Attachment A),[423] while the core budgetary part of the documents is included in Attachment B. This Attachment is particularly technical with a table (Table I) outlining the authorizations for every item included in the Budget. It can be said that Table I represents the core of the Budget, including a comparison with the data of the previous year and the final decisions proposed for the year. Every draft Budget contains extremely specific details (from appropriations for staff, operating expenditures, documents) and defines the financial analysis, underlining the Secretariat's requests.

§2. Adoption of the Budget

292. The Budget attributes the necessary appropriations to the planned activities for the functioning of the Agency. Since the establishment of the IEA and the adoption of the concept of Programmes of Work and Budget, there have been several significant changes and developments introduced on different levels and particularly during the third decade of its establishments. Consequently, these changes affected the procedures and formation of the Programme of Work and Budget. Traditionally and pursuant to the OECD Council Decision on the Establishment of the IEA, Article 10 (b), and the I.E.P. Agreement, Article 64.3, IEA's Budget used to be adopted on an annual basis and by the majority vote, pursuant to the I.E.P. Agreement majority requirement, although the Budget used to be adopted particularly during the first two decades almost always by consensus. Consensus was important and made voting easier as the voting rules as set forth in the I.E.P. Agreement were considered very complex particularly that they are not counted as 'one country, one vote'.[424] Instead, the voting weight was assigned for the IEA Member State, according, to a certain extent, to the oil consumption figures of 1973. This has led over the years for a call to change the way voting rights were allocated to at least reflect more up-to-date figures, and include other criteria.[425]

293. Before these changes, the procedure to adopt the Budget relied on a draft from the IEA Administrative Unit, in coordination with the Office of the Deputy Executive Director. The first step consisted in the approval by the Executive Director. The Budget was then joined with the Programme of Work in order to be given to Delegations by 1 October of each year. A discussion between the Executive Director and the Energy Advisors in Delegation followed. The draft was then put under the attention of the Budget Committee. During the next meeting, held in November, the Committee analysed the Budget Items, the planned financial tripartition and the additional resources to cover unexpected expenditure of the previous

423. Attachment A includes also projects, conferences, workshops and seminars organized by the IEA.
424. Graaf and Lesage, *supra* n. 34 at 306.
425. *Ibid.*

year.[426] Recommendations and observations to the Governing Board could also be made. The Budget Committee also considered the general financial administration in relation to the ability of the Secretariat to provide the necessary changes in the case of new challenges and situations. The Secretariat, as already highlighted, should always keep the pace in the ever-changing landscape of the Agency.

294. In some situations, one or even more members show their disapproval on particular issues, underlining their decision to reserve their positions. In similar cases, the Secretariat usually tries to find a bilateral compromise, with the goal of presenting the draft to the Governing Board with the widest consensus. After all these steps, the Governing Board starts a deep reviewing process.

295. In December, the drafts were considered in relation to the Secretariat's proposals and the Budget Committee's report. The approved draft Budget was then put under the attention of the OECD Council for adoption into Part II of the OECD Budget.

296. It is worth noting that this transmission to the OECD Council has nothing to do with the idea of a formal adoption. Since the decision by the OECD Council is taken after the agreement by the IEA members, this step has mainly an *informative* nature.[427] Such a formality represents a sort of confirmation of the relationship between the IEA and the OECD, as described in Article 10 (a) of the Council Decision which establishes the IEA. The deadline by which the Programmes of Work and Budget should be confirmed is December 31 of the previous year. In this way the IEA could start the new year adapting all the necessary things to the circumstances and to the annual goals. Hence, the Budget was confirmed in early December. Although consensus was not required,[428] the Budget is usually approved by consensus. Regarding Article 10 (a), it states that 'each participating country's share in financing such expenditure shall be fixed by the Governing Board'.[429]

297. It is necessary to highlight that, during the last decades, some changes have occurred in relation to the Programme of Work and Budget. Most of the Member States had to face internal fiscal difficulties, with obvious consequences also on the Agency dynamics. A general demand for more transparency has also arisen. As a response, some changes have been adopted.

426. This sort of unexpected expenditure often occurs, e.g., due to a bigger demand for publications by the Agency.
427. To better understand the informative nature of this transmission, consider this example of 1994, according to which 'the Agency's Programme of Work [IEA/GB(93) 44, Annex I and Corrigendum] is hereby transmitted to the Council *for information*; and the Agency's 1994 Budget [IEA/GB(93)63, Attachment B and Corrigendum] is hereby submitted to the Council for *adoption*' [emphasis added]'.
428. According to Art. 64.3, a simple majority of 60% of the total combined voting weights and 50% of the general voting weights is sufficient to get the Budget approved.
429. Craig S. Bamberger, *The History of the International Energy Agency, 1974-1994 Volume I Origins and Structure* (OECD/IEA 1994), 295.

298. First of all, the traditional consensus has been overcome in 1994. On that occasion, the Budget was adopted by the necessary majority, rather than by consensus. This result was due to the vote of some member countries, which wanted the Budget to be close to the rate of inflation in France. The entire mechanism of the Programme of Work, after all, had been criticized before that year.[430] As a consequence, the Governing Board decided to review the item in order to approve the Programme of Work and the Budget of the Agency.[431] This review was based on the goals to secure more transparency along with representing a demonstration of the flexible nature of the Agency. Objects of this review were: whether the two tools (the Programme of Work and the Budget) should be more integrated with each other; the possibility of anticipating the process of drafting; the opportunity of medium-term goals by introducing biennial tools (rather than annual); considering the opportunity of giving more importance to the Standing Groups and Committees and the idea of giving them budget envelopes. Moreover, in that occasion a new calendar was put under attention.[432] This calendar was endorsed.[433]

299. The Secretariat then wrote a note[434] with a draft concerning the new item to adopt both the Programme of Work and the Budget of the Agency. This proposal was adopted by the Governing Board, which, once again, confirmed its objectives, increased the level of transparency and information of the procedure and also the level of integration between the two tools. These new procedures were basically inspired by the idea to avoid excessive bureaucracy and assuring a good level of flexibility. This important principle was orientated to the idea that the Secretariat, in case of a change of circumstances, had to report to the Governing Board as soon as possible, including the proper Committees and Standing Groups. The Budget, during that analysis, was decided to remain on an annual basis but a medium-term perspective was included for the first time in the Agency mechanisms. A medium-term strategy was established to be adopted every four years. Such a change represented an extremely valuable step in the perspective of a new form of strategy by the Agency. Planning with a medium-term horizon opens to new opportunities and considerations.

---

430. In 1993, the Secretariat reported the opinions of some delegations which had asked for reviewing the phases of preparation and monitoring the Programme of Work and Budget of the IEA. As a response, the Governing Board confirmed in that occasion its new goal for the year to come (1994) of looking into the Budget preparation. *See*: IEA/GB(93)65, Item 2(f)(xviii).
431. *See*: IEA/GB(94)15.
432. According to this new proposal, the first discussion was planned to be in June; the month of July was supposed to be dedicated to the draft circulation and the final consideration was planned for the month of September.
433. IEA/GB(94)25, Item 5. Moreover, according to Annex I, this calendar was approved with some requirements: 1) in case the Standing Groups and Committees began their consideration of the Programme of Work during Spring, they should discuss resource implications; 2) the June discussion of main directions of the POW and of resource implications would occur in the Governing Board and the respective Chairmen would report on discussions in the Standing Groups and Committees; 3) Standing Groups'/Committees' comments on the proposed drafts could take place from July to September; in case of no scheduled meetings, Chairmen should canvass their delegates; 4) the mid-October referral to the Committee on Budget and Expenditure would include 'guidance for its consideration of the resources required'.
434. IEA/GB(94)28.

300. The following Programme of Work and Budget were confirmed according to the new methodology.[435]

301. Another milestone of the history of the IEA is represented by 2002. Since April 2002, the Budget process has been voted to become biennial.[436] This new perspective derives from the influence of the OECD biennial budget process. This biennial term gives the chance to make more stable planning, organizing the activities (and the necessary resources) with a larger time horizon. During 1994, in reality, both the Programme of Work and the Budget were still on an annual basis. The first biennial cycle was adopted in June 2001 by the OECD. Following the example of the OECD, the Governing Board then voted to adopt the same biennial basis. The biennial Programme of Work and Budget were defined as follows: 1) by 1st October of every second year a new Programme of Work and Budget had to be drafted; 2) a second-year draft Budget should be adopted at the same time of the Programme of Work for the biennium, along with the first-year Budget; 3) similarly, the Executive Director is asked to prepare a provisional second-year Budget of the biennium, along with a list of the necessary changes to be adopted for the Programme of Work for the second year of the biennium by 1st October. These proposed changes, in case of approval by the Governing Board, have to be confirmed and become effective by the beginning of the new year; 4) regarding the Budget for the second year of the biennium, it has to be confirmed and effective by the same deadline (1st January). Before that time, the decision should be taken by unanimity; 5) the biennial system has to be reviewed every two cycles.[437]

302. Of the notable periods during which important developments happened was towards the early years of the third decade after the IEA's establishment. Of the purposes behind the changes is to: (i) improve the transparency and operation of the procedures of the IEA Programme of Works and Budget, (ii) develop greater integration between the Programme of Work activities and the Budget resources, (iii) avoid micromanagement and unnecessary administrative burden during the procedures, and most importantly (iv) maintain flexibility to respond efficiently and promptly to any emerging priorities and needs.[438] Consequently, a new reformed methodology was formulated, upon which the IEA adopted its 1995 Programme of

---

435. IEA/GB(95)1.
436. IEA/GB/C (2002)1, Item 9(c).
437. Bamberger, *supra* n. 420 at 92.
438. Traditionally and before the introduction of the changes to the formation and adoption of the IEA Budget, the Budget used to be prepared and adopted on a yearly basis. The procedure would kick off with the preparation of a first draft of the Budget by the IEA Administrative Unit in coordination with the Office of Deputy Executive Director once the Programme of Work is outlined and is clear. This first draft would be prepared in consultation as well with senior officials of the Secretariat and others. Then, the draft is approved by the Executive Director before its elements are joined with the Programme for work and subject to further consultations by different bodies including the Budget Committee. The said committee examines the draft and provides observations and recommendation before reporting to the Governing Body which adopts the Budget together with the Programme of Work in December of each year, and then transmitting it to the OECD Council to adopt it into the OECD Budget Part II. For more information of the initial procedures and practice, *see* Scott, *supra* n. 400 at 288-290.

Work and Budget.[439]Another development considered to be of the most significant developments is the adoption of a two-year budget. Since 2002, the IEA followed the model of the OECD Budget and started adopting biennial Budget and Programme of Work. Talks and discussion in changing into a biennial Budget and Programme of Work have arisen approximately a decade before its actual adoption by the Governing Board, particularly when the OECD had adopted a biennial Programme of Work process in 1994, but the Governing Board deferred from shifting up until the Committee on Budget and Expenditure was actually ready to do so and suggest that to the Governing Board. Consequently, the Governing Board decided to implement a biennial Programme of Work and Budget process as of 2003-2004.[440] Therefore, the Governing Board agreed on adopting the provisional budget of the second year at the same time of the adoption of the first year's Programme of Work and Budget. It is important to note that changes to the provisional budget of the second year which were already approved are permitted only upon the unanimity of all the members, which is different from the previously adopted standard of the majority vote.[441] Consequently, and to make that effective, it was essential for all of the IEA Member States to waive their treaty rights to adopt the annual budget by majority vote as per the I.E.P. Agreement.[442] Many changes were introduced over the years particularly due to the mandate expansion and the enlargement of the scope of the IEA activities to reach, *inter alia*, environmental and economic affairs, which inevitably led to the steady growth of the amounts of the IEA Budgets over the years.

§3. The IEA Operates Within the Financial Framework of the OECD

303. In order to understand the actual link to the OECD, it is necessary to be aware of the historical roots at the base of this relationship. During the negotiations on the I.E.P. Agreement, the OECD had a crucial role in shaping the IEA. This contribution dealt with defining the structure of the Agency and the formal terms in order to create it. Such a first link between the OECD and the IEA dates back to 1974, in the occasion of the Washington Energy Conference and the Energy Co-ordinating Group (ECG). A support by the OECD was absolutely fundamental back then. By referring to the I.E.P. it is meant the agreement that defines the relationship between the IEA and the OECD. Such a tool works along with the power of the Governing Board and the Council. More specifically, the I.E.P. Agreement includes the obligations and goals of the Agency. The Council has a different perspective: it deals with the internal mechanism between the IEA and the OECD. The Governing Board, on the other hand, provides the implementing actions in relation to the powers of the Agency.

439. Bamberger, *supra* n. 420 at 75.
440. *Ibid.* at 91.
441. *Ibid.* at 95.
442. *Ibid.*

304. As previously mentioned, Article 10 of the OECD Council Decision on Establishing the IEA proclaims that the Budget of the IEA shall form part of the Budget of the OECD and expenditure of the IEA shall be charged against the appropriations authorized for it under Part II of the Budget of the OECD, which shall include appropriate budget estimates and provisions for all expenditure necessary for the operation of the IEA. It is clear that this article describing the technical function of the Budget subjected it to the financial framework of the OECD. In effect, the IEA enjoys a full general autonomy on all levels, let alone on the financial stage. As the IEA Budget was integrated into the OECD Budget, a startling risk of subordination of the IEA to the OECD mounted. This occurrence is exacerbated by the fact that the Budget is adopted by only the majority, entailing uncertainty with respect to the approval of the Budget in the OECD. Actually, any non-member IEA or any IEA member on the minority side of the Budget could vote to reject the Budget. This could militate to the failure of reuniting the majority and so failure of approving the Budget. To put an end to this IEA autonomy jeopardy, it was resolved that only the IEA members who voted for the Budget in the Governing Board give their agreement to it in the OECD. This special formula was construed in Article 10 (b) of the Council Decision. This safeguard protected the budgetary autonomy of the IEA. At the outset of the IEA, this provision had much more interest when a number of OECD members had not yet joined the IEA and so could block the adoption of the IEA Budget. Today, this provision is of a lesser practical significance but remains an assurance for the IEA in case in the future any disorder in the memberships appears. What enforces more the financial autonomy of the IEA is the creation of the IEA Budget Committee. This ensures that the IEA is advised by its own proper committee rather than by a committee related to the OECD.

305. On another note, although the IEA is an autonomous agency, it was instituted within the framework of the OECD. Thus, the OECD provides to the IEA regulatory and operational services. The relationship between the IEA and the OECD is based on historical roots. In 1974, the emerging IEA needed a structure, by which we refer to concrete elements, like staff, facilities, expertise and so on. The OECD offered this basis to let the IEA function immediately. This is the main reason why the new agency was decided to be considered within the OECD as an 'autonomous agency within the OECD framework'.

306. The definition and consequently the relationship are not easily understandable. Effectively, the IEA does apply the financial regulations of the OECD but only to complement its statutory lack or inexperience. This application of the OECD provisions marked only routine affairs of the IEA such as cash management, making disbursements, maintenance of accounts, inventory, etc. Also, the OECD made some services to the IEA, such as assistance in the Budget preparation, contracts reviews, etc. Again, these services do not have any energy significance. Hence, this slight reliance on the OECD does not alter the energy policy strategy of the IEA and so does not affect the financial autonomy of the IEA. After all, it is the Governing Board who is solely conferred plenary powers with respect to the IEA financial administration. Yet, some critics view the institutional link between the IEA and the OECD as a weakness which might actually negatively affect the IEA's budget, autonomy, and image.[443] Furthermore, such institutional linkage could impose on the IEA some practical limitations particularly where the IEA's budget forms a part of the OECD's budget. For instance, OECD charges such as costs incurred by the OECD for managing staff contracts might be considered as demands on the IEA.[444] These kinds of costs are out of the Governing Board control.

307. The influence of the OECD does not affect only financial sources. Becoming a new member country of the IEA can be more difficult because of the prerequisite of the OECD membership. The idea to break this historical linkage, on the other hand, may not be the solution. First of all, the IEA and the OECD have found a sort of balance, with complementary expertise and a good level of cooperation.

308. All this considered, it seems to be the case to avoid new negotiations to change the treaty. This idea does not only refer to the linkage with the OECD itself. The risk of this change lies in the possible reacting pressure to change other parts of the treaty. Among all, one of the most criticized parts of the text is the voting weight allocation, a system that does not reflect the current geopolitical scenario.

§4. Assessed Contributions for Member Countries

309. The OECD principles and procedures are clearly part of the IEA financing procedure. The Governing Body adopts financial regulations, depending on the circumstances. What is clear is that the application of the OECD procedures is the preferential procedure, if there is no conflict with the Governing decisions.

310. The decisions are traditionally made by majority vote under the I.E.P. scheme. After the approval of the Budget, it becomes part of Part II of the OECD Budget for the year with the consensus of the OECD Council. This means that there is a kind of double check in the sense that the members of the Council who take the decision are the same of the IEA Governing Board. According to Article 64.1 of the I.E.P., the Governing Board selects a scale of contributions every year. Every country has a contribution rate (with a minimum and maximum) mainly based on its GNP. Such a contribution is defined by a percentage of the total Budget amount. Starting from the total, every country contribution is made clear. This definition of the contribution is mandatory. It means that once the country contribution is defined it has to be assessed by the Governing Board. Aside from these mandatory contributions, there are also other important financial sources: voluntary contributions and grants. Although they represent a quite small part of the total budget, they have their importance. This kind of contribution is traditionally linked to a specific goal included in the Programmes of Work. Moreover, an authorization of the Governing Board is required. This approval can be made either through a written procedure or during the meetings.

443. de Graaf, *supra* n. 363 at 236.
444. *Ibid.* at 236.

311. Article 65 of the I.E.P. Agreement states that also special activities conducted by more than a member country can be financed. In such a circumstance, the financing of the projects/activities is entirely defined by the countries themselves. They can simply arrange a solution, independently.

312. In principle, the IEA receives financial resources through different kinds of resources including assessed contributions of IEA Member States, assessed contributions of OECD members (until 1994), voluntary contributions and grants, and returns from sales of publications as well as from services and assistance through exchanges in kind.[445] The financing arrangement of the IEA is in large based on the contributions of the countries to the expenditure. For example, about a third of the IEA financial resources in 2017 were derived from voluntary contributions of governments. For other projects undertaken by the countries and in which the IEA is not a party, the countries do finance themselves for these projects. Actually, these contributions are the dominant sources of the IEA funding. They are the largest portion of its resources. Another option consists in some funding from private sources.

I. Contributions to the IEA Expenditures

313. The contributions of participant countries to the expenditures of the IEA rely on a twofold statutory reference: on the one hand Article 10 of the OECD Council Decision on Establishing the IEA stipulates that each participating country contributes to the expenditure necessary for the operation of the IEA. On the other hand, Article 64.1 of the I.E.P. Agreement states that the expenses of the Secretariat and all other common expenses shall be shared among all the participating countries. Article 10 of the OECD Council Decision on Establishing the IEA specifies that the countries' share in financing the expenditure necessary for the operation of the IEA shall be fixed by the Governing Board. Regarding the apportioning of the expenses, including the expenses of the Secretariat and all other common expenses, Article 64.1 of the I.E.P. Agreement determines that the scale of contributions is elaborated according to the principles and rules set out in the Annex to the 'OECD Resolution of the Council on Determination of the Scale of Contributions by Member Countries to the Budget of the Organization' of 10 December 1963. Yet, following the first year of the application of the I.E.P. Agreement, Article 64.1 further states that the Governing Board is required to review the aforementioned contributions and unanimously decide on any changes.

314. Yet, Article 64.1 has been seen as a complicating factor particularly that the aforementioned principles and rules set out in the Annex might be very likely subject to amendments by the OECD, and consequently such amendments should be made through a treaty amendment which should be unanimously agreed by the members and subject to the constitutional procedure of each member. In fact, the rules and principles set forth in the Annex were subject to several amendments including during 1987 and 1991, and they were applied although there was no

445. Scott, *supra* n. 400 at 296.

record of Governing Board consideration on these decisions.[446] Notwithstanding the foregoing, the 1963 OECD formula takes into account the size of economy of the participant countries. Accordingly, the IEA adopts such formula, and it actually as well relies on the national income statistics of the countries to determine their capacity to pay.

315. The OECD proceeded to make several amendments to the principles and rules annexed to the 1963 resolution. In 1999, a new provision was introduced regarding the scale of contributions. It stated that no country shall pay more than 25% nor less than 0.10% of the total Budget of the IEA. When a new member country accedes to the IEA, the scale of contributions, i.e. the share of all prior member countries, will be adjusted proportionately. When such a resolution was adopted, the OECD Secretariat was of the view that this new amendment and criterion shall apply to Part II of the Budget the same as Part I in the event where a new member join. Yet, Article 10 of the OECD Council Decision confirms plenary power of the Governing Board in fixing each participating country's share in financing the Budget, with the decision of the Governing Board deemed final.[447] With respect to the procedures applied by the IEA to adopt the scales of contributions, several procedures have been taken throughout the years including through Governing Board meetings, or through Governing Board written procedures.[448]

316. The method of contributions is clearly linked to the number of member countries. If they change, the method needs to be modified. In the event of a new membership, two kinds of scales of contributions can be used. On the one hand, the scale of the year before the new membership can be adopted; on the other hand, a second scale including the new member can be adopted until the end of the year. Historically speaking, the first six members of the IEA share with the other members the established amount of resources decided for the year. This happened because the IEA did not decide to increase the effective annual resources. Such a method was not followed for the other two members (Finland and France). Since Finland joined the Agency before the approval of the Agreement, a second scale was not necessary. For France, which joined in the middle of the year, the amount of resources was increased since there were increasing and demanding new activities. During the same year, a new method of contribution was adopted: the percentages of 'Advance Payments of Participating Countries'.[449] Through this method, the uncertainty of the membership proceedings of France was solved. When the proceeding became effective in August 1992 and the Governing Board adopted the scale of contributions, the percentage amounts of the scale were the same defined in the Advanced Payments decision.[450]

446. Bamberger, *supra* n. 420 at 105.
447. *Ibid.* at 105.
448. *Ibid.* at 108.
449. IEA/GB(92)25, Item 11, 11 May 1992. For a more detailed explanation of this method, *Ibid.* at 301.
450. IEA/GB(92)45, Item 7(a)(ii) and (iii).

II. Funding of the Projects

317. The IEA members can launch many projects, either between them or between them and other non-member countries. As per Article 10 (a) of the Council Decision and Articles 64.2 and 42.3 of the I.E.P. Agreement, any special expenses incurred in connection with special activities shall be shared between the participating countries taking part in such special activities and the proportions shall be determined by unanimous agreement between them. Accordingly, the IEA is not involved in funding any of such projects. All of the funding is thus entirely in the hands of the participants in the projects. Members that do not participate in the projects are not required to contribute.

318. In addition, the participants enjoy jointly a full financial autonomy in the conduct of the project as their contributions are straightforwardly directed to the projects. They are not addressed to the IEA for the latter to allocate them to the projects. The IAs are generally the platform of the projects. Therefore, the participants' financial commitment levels are determined upon mutual agreement in these IAs. Generally, each participant is responsible for its own participation in the programme. Related tasks are borne solely by the countries carrying them out. Some other common tasks are jointly shared between them. Among the criteria that the IEA referred to in order to determine the share of contributions are: percentage of the participant country's national GDP, a percentage of the member's IEA contributions, percentage of the relevant national expenditure on R & D or a combination of these measurements. All of the members' contributions are transferred to a 'common fund' account, which is established in the IA. The IA further provides audits and other safeguards of financial integrity.

A. *Voluntary Contributions to Support and Strengthen a Wide Range of Activities in the IEA Programme of Work and Budget*

319. Back in 1975, the financing system of the IEA was based on the income deriving from the scales of contributions for the first category and, for the second one, the OECD decided to provide from Part I of the OECD Budget the cost of thirty-nine personnel posts. This practice was followed for years, until 1994.[451]

320. Concerning the third category, voluntary contributions and grants, it has to be noticed that it was not part of the I.E.P. This category derives from practice at an international level. It was first included in the Decision, by the Council, to establish

451. Scott, *supra* n. 400 at 290.

the Agency. Article 10 (c) deals with this topic. The Governing Board is entitled pursuant to Article 10 (c) of the Council Decision to receive on behalf of the IEA voluntary contributions and grants.[452] Voluntary contributions could come from different sources including individual states, or even non-state actors such as corporations.

321. According to the OECD, there is a distinction between voluntary contributions and grants; by voluntary contributions it is meant they derive from OECD member countries, while by grants it is meant they come from OECD non-member countries. In its own practice, the IEA makes no such distinction, using the two terms interchangeably. The reliance upon voluntary contributions, in this wide sense, has become more and more important by the passing of time. This reliance was officially recognized in February 1996. In that occasion, the Governing Board had failed twice to agree on a Budget for the Financial Year 1996; as a consequence, the Governing Board took a decision which 'urged Members to consider how voluntary contributions might be used to dampen any precipitous reduction in Agency resources'.[453] From that year, every decision of the Governing Board has included this exhortation.[454] The percentage of voluntary contributions can be considered not only by looking at the value of grants recorded in the conclusions of the Governing Board but also by considering the grants accepted by written procedure at the end of every year, the amount received by the Agency and the percentage of grants in the overall appropriations of the Agency.[455]

322. It is worth noting that voluntary contributions should be in line with some principles. First of all, these contributions should meet the existing Programme of Work item. In case of grants, a documentary basis is required, but it is different from grant to grant. On the one hand, some donors need no documentation, while, on the other hand, some very detailed contracts are necessary for some donors. It also happens that the Secretariat finds a compromise with the donor concerning the terms of the grant.

323. A statement about the principles which should be adopted when dealing with voluntary contributions was distributed by the Secretariat in 2001 to member delegations.[456] First, the statement highlighted that all the grants should be linked to activities connected to the Programme of Work of the Agency. Second, the copyright to its work must be retained by the Agency.[457]

---

452. It is worth to mention that the OECD, and unlike the IEA, distinguishes between voluntary contributions and grants. OECD considers the voluntary contributions to be from OECD member countries and grants to be from OECD non-member countries. However, and in practice, the IEA does not make such distinction between the two terms.
453. IEA/GB(96)13, Item 3(a)(viii).
454. As an example, *see*: IEA/GB/C(2003)6, Item 5(a)(v).
455. As an example, the value of grants during 1993 was two, for the total amount of EUR 23,934 while voluntary contributions ten years later, in 2003, were thirty-five for the total of EUR 1.739,870.
456. Craig S. Bamberger *The History of the International Energy Agency, 1974-1994 Volume IV Supplement to volumes II, III and IV* (OECD/IEA 2004), 112.
457. In some cases, the use of products by the donors is admitted.

324. The statement underlined the nature of the contribution: it must be a grant, rather than a payment for services.[458] Some principles connected to the Agency itself are also of extreme importance. The Agency should always be independent; this means there must be no connection between the activity financed by the contribution and the donor; no details concerning the staff working on the activity should be shared with the donor; furthermore, the donor cannot withhold payment based on judging the Agency's work.

325. Another interesting frame is worth noting: the OECD's immunity. This means that there is no domestic court jurisdiction over potential disputes and audit of the OECD's accounts by external agencies is not admitted.

326. The steps for a grant to be accepted are first a review by the Legal Office, second a decision by the Executive Director and third the examination by the Governing Board. The Governing Board discusses the proposed grant during its next meeting or by written procedure. This second method, the written procedure, has no value limitations on contribution, but it is available only if a decision is needed in advance of the next scheduled meeting of the Board and discussion by the Board is not necessary.

327. Traditionally, every single grant was proposed to the Governing Board in a separate note but, since the number of grants was increasing, in 1995 the Secretariat started proposing all of them in bloc. Furthermore, it may happen that a member country asks for more information concerning a possible contribution or donor.

328. By looking at the data, all the proposed grants have been admitted by the Governing Board. Only one proposal had to be further negotiated with the donor and then proposed again to the Governing Board.[459]

329. Voluntary contributions are usually earmarked for specific tasks. They have been disbursed for a wide array of activities. They usually are remitted from member countries. Very rare have been the cases in which a bank, a commission or a non-member country has voluntarily contributed. The contributions take several forms such as amounts of funds, contributions in kind, secondment of individuals and a loan of governments. The approval of the Governing Board is required prior to receiving any contribution. This allows the IEA member governments to exercise a control over the source, destination and amount of any offer of voluntary contribution or grant.

330. If we consider 2002,[460] for example, contributions of the total value of EUR 2,295,351 were accepted by the Governing Board during the year; they mostly

458. In reality, according to Art. 10 (c) of the OECD Council Decision, the Governing Board has the power to accept payments for its services, but this authority has never been used.
459. Bamberger, *supra* n. 457 at 113.
460. *Ibid.* at 109.

derived not only from member countries but also from the private sector. By analysing the data of 2003, it emerges that voluntary contributions were focused on renewable energy (EUR 533,419) and the Climate Change Technology Initiative (CTI) (EUR 394,840).[461]

331. The idea to create a CTI dates back to 1995. During the first session of the COP-1 to the UNFCCC, some Member States, along with the European Commission, suggested the creation of this initiative. In the beginning, the initiative had a temporary nature. Its activities were included in the Programme of Work of the IEA; these activities were mainly founded, thanks to voluntary contributions. During this initial phase, the CTI was then not a topic of interest for all the member countries. The idea to create a special activity within the IEA was part of a proposal. This proposal[462] suggested the creation of a special activity as part of the IEA, but maintaining a sort of independence. Such an independent perspective was based on the same autonomy of the IEA itself within the OECD. The idea was a budget to be defined by the CTI members on a unanimous basis. This budget had to be defined before every fiscal year. According to the proposal, the 'core' contributions were defined *ex ante*, followed by supplementary contributions.

332. This proposal would have been similar to a decision of the Governing Board in order to create an Implementing Agreement. Rather than empowering an external party, it was essentially based on the power of the IEA Secretariat to be the main actor for the special activity. As a consequence, the CTI members would have to reimburse the IEA. It is clear that the IEA members would not be ready to face CTI needs within the Budget of the institution.

333. On the other hand, the idea to locate the CTI within the IEA would have been essentially based first on the creation of a special activity by the Governing Board. As defined in Article 65.1 of the I.E.P.,[463] IEA members have the possibility to abstain from taking part in special activities. This decision by the Governing Board is considered as a possible solution to avoid legal problems. By looking at the second part of the decision, a link between the CTI and the IEA would be created. In this link, the role of the IEA Secretariat is underlined; this role consists in supporting the CTI ad the CTI's programme of work and budget.

334. This proposal has been endorsed by the Governing Board, but in accordance with the adequacy of member country participation and resources.[464] It was

461. *Ibid.* at 109.
462. IEA/GB(2000)27.
463. Art. 65.1 I.E.P.: 'Any two or more Participating Countries may decide to carry out within the scope of this Agreement special activities, other than activities which are required to be carried out by all Participating Countries under Chapters I to V. Participating Countries which do not wish to take part in such special activities shall abstain from taking part in such decisions and shall not be bound by them. Participating Countries carrying out such activities shall keep the Governing Board informed thereof.'
464. IEA/GB/C(2000)5, Item 8.

then understood that the member country commitment and finance were not enough to face the creation of the CTI as a special activity of the IEA.

335. With a Secretariat note regarding the background of the CTI,[465] the Board gave directions about the CTI, in particular about its recognition as an Implementing Agreement.[466] In July 2003, an Implementing Agreement was approved by the Board.[467]

336. Some states favour reliance on voluntary contributions for several reasons. Some see them as a flexible mechanism for responding to crises, while others consider them as an instrument that ensures important needs are met. Moreover, some states might actually contribute in the finance of the IEA through the voluntary contribution to acquire in return analysis and use the IEA as a low-cost think tank on issues that may not be high priorities for the IEA members as a whole.[468] In principle, proposed voluntary contributions shall be reviewed by the IEA Legal Office before their actual adoption to confirm their compliance with a set of principles including, *inter alia*, to confirm that the purpose of such contributions is to contribute to an existing current Programme of Work item rather than a work from outside.[469] Yet this principle is not required by law but rather is adopted as a matter of police.[470]

337. Some states actually criticize any disproportionate reliance on voluntary contributions whereby the consensual nature of the Governing Board could be undermined, and IEA's priorities might be distorted.[471] Voluntary contributions could actually shape the work of the IEA particularly where extra amounts are provided by individual Member States such as, for instance, the US and Japan. It could be safe to say that such two big countries have a huge impact on the plans and work of the IEA implementing programmes of interest to these particular countries at large.[472] It is vivid, similarly to the effect of financial contributions on different sectors, that money plays a huge role in determining how a certain organization evolves. Having said that, it has been reported that some bodies including staff and governing board members have disagreed in certain occasions on the degree to which the voluntary contributions could form the IEA funding.[473]

465. IEA/GB(2002)21.
466. IEA/GB/C(2002)2, Item 6.
467. IEA/GB/C(2003)5, Item 6(c).
468. *Florini*, *supra* n. 26.
469. The IEA Legal Office would bring any outstanding issues before the Executive Director for decision, after which an accepted grant is proposed to the Governing Board for acceptance.
470. Bamberger, *supra* n. 420 at 111.
471. Florini, *supra* n. 26.
472. *Ibid.*
473. *Ibid.* The author is not aware of specific incidents.

III. Are the Finance Mechanisms Sufficient or Is There a Need for New Funding Sources?

338. Although the assessed contributions of the IEA Member States and the voluntary contributions make most of the IEA funding, yet the IEA has been relying as well on additional sources such as sales of publications and the sales of its intellectual property products. Moreover, it relies on payments for the services it renders, a source foreseen in Article 10 (c) of the Council Decision. These are widespread and universally applied by international organizations; however, they are very tiny contributions to the IEA funding compared to the other primary sources. Notwithstanding the foregoing, the core budget of the IEA has not grown in line with demands placed upon. The demands are not anticipated to decrease particularly in light with the increasing energy and environmental challenges facing the world in the present time and are predicted to remain for at least few decades to come, and topics requiring data collection and analysis continue to grow. It is quite clear that this agency is taking more and more importance in the perspective of an energy transition, and it will probably be involved in new projects regarding renewables and new cooperations with other institutions. A first step which is surely necessary is a sort of restyling of the IEA;[474] it happens that the common sense often links this agency to fossil fuels, decreasing the quality of the image of the institution in the climate change context. Hence, there is a strong need for some investments in a new strategy of communication and approach to the energy field. The IEA should focus on more sustainable trends, changing, somehow, once again; according to the data, this change is happening. By looking at the Public Energy Technology RD&D Budgets, it is shown that the IEA member countries are turning to greener investments. In 2018, the total public energy RD&D budget for IEA members was around 18.9 billion; such an increase was mainly based on investments in the low-carbon energy technologies. Yet, low-carbon technologies in the IEA area registered an increase in 2018, reaching 94% of total RD&D budgets.

339. In a comparative perspective among the IEA member countries, the US and Japan are the main investors in the energy RD&D, followed by France, Germany, the United Kingdom and Canada, Korea and Italy.[475]

340. These investments have been changing with the passing of time. If we consider the energy sector in 1974, for example, nuclear power had a crucial role (around 75% of total public energy RD&D). From that year, it started to decrease in importance in the RD&D budget, reaching 22% in 2018.

341. Other investment trends are of interest: in 2018, 20% of worldwide investments were focused on Asian economies, while 10% dealt with oil and gas in North America. The general trends affirm a tendency to improve business models, trying to identify new opportunities to invest in energy efficiency and renewables. Despite

474. de Graaf, *supra* n. 363 at 240.
475. Energy Technology RD&D Budgets, Overview 2019 First Edition, 4 https://webstore.iea.org/energy-technology-rdd-budgets-2019-overview accessed 13 April 2019.

these trends, other factors should be taken into consideration: market dynamics and policies are not facilitating investments in low-carbon power and, more in general, energy efficiency. The risk is that policies not in line with the real needs would slow down the investments necessary to turn to a low-carbon era. More specifically, investments would be of interest in those areas with the highest constraints (sub-Saharan African, e.g.).

342. As a consequence, it is clear that an energy transition will require proper policies, designed in order to decrease the risks of investors and to organize an efficient allocation of these risks. This is confirmed by the fact that energy supply spending has focused on shorter lead times projects; such a tendency clearly highlights that investors favour better managing capital at risk. Some sectors of the energy market have registered an increase: this is the case of renewables whose investment is around 55% since 2010.

343. Moreover, the energy sector, as previously underlined, is only the most important topic for the IEA, among many others. Therefore, the IEA should always seek to develop current resources and develop new ways of acquiring funding resources. Resources, as usual, represent the fundamental starting point to make things possible.

344. The OECD's Director of Legal Affairs has affirmed informally his concurrence with his predecessor's view that Article 10(c) of the 1974 Decision of the Council Establishing an International Energy Agency of the Organisation authorizes the IEA to enter, in its Budget, appropriations in the amounts of voluntary contributions or grants, without submitting those appropriations to the OECD Council for adoption under Article 10(b) of the Council Decision.

Chapter 6. Data and Publications

345. Data and publications are the core product of the IEA's work. The Agency produces numerous annual, quarterly, and monthly publications, based on data from industry, governments and other key stakeholders. Due to the up-to-date statistics and in-depth analysis the publications provide, the IEA gained the importance and influence in the international energy arena and among the policymakers. The reports are one of the main tools the IEA uses to convey its position and reveal global trends to decision-makers and broader audience. With the increasing importance of data and analysis it provides, the Agency has more responsibility on its forecasts and recommendations. By being initially an institution set to handle the oil crises and provide more transparency in the oil and coal-dominated energy system, it had hard time to adapt to the new energy system with fast-changing renewables. By failing many times to adapt its forecast to the non-linear development of PV cost, the Agency gained the flame of being conservative in terms of renewable energy promotion, despite the active work done in this sector.

346. This chapter gives an overview of the data and main publications produced by the IEA. Throughout this chapter, the reader could observe that the IEA produces numerous reports on different fields and it is easy to get lost in this vast amount of information. The chapter attempts to guide a reader through these publications providing the general overview of reports and the methodology used for the analysis. The classification used in this chapter is based on the same division of publications used in the IEA's website: *data and statistics*, *WEO*, *oil market*, *market report series*, *world energy investments, special country reports* and *technology roadmaps*. This chapter is based mainly on the secondary data obtained in the IEA's website, scientific articles, books and news websites.

§1. Statistics and Data

347. Since the establishment of the IEA in 1974, the IEA has been gathering information on policies, statistics and measures supporting the transparency in the energy sector. In the beginning, the IEA staff was merged with OECD energy staff to gather data and statistics, but mainly focusing on oil and coal data collection at first. The data was gathered not only for member countries but also on developing countries, with the first report issued in 1978: 'Basic Energy Statistics and Energy Balances of Developing Countries, 1967-1977'.[476] Throughout the years the data accuracy and number of reporting countries grew, due to the growing importance of the Agency to the global energy system. As of 2018, the IEA has a network of statistics contacts in 120 non-OECD countries and 30 member countries and stores information on almost 2,000 policies[477] (Figure 14).

476. R. Scott, *The history of the International Energy Agency: The First 20 Years. Volume One*, Volume one. OECD/IEA, 1994.
477. Duncan Millard, 'Developing and Enhancing Worldwide Energy Data', Washington DC, 2018.

Figure 14 Map of OECD and Non-OECD Countries Where Data Is Collected

Source: D. Millard, 'Developing and Enhancing Worldwide Energy Data', Washington DC, 2018.

348. The IEA collects up-to-date data on various energy sources with data available for many years. Such credibility, quality and efficiency in data collection is recognized and actively used in the reports prepared by international organizations,[478] governments[479] and civil society organizations.[480] Due to its well-established network and the fact that member countries should timely report their energy data, the IEA holds the first-handed data before any other agency has it on such a large scale. For instance, it collects the data on all fuel consumption for the first ten months of each year and resulting emissions from them. Therefore, the IEA was the first to report that despite many years of climate change policy in place, 2018 reached historically high emissions levels.[481] Fortunately, not all the IEA's data provide negative information. For instance, the Agency has data on the electricity access worldwide and the recent report showed that for the first time ever, the total number of people without electricity access fell below 1 billion according to new data from the *WEO* 2018.[482]

349. Since its establishment, the IEA was using the questionnaires to collect the data on different energy resources, starting first with coal and oil information and gradually including natural gas and later heat, electricity and renewables. Such

478. UNDP, 'The Energy Access Situation in Developing Countries', 2009.
479. Brazilian Ministry of Mines and Energy (MME), 'Energia no Mundo,' 2017.
480. Greenpeace, 'Energy [R]evolution: Towards a Fully Renewable Energy Supply in the EU 27,' 2010.
481. IEA, 'World Energy Outlook 2018,' Paris, 2018.
482. Cozzi, *supra* n. 234.

methodology came from the OECD, which provided a framework for the foundation of the IEA's work.[483] In OECD countries, the data are collected by official bodies (often the national statistics office in each country) using joint questionnaires, which are intended to provide a standardized methodology across countries and reporting entities, as opposed to self-reporting:[484,485]

- Five annual joint questionnaires on coal, oil, natural gas, electricity and renewables.
- Annual collection on energy efficiency, RD&D and forecasts.
- Quarterly questionnaires on prices and taxes.
- Monthly questionnaires on oil, natural gas and electricity.

350. For non-member countries, data collection is done on voluntary bases and largely relies on the network the IEA established through many years with 120 countries.[486] Yet, as it is a voluntary data collection, the information could be incomplete and different definitions might be used, which are hard to merge. Moreover, when comparing data from other international or national organizations with the IEA's data, often the divergence in numbers appears due to the difference in definitions and conversion factors they use. For instance, across three agencies (EIA,[487] IEA and OPEC), the biofuel and processing gains are treated differently, making it difficult to compare the individual country supply level.[488]

351. The oil data from non-member countries of IEA were often incomplete, affecting the market stability and long-term price uncertainty.[489] In 2001, JODI was created, which brings together the IEA and five other international organizations[490] to raise awareness of all oil market players to the need for more transparency of oil market data.[491] Later a joint database was created and since 2006,[492] the IEA started using JODI's standardized questionnaires to collect monthly energy data.[493] JODI's database is hosted by the IEF, but its creation was heavily pushed by the IEA, which offers the possibility to partner with new global players to improve its data.[494] The

483. Scott, *supra* n. 477 at 33.
484. Millard, *supra* n. 478.
485. IEA, 'Statistics Resources.' [Online]. Available: https://www.iea.org/statistics/resources/questionnaires/faq/#four. [Accessed: 30-Oct-2018].
486. Millard, *supra* n. 478.
487. US Energy Information Administration (EIA).
488. Robert McNally, 'The Critical Importance of Improving Oil Data', 2017.
489. Blake C. Clayton, *Market Madness: A Century of Oil Panics, Crises, and Crashes*. 2014.
490. Asia-Pacific Economic Cooperation (APEC), Statistical Office of the European Communities (Eurostat), Latin American Energy Organization (OLADE), Organization of the Petroleum Exporting Countries (OPEC), and United Nations Statistics Division (UNSD). For more information visit: https://www.jodidata.org/ accessed 13 April 2019.
491. JODI, 'JODI OIL manual: 2nd edition,' page 11.
492. JODI, 'JODI Manual,' 2006.
493. JODI, 'JODI world Data Bases,' *Joint Oil Data Initiative (JODI)*. [Online], https://www.jodidata.org/about-jodi/jodi-world-databases.aspx. accessed 13 April 2019.
494. de Graaf, *supra* n. 363 at 233-241.

data are collected for more than hundred countries and available since 2002. Mainly, data consists of the following categories:[495]

- *Product categories*: crude oil, NGL, other (refinery feedstocks + additives/oxygenates + other hydrocarbons), total (primary products), LPG, Naphtha, motor/aviation gasoline, kerosene, of which: kerosene type jet fuel, gas/diesel oil, fuel oil, other oil products and total oil products.
- *Flows*: production (general and from other sources), trade, products transferred/backflows, direct use, stock change, statistical difference, refinery intake, closing stocks, refinery output, receipts, products transferred, interproduct transfers, demand.
- *Data in three different units*: barrels, tons and litres.

352. As all five organizations were previously collecting data on oil, the questionnaires were adapted to include all the information gathered before, but at the same time simplifying it in order to have a small and easily understandable questionnaire. Definitions were merged between the agencies and kept to the minimum including the absolute essentials.[496] While it started the work with the collection of information on oil, JODI later included the collection of data on gas and the IEA uses also the JODI's questionnaire on gas.[497] However, as recognized on the JODI's website, not all the data for all the flows, products and countries are always available, especially for Non-OECD countries. Apart from this cooperation and collection of data from the Member States, the IEA developed also a bilateral cooperation with national administrations of non-member countries, industry organizations and other international organizations to gather data. For instance, for renewable energy policy measures, the IEA works together with IRENA since 2012 on collaborative data gathering.[498] As for the bilateral cooperation with governments, IEA has established in-depth bilateral cooperation with China, Argentina[499] among other major economies to collect data.

353. The main advantage of the IEA's data is the possibility of comparing the same data across many countries. That became possible, as the specific methodology was elaborated to present the data with a common energy unit. The questionnaire is sent in the form of an excel file to the governmental bodies responsible for the statistics. The information provided by the government is checked twice: first, the file consists of basic arithmetic and consistency checks to make corrections on filled data already by the countries before sending it back to the IEA. The second check is done by the IEA's statistical division for arithmetic errors, time series discrepancies and consistency.[500] Finally, the statistical division runs energy balances

495. JODI, 'JODI OIL Manual: 2nd edition.'
496. *Ibid.*, p. 15.
497. JODI, 'JODI Gas Manual: 1st edition.'
498. IEA, *supra* n. 261.
499. IEA, 'IEA and Argentina Agree to Cooperate on Energy Statistics,' 2017. [Online], https://www.iea.org/newsroom/news/2017/march/iea-and-argentina-agree-to-cooperate-on-energy-statistics.html. accessed 13 April 2019.
500. IEA, 'Frequently Asked questions,' Paris, 2018.

and calculates efficiencies to identify problems in either inputs or outputs to the various transformation processes.[501] This complex procedure ensures a certain level of quality for data reported by countries, as it 'is important for the accuracy of the analysis and the forecast'. Another step to ensure quality is direct work with the statistical division of governments and institutions, which report the information. For instance, the IEA has as well manuals translated in various languages[502] and the Agency often organizes statistics workshops on how to correctly interpret and gather data. As of 2018, the IEA directly trained 496 statisticians worldwide and over 4,500 online.[503] It has an online platform with training on price, data analysis and reporting, and the Agency organizes various online webinars to cover the range of energy statistics.[504] It is interesting to note that the video training is translated and available online in English and some in Mandarin, emphasizing the importance the IEA gives to data from China.

354. There are still many challenges on data collection, according to Duncan Millar, chief statistical of the IEA.[505] The confidentiality concerns as well as incomplete and inaccurate data supply remain important obstacles. Yet, with the emergence of renewable energy sources, new challenges arise:

- Many small-scale renewable systems produce the off-grid generation, but it is hard to measure it, as it is not covered in the official data.
- With the increased possibility of producing and consuming the electricity by the same entity, the question arises on how to measure the self-use.

355. All the data is published online and partially available for free. For some annual, quarterly and monthly data sets, users have to get annual subscriptions or pay-per-view access. Apart from the online access, the data are available in the form of publications, such as the *Key World Energy Statistics Report, World Energy Balance* and other publications.[506] For instance, the *Key World Energy Statistic Report* 2018 gives an overview on how a particular energy indicator has changed over time comparing current data to the data of 1973, showing changes the energy sector went through in the past forty-five years.

501. Duncan Millard, 'Commentary: Understanding and Using the Energy Balance,' *IEA*, 2017, https://www.iea.org/newsroom/news/2017/september/commentary-understanding-and-using-the-energy-balance.html accessed 13 April 2019.
502. For more information please visit: https://www.iea.org/statistics/resources/manuals/ accessed 13 April 2019.
503. Millard, *supra* n. 478.
504. For more information please visit: https://www.iea.org/statistics/#training accessed 13 April 2019.
505. Millard, *supra* n. 478.
506. For more information please visit: https://webstore.iea.org/statistics-data accessed 13 April 2019.

I. World Energy Outlook

356. The WEO is the IEA's flagship publication, which provides strategic insights on future patterns of global energy systems. The report presents the analysis on demand and supply by energy source and by country, providing in-depth understanding of the current situation of global energy systems and its future possible developments. The overview of the entire energy sector is provided with insights on fossil fuels, renewable energy and energy efficiency, new technologies and its implication for the energy market. The report provides a comprehensive overview of the global energy sector and serves as an umbrella for other IEA's reports to be aligned with its analysis. The first WEO was published in 1977 and it has been an annual publication since 1998,[507] usually released in November of each year. The WEO looks at all the fuels and gives an overview of the global energy system trends and forecast. Since 2011, the WEO has a second part – special issue, which has a closer focus on a single sector or region, defined by the IEA's team and related to the trend which they saw this year. For instance, the first special issue in 2011 'Are We Entering a Golden Age of Gas?',[508] foresaw the thrive of natural gas in the future. From the last special issues, the Agency focused its attention on renewable energy in 2016, Southeast Asia energy in 2017 and electricity in 2018.[509] While the report, in general, gives the readers an overview of the energy sector, it highlights as well the challenges the world faces with the trend on tackling different problems with topical focuses such as air pollution and access to electricity. Finally, it forecasts the future energy sector's development, if nothing will be changed and proposes the scenario as well on what should be done from the energy sector perspective to achieve internationally agreed goals on climate change and sustainable development.[510]

A. How Data Are Gathered?

357. The WEO is produced by the Energy Demand Outlooks Division and the Energy Supply Outlooks Division in consultation with other entities within the IEA[511] based on the particular topical focus selected for each issue. The authors of the WEO gather existing data, analyse and produce the first draft. In addition to that, the report uses many informal data sources as first-hand information through workshops and meetings with key stakeholders. For instance, the EBC provides the information from leading energy companies around the globe. As gas becomes a more

507. IEA, World Energy Outlook, https://www.iea.org/weo/aboutweo/ accessed 13 April 2019.
508. IEA, 'Special issue of the World Energy Outlook: 'Are we entering a Golden Age of Gas?', 2011.
509. IEA, Analysis, https://www.iea.org/weo/weospecialreports/ accessed 13 April 2019.
510. Sustainable Development Goals, https://www.un.org/sustainabledevelopment/sustainable-development-goals/.
511. IEA, World Energy Outlook, https://www.iea.org/weo/aboutweo/ accessed 13 April 2019.

and more important energy source in the modern energy system, the 'Unconventional Gas Forum'[512] provides as well important insights for the WEO. There are many other forums, which are discussed in more details in Chapter 6, which are as well important data source for the monograph depending on its yearly focus.

358. After the first draft is completed, it undergoes an extensive peer review process by leading international experts in the relevant fields from governments, industry, research institutions and other organizations.[513] Although country representatives are invited to give comments and suggestions, which are useful for the analysis, the authors of the reports have a certain degree of flexibility in determining their directions with little editorial interference from Member States.[514] Finally, the WEO team organizes a high-level workshop[515] on every issue of the WEO, bringing together decision-makers and leading experts from around the world to provide a strategic guidance on the analysis.[516] Yet, the choice of experts acknowledged in the report is unclear and not specified in the report. After the suggestions from the workshop's participants and other experts are received, they are incorporated into the report.[517]

B. Forecast Methodology

359. The detailed projections are generated by the WEM, a large-scale simulation tool, developed at the IEA over a period of more than twenty years that is designed to replicate how energy markets function.[518] The WEM is a partial equilibrium model covering all fuels and regions that replicates how global energy markets function over the medium to long term.[519] The model is constantly reviewed and updated to ensure its completeness and relevancy. The WEM consists of three main modules: final energy consumption (covering residential sector, services, agriculture, industry, transport and non-energy use); energy transformation including power generation and heat, refinery and other transformation; and energy supply. Outputs from the model include energy flows by fuel, investment needs and costs, CO_2 emissions and end-user pricing. The model uses following key assumptions: population growth, based on UNDP data, macroeconomic indicators (economic growth, based on IMF forecast and GDP) and data on prices (fossil fuel, CO_2 prices,

512. The Forum is organized by IEA since 2012 and aimed at constructing a common platform for different stakeholders' best practices and regulatory action on unconventional gas development. For more information: https://www.iea.org/ugforum/ accessed 13 April 2019.
513. IEA, 'World Energy Outlook 2018', Paris, 2016.
514. Harald Heubaum & Frank Biermann, *Integrating Global Energy And Climate Governance: The Changing Role of the International Energy Agency,* 87 Energy Policy 229-239 (2015).
515. IEA, IEA Holds High-Level Workshop on the Future of Electricity (2017), https://www.iea.org/newsroom/news/2018/april/iea-holds-high-level-workshop-on-the-future-of-electricity.html accessed 13 April 2019.
516. International Energy Agency (IEA), 'World Energy Outlook 2013,' Paris, 2013.
517. IEA, World Energy Outlook 2018: The Future is Electrifying (2018), https://www.iea.org/workshops/world-energy-outlook-2018-the-future-is-electrifying.html accessed 13 April 2019.
518. IEA, World Energy Outlook, https://www.iea.org/weo/aboutweo/ accessed 13 April 2019.
519. IEA, 'Market Report Series: Energy Efficiency,' Paris, 2018., page 25.

end-user prices, subsidies).[520] Therefore, the scenarios, which WEM generates are largely based on the historical trends combined with exogenous assumptions and coefficients for the evolution of technology, prices, and policies.[521]

360. Klaus Mohn, for instance, reviewed the methodology and WEM behind the IEA's *WEO* and came to the conclusion that important aspects of the IEA's scenarios are driven by critical exogenous assumptions[522] and do not include the variation of economic growth between the scenarios.[523] The finding means that the result derived from the model is just one of the possibilities of the world energy system development and should be read with caution. In theory, the WEO serves as the base report to which all other reports alight their definitions and data. Yet, it 'is possible to see the differences in definition between different reports within the IEA'. For instance, biofuel demand is measured differently in IEA's OMR versus WEO. IEA's OMR estimates measure biofuel by their physical volume, but the Agency's WEO uses the gasoline and diesel equivalent volume for biofuels.[524] The different definitions impact the data input in the model and provide different conclusions, as a result.

C. Scenarios

361. The WEO uses the scenario approach to examine future energy trends using the WEM for simulations. The IEA has two kinds of scenarios: Business As Usual (BAU) and alternative scenarios. BAU scenarios demonstrate the trends of the energy sector if nothing will change, taking into account mainly the current policy. The alternative scenarios take into account the international climate and sustainable goals and show how the energy sector should change if the world wants to achieve these goals (*see* Table 4).

Table 4 The Overview of Main Scenarios Used in the World Energy Outlook

BAU	*Name*	*Description*
	Current Policy Scenario	Considers the impact of those policies and measures that are firmly enshrined in legislation

520. IEA, 'World Energy Model,' 2018.
521. M. Klaus, 'Undressing the Emperor: A Critical Review of IEA's WEO,' *UiS Work. Pap. Econ. Financ.*, 2016.
522. These are mainly costs of CO_2 emissions, plans and measures for energy and climate policies, technological progress by industry and region, and assumptions for macroeconomic developments (i.e., economic growth).
523. Klaus, *supra* n. 522.
524. McNally, *supra* n. 489.

BAU	*Name*	*Description*
	New Policy Scenario	Includes the policy directives, composed of existing energy policies and announced policy positions, including national-level commitments adopted under the Paris Agreement on climate change
Alternative	*Sustainable Development Scenario*	Proposed pathway of the world energy system to achieve internationally agreed objectives on climate change, air quality and universal access to modern energy

Source: own based on iea.org.

362. BAU: Prior to 2010, the *Reference Scenario* was a predominant pathway in which policy assumptions would reflect the present countries' regulation.[525] In 2010, the Reference Scenario was transformed into the *Current Policy Scenario* and was complemented by the *New Policy Scenario* compiled based on what the IEA deems as credible policy directives, composed of existing energy policies and announced policy positions, including national-level commitments adopted under the Paris Agreement on climate change.[526] It is important to mention, though, that these scenarios are not projections or forecasts, but rather the scenarios on how the energy sector would be evaluated if nothing is changed.

363. Alternative scenarios: The *450 Scenario*[527] made its first appearance in 2010, as a pathway to limit climate change to below 2°C. The scenario was mainly based on the pledges announced at the Copenhagen Accord and Cancun Agreements, and IEA showed how the current energy system has to change to achieve these targets. However, this approach focused mainly on GHG emissions and had to be upgraded once the United Nations' (UN) SDGs were set by the UN General Assembly in 2015. To assist with SDG's implementation, the *Sustainable Development Scenario (SDS)* was introduced in the WEO-2017. The SDS scenario aims to achieve the main energy-related components of the '2030 Agenda for Sustainable Development'[528] adopted in 2015 by the Member States of the UN. Compared with the 450 scenario, the latter represents a more integrated approach to achieve internationally agreed objectives on climate change, air quality and universal access to modern energy. In addition to these scenarios, the Agency has many other scenarios

525. IEA, 'World Energy Outlook 2010,' Paris, 2010.
526. IEA, *supra* n. 520 at 25.
527. The number 450 stands there for the limitation of the long-term concentration of greenhouse gases in the atmosphere to about 450 parts per million of carbon-dioxide equivalent (ppm CO_2-eq). For more information: https://www.iea.org/weo/energyandclimatechange/ accessed 13 April 2019.
528. Sustainable Development Goals, https://sustainabledevelopment.un.org/post2015/transformingourworld accessed 13 April 2019.

and cases, which are more report specific.[529] For example, the FES – introduced in the WEO 2018 especially to explore key areas of uncertainty for future electricity demand.

D. Rising Criticism

364. Both WEO and *Key World energy statistic reports* are the main flagships of the Agency, which endow the Agency with significant agenda-setting powers.[530,531] As mentioned before, many decision-makers use the data and most importantly the Agency's forecast for future investments and priority setting in the energy system. With such increasing importance, the Agency has also the growing responsibility on the paths and ideas it promotes. Researchers, journalists and NGOs would argue that the IEA's scenarios are rather conservative and could be more challenging, especially as WEO provides a guideline for many policymakers.[532] In 2008, the Energy Watch Group accused the IEA of deliberately underestimating the potential of wind, solar and sea power, while promoting oil, coal and nuclear as 'irreplaceable' energy sources.[533] This accusation is made due to the fact that the annual WEO reports 'between 1994 and 2014 have been publishing misleading projections on solar photovoltaic (PV) and wind energy'.[534] Another NGO – Oil Change International – similarly referred to the preferences of the Agency towards oil and gas, effectively encouraging governments to overshoot emissions targets and worsen climate damage.[535] Research community as well investigated the WEO predictions and pointed out some mismatches in the scenarios, especially in the case of PV technology. Auke Hoekstra made a graph where he shows that new policy scenarios and reference scenarios (which are based on the existing policies), both failed to predict the real addition of PV installations worldwide underestimating its rate of growth (*see* Figure 15).

---

529. For more scenarios please *see* the page: https://www.iea.org/weo/weomodel/ accessed 13 April 2019.
530. Klaus, *supra* n. 522.
531. Roehrkasten, *supra* n. 97.
532. Carrington and Stephenson, *supra* n. 309 at 103-113.
533. de Graaf, *supra* n. 363 at 233-241.
534. Energy Watch Group, New EWG Study: International Energy Agency Holds Back Global Energy Transition (2015), http://energywatchgroup.org/new-ewg-study-international-energy-agency-holds-back-global-energy-transition accessed 13 April 2019.
535. G. Muttitt, Oil Change International Responds to International Energy Agency's 2018 World Energy Outlook (Oil Change International, 2018), http://priceofoil.org/2018/11/12/oil-change-international-responds-to-international-energy-agencys-2018-world-energy-outlook/ accessed 13 April 2019.

Figure 15 Annual PV Additions: Historic Data Versus IEA WEO Predictions

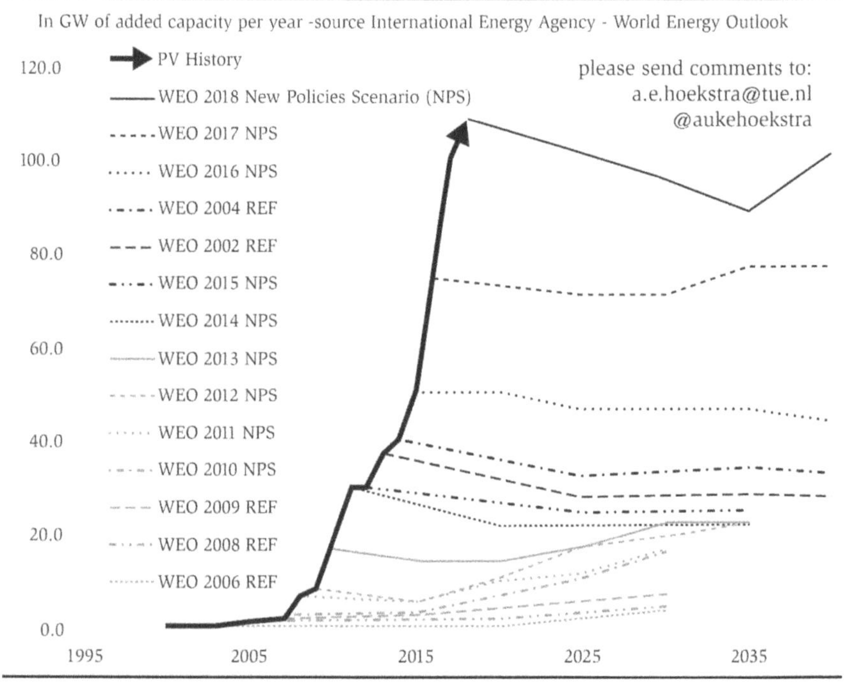

Source: Tweet by Auke Hoekstra at Eindhoven University of Technology extracted from https://twitter .com/ (13 January 2019).

365. Gerry Carrington and Janet Stephenson (2018) as well examined the solar PV projections in twenty-six recent global energy scenarios, contrasting them with academic studies and other analyses,[536] and found that they all fail to account fully for the technological developments and to recognize non-linear rates of solar PV growth. The authors argued that the WEO's scenarios are among the most conservative of the twenty-six reviewed scenarios. They concluded that a scenario with low PV capacity projections such as the IEA's one is likely to deter investments in the PV innovation and development that would otherwise occur.[537] On the other hand, the IEA argues that the policy scenarios, it refers to, are just scenarios and not

536. Nine are developed by the IEA, five are by the World Energy Council, three are by Greenpeace, one by Carbon Tracker (a think tank based in the UK), the World Wide Fund for Nature and the US's Energy Information Administration.

537. Carrington and Stephenson, *supra* n. 309 at 103-113.

the predictions.[538] Meaning that they are based on the existing policy measures and represent the BAU paths, referring to the market and policy information they have on hands. However, it 'is interesting to observe that among all the investigated forecasts the IEA had the most conservative assumptions about the PV'.

366. At the same time, scholars acknowledged some changes, which the IEA undertook towards a more positive view in the renewable energy future. This shift was mainly due to the two solar technology reports[539,540] published in late 2014 which together spell out an ambitious vision for solar energy to become the world's largest electricity source by 2050 and contribute to a significant reduction in CO_2 emissions.[541,542] The reassessment of solar technology potential was due to the price decrease in PV technology, greater uncertainty in regard to nuclear power and Carbon Capture Storage (CCS), and increasing importance of solar thermal technology due to its storage possibility.[543] Indeed, for fossil fuels and other more slowly changing energy sources, the WEM seems to respond correctly and design better scenarios, while it constantly fails for PV prediction. The main reason for that could be that the model is more suitable for conventional energy sources, which dominated since the design of the model and it has a hard time to adapt to the fast-changing learning curves of new technologies. While the learning curves of other technologies usually develop slower, the PV and Wind have unique pathways and the model failed to adapt to its fast-changing situation. Another important criticism, raised in the literature and media, concerns the projections on oil production made by the IEA. In 2009, *The Guardian* published an article accusing the IEA on the accuracy of the organization's latest *WEO* on oil demand and supply: 'The senior official claims the US has played an influential role in encouraging the watchdog to underplay the rate of decline from existing oil fields while overplaying the chances of finding new reserves.'[544]

367. These allegations casted a dark shadow over the launch of the IEA's yearly WEO in 2009.[545] In March 2010, a scientific article was published in which the IEA's analysis on oil depletion was challenged by researchers. The team headed by the Swedish Professor Kjell Aleklett claimed that oil production is more likely to be 75 million barrels a day by 2030 than the 105 million barrels a day as projected by

538. J. Watts, *IEA Accused of Undermining Global Shift From Fossil Fuels* (The Guardian, 2018), https://www.theguardian.com/environment/2018/apr/05/iea-accused-of-undermining-global-shift-from-fossil-fuels accessed 13 April 2019.
539. IEA, 'Technology Roadmap – Solar Thermal Electricity 2014,' p. 52, 2014.
540. IEA, 'Solar Photovoltaic Energy,' 2014.
541. Heubaum and Biermann, *supra* n. 515 at 229-239.
542. IEA, *How Solar Energy Could be the Largest Source of Electricity by Mid-Century* (2014)., https://www.iea.org/newsroom/news/2014/september/how-solar-energy-could-be-the-largest-source-of-electricity-by-mid-century.html. accessed 13 April 2019.
543. IEA, *supra* n. 540 at 52.
544. Terry Macalister, *Key Oil Figures Were Distorted by US Pressure, Says Whistleblower* (The Guardian, 2009), https://www.theguardian.com/environment/2009/nov/09/peak-oil-international-energy-agency accessed 13 April 2019.
545. de Graaf, *supra* n. 363 at 233-241.

the IEA in the 2008 edition of its WEO.[546] Another article, written by Miller, as well referred to the IEA's oil projections as too optimistic and pointed out that the criticism was not addressed by the Agency.[547] In response, Christophe E. McGlade called into question the reductions in future global oil production, that Aleklett argued is necessary, pointing out to incorrectly applied depletion rate for all fields within the region to different subset of fields.[548] Therefore, some researchers argue about the reduction of oil production, others claim the contrary, yet the scientific community usually would refer to the WEO scenarios as pessimistic for renewables and optimistic for fossil fuels.

II. Oil Market Report

368. The first issue of the monthly and *Annual* OMR dates back to 1983, yet containing mainly the information on OECD countries.[549] The 'truly global' report starts to be published only after 1991, as a result in part of the breakdown of barriers between Eastern and Western Europe and the availability of adequate data.[550] The monthly OMR is published under the responsibility of the Executive Director of the Agency, which is available online and the oldest issue dates back to 1990.[551] The monthly report covers topics such as supply and demand, stocks, prices and refinery activities and gives a more detailed and up-to-date information on the main changes happening in the oil market on a monthly basis. The report is available to the subscribers through the online service[552] and is confidential before the release, as it contains market-sensitive information. The *Annual OMR* started to be published in 1984 (1983 data) and after 1991 was replaced by an *Annual Statistical Supplement to the Monthly Oil Market Report*.[553] The latest issue available online dated back to 2004 and provided an overview through a longer historical perspective of the oil demand, supply, trade, stocks, prices and refining data than is normally included in the monthly issue. It contains tables examining the above sections on a quarterly basis by country, aggregated by OPEC, non-OPEC countries and by geographic region.[554] The information is presented in the form of tables with monthly, quarterly and annual data including the historic overview. The information

546. Kjell Aleklett et al., *The Peak of the Oil Age – Analyzing the World Oil Production Reference Scenario in World Energy Outlook 2008,* 38(3) Energy Policy 1398-1414 (2009).
547. Richard G. Miller, *Future Oil Supply: The Changing Stance of the International Energy Agency,* 39(3) Energy Policy 1569-1574 (2015).
548. Christophe E. McGlade, *Comment on the 'Uppsala Critique'*, 67 Energy Policy 154-158 (2014).
549. Scott, *supra* n. 477 at 322.
550. *Ibid.* at 60.
551. IEA, Oil Market Report, https://www.iea.org/oilmarketreport/reports/ accessed 13 April 2019.
552. Note that the monthly reports could be available for non-subscribers free of charges two weeks later their issue following the link https://www.iea.org/oilmarketreport/ accessed 13 April 2019. While some statistical data accompanies each Oil Market Report, monthly data charts are also available through an interactive website https://www.iea.org/oilmarketreport/omrpublic/currentreport/#Overview.
553. Scott, *supra* n. 477 at 322.
554. IEA, 'Annual Statistical Supplement 2017,' Paris, 2017.

is presented largely for the OECD members with fewer data available for non-OECD countries, due to the fact that the data collection from non-Member States is voluntary.

369. A good complement to the monthly overview of the market and the statistical supplement is the annual report on oil market, which presents a broader analysis of available data with medium-term forecast of market development. The first issue of the *Medium-Term Oil Market Report*[555] available online dates back to 2007 and provides more in-depth analysis of trends regarding demand and supply, biofuel, refinery activities and crude trade. The issue was a part of market report series, which will be discussed in detail in the next section. Since 2017, the report is renamed *Oil 2017: Analysis and Forecasts to 2022.*[556] Similar to monthly reports, it covers demand, supply, stock, prices and refining information among other important data, yet with annual analysis.[557] An important part of the report is the forecast of the oil demand and supply for a further five years based on regular monitoring of macroeconomic and energy market conditions, technology, and policy developments. The OMRs are produced by the Oil Markets Division headed by Neil Atkinson, as of 2018.[558] Similar publication on oil market is provided by OPEC. Both the IEA and OPEC capture market-moving events and offer in-depth analyses in their respective reports. The IEF compares the data and forecast for short, medium and long-term oil market outlooks. As of 2018 report, the overall overview of both agencies' data and forecast presented little difference between each other, which was possible to achieve due to the data harmonization and comparability of outlooks that was promoted by the IEF and JODI initiative, discussed above. However, the agencies still have some minor divergence in data due to various criteria, as, for instance, the regional grouping and definitions used for bunker fuel.[559]

A. *How Information Is Gathered?*

370. Since the beginning, the IEA established the reporting system where the information is supplied by IEA member country governments, largely on the basis of information they receive from oil companies.[560] Prior to 2004, the IEA used its own *MOS* questionnaire, sent electronically to its member countries. Initially data was gathered on forty-two key data points: seven product categories (crude oil, LPG, gasoline, kerosene, gas/diesel oil, fuel oil and total oil products) and six flows

555. IEA, 'Medium-Term Oil Market Report,' 2007.
556. IEA, 'Oil 2017: Analysis and Forecasts to 2022,' 2017.
557. IEA, 'Oil 2018: Analysis and Forecasts to 2023,' 2018.
558. A. Halff, The IEA's Medium-Term Oil Market Report (Webinar online. *CSIS Energy and National Security Program*, 2014), https://www.youtube.com/watch?v=k3rIkNYu1IM accessed 13 April 2019.
559. International Energy Forum in Partnership with Resources for the Future, Introductory Paper: A Comparison of Recent IEA And OPEC Outlooks, 2018.
560. Scott, *supra* n. 477 at 304.

(production, imports, exports, stock changes, closing stocks and demand). Since 2004, the IEA started using JODI's questionnaires, which was mentioned in section §5.I.[561]

371. Submissions are made during the seven-to-eight-week period following the month to which the figures relate (i.e. three months before the release of the report) and may include revisions to earlier months.[562] Each OECD producing country submits oil production data to the IEA, but these aggregate data are supplemented by information on individual fields provided by governments, oil companies and consultancies. These data consist of demand and production information broken down by product category, such as gasoline, jet/kerosene, and diesel.[563] Preliminary stock data are available for the EU plus Norway, Canada, Japan, Korea, Mexico and the US, while preliminary EurOil stock data are used to calculate the remaining EU countries' stock positions. Finally, a market assessment of the pricing trends based on crude oil and oil future is presented based on information from capital markets and commodities exchanges, on a month-to-month basis.[564] Monthly statistics are also adjusted after member countries publish their annual demand data, which by definition come with a lag but offer greater details and are more reliable than monthly estimates.

372. There is no formal submission system for non-OECD data. Information is gathered from a variety of governments, oil companies, consultancies and journalistic sources. However, as the data collection is based on the voluntary bases, the timeliness and degree of detail is highly variable, as recognized by the IEA itself[565] and JODI.[566] Data is available on average for ninety-one countries (taking the average of data availability since 2002[567]). Relatively up-to-date information is available for roughly 60% of non-OECD demand, in some cases as quickly as for OECD data, but for others, up to six months or longer. As of the 2018 Report, non-OECD information is presented for Demand in China, India, Iraq, Saudi Arabia, Brazil, Argentina, Egypt, Pakistan, and Venezuela;[568] non-OECD information for supply is presented for Saudi Arabia, China, UAE, Kuwait, Qatar, Iraq, Iran, Libya, Nigeria, Angola, Congo, Equatorial Guinea, Gabon, Russia, Kazakhstan, Azerbaijan. Non-OECD data were collected for Refining capacity for Iran, Algeria, UAE, China, Iran, Venezuela, Brazil, Azerbaijan, Belarus, Russia.[569]

---

561. JODI, 'JODI OIL manual: 2nd edition.'
562. *Ibid.*
563. IEA, *supra* n. 558 at 7.
564. IEA, 'Monthly Oil Market Report: December,' 2018.
565. IEA, 'Annual Statistical Supplement to the Monthly Oil Market Report,' 2006.
566. JODI, 'JODI World Data Bases,' *Joint Oil Data Initiative (JODI)*, https://www.jodidata.org/about-jodi/jodi-world-databases.aspx. accessed 13 April 2019.
567. *Ibid.*
568. IEA, *supra* n. 558 at 10-14.
569. *Ibid.*

B. What Are the Assumptions for the Forecast?

373. As stated in the user guide of 2006,[570] the aim of projecting future demand and supply is to produce estimates of 'most likely' (model) levels under normal conditions.[571] Meaning that these are projections, which are made taking into account currently known conditions and most likely to be true if no other conditions emerged. The monthly OMR gives the forecast on demand, supply and price of oil for the next six to eighteen months. Since 2017, the annual market report provides the forecast for the next five years.[572] The key assumptions used for the projects of oil demand are: economic growth, which is based on the IMF's projections, changes in oil's share of the energy mix, changes in efficiency of oil use, oil prices (both in absolute terms and relative to competing fuels) and the weather. Two other factors, which can affect the monthly pattern of sale, are the number of working days and the possibility of strikes.[573] Oil supply projections for individual countries are developed by a bottom-up approach using monthly information on over seven hundred fields, areas or other elements for over ninety countries (as of 2006). The current and expected upstream operating environment is also taken into account.[574]

III. Market Report Series

374. In 2006, the IEA introduced a new series of market reports – annual reports that forecast market trends for the next five years concerning the primary energy sources for global markets. First publications were focused mainly on oil, coal and gas, and only in 2012 renewables and energy efficiency became also the focus of the reports' scope.[575] Renewable energy sources were constantly growing over the last five years, leading the IEA to acknowledge 'the coming-of-age of the renewable energy sector'.[576] The aim of the market reports is a greater transparency, as stated on the website and it generally gives a broad overview of the recent trends and future prospects in terms of 'global demand, supply, processing and trade for oil, coal and gas as well as analysing the current drivers and barriers influencing

570. The latest publication available which explains the forecast methodology, since 2007 the Glossary and User's Guide became the separate web-based publication at https://www.iea.org/oilmarketreport/ accessed 13 April 2019.
571. IEA, *supra* n. 566.
572. IEA, *supra* n. 557 at 14.
573. IEA, *supra* n. 566.
574. *Ibid.*
575. For more information please visit: https://webstore.iea.org/market-reports?pagesize=24&viewmode=list accessed 13 April 2019.
576. IEA, 'IEA Sees Renewable Energy Growth Accelerating Over Next 5 Years' (2012), https://www.iea.org/newsroom/news/2012/july/iea-sees-renewable-energy-growth-accelerating-over-next-5-year.html. [Accessed: 02-Mar-2019].

deployment of renewable energy worldwide'.[577] All reports provide the forecast for a particular market development for the next five years and are usually in line with the *WEO*.[578]

375. Basic assumptions, which are used in the report, are related to the political situation and to the economic factors, such as: GDP growth rates, provided by IMF, population growth and prices. Another common step for all reports is the peer review process before the publication with many experts from public and private sectors. However, this rule excludes the annual market report on oil,[579] supposedly due to the confidential information, which could be sensitive for the market.

376. For the coal, gas and oil sectors, the reports cover mainly demand, supply and trade with more energy-specific sections, similar to the *Annual Market Report on Oil* discussed above. Also, the reports provide the forecast of global demand and supply for the following five years, identifying trends in market development and policy at the national or regional levels. The reports related to the gas sector are available online with publications dating back to 2006. These reports were prepared first by the Energy Diversification Division, which later was renamed Gas, Coal and Power Markets Division (GCP) in cooperation with other divisions of the IEA.[580],[581] These reports examine the evolution of the gas market in the previous year and provide a detailed analysis on the supply and trade development, infrastructure investments and demand forecast. The reports provide also insights on important events which impact supply and demand; investments in infrastructure, regulation changes, individual country focus and trade. The trade overview is divided into the analysis of pipeline gas and LNG. As for the latter, one of the key metrics the Agency follows annually (since 2014) is the evolution of the LNG's contract flexibility, which enables tracking the trends on a more detailed level, such as short-term volumes contracts, its average duration, etc.[582] With this information in hands, authors simulate the forecast of gas energy sector for the next five years, using mainly the following assumptions: GDP growth rate, oil and coal prices, while gas price assumptions are based on the gas forward curves. Apart from these assumptions, little information is available on how gas market modelling is done.

377. The earliest publications on the Coal Market were available online since 2011 and were prepared as well by the Gas, Coal and Power Division (GCP).[583] Also, the report is prepared together with support from the universities and CIAB. Similar to previously discussed reports, the coal market report gives an overview of

577. Market Report Series, https://www.iea.org/publications/marketreportseries/ accessed 13 April 2019.
578. IEA, 'Medium-Term Renewable Market Report 2015,' 2015.
579. IEA, *supra* n. 557. .
580. IEA, 'Natural Gas Market Review 2009,' 2009.
581. IEA, 'Market report series: Gas 2017,' 2017.
582. J.-B. Dubreuil, The IEA's Gas 2018 Medium Term Market Report and Global Gas Security Review 2018. Presentation online, *the Center on Global Energy Policy* (2018), https://www.youtube.com/watch?v=oABkUpaQ_zw.
583. IEA, 'COAL 2017: Analysis and forecast to 2022,' Paris, 2017.

the recent trends in demand and supply, then discusses the trade-related issues, investments and finally proposes the projections for demand and supply for the next five years.

A. *Methodology for Coal Market Forecast*

378. The medium-term forecast sheds a light on how the coal market would react in the next five years, based on the current policy and data the Agency has. Several parameters are taken into account, such as export capacities, costs and coal demand, enabling to estimate the future trade between exporting and importing countries. As of 2017, the Agency uses two models for different kinds of coal trade forecast with more detailed information available in the methodological part of the report.[584] The results of the simulation produce the actual forecast and then the country-level analysis is provided. Thus, the trade flows between exporting and importing countries are estimated for the next five years, based on data about the future development of coal demand, transport, production costs and capacities. The main policies concerning coal, such as export quotas, taxes and royalties, are assumed to stay constant during the outlook period unless changes have been firmly committed.[585]

B. *From Coal, Oil and Gas to Renewables and Energy Efficiency*

379. In 2012, among the usual annual reports on gas, oil and coal, renewable energy was for the first time the focus of market report series. Since 2012, the IEA publishes annually the market report on renewables, recognizing its increasing role in the global power mix. The first edition of the report forecasted renewable energy generation and capacity across eight technologies – hydropower, bioenergy for power, onshore wind, offshore wind, PV, Concentrating Solar Power (CSP), geothermal and ocean.[586] Since 2016, the scope of the report covers also the trends on renewables technologies for transport and heat production technologies, as they are responsible for a large part of global final energy consumption.[587] Apart from the official IEA statistics, which provides the basis for much of the data analysis, the report has other sources, including the suggestions from the research community, industry associations and consultancies, which are mentioned in the acknowledgement part.[588] Throughout the years, it 'is possible to see much more countries and institutions from not only OECD countries but also non-OECD members, providing comments and inputs for the report, mentioned in the acknowledgement'.

---

584. *Ibid.* p. 100.
585. IEA, 'Medium-Term Coal Market Report 2015,' 2015.
586. IEA, 'Medium-Term Renewable Market Report 2012,' 2012.
587. IEA, 'Medium-Term Renewable Market Report 2016,' 2016.
588. IEA, 'Medium-Term Renewable Market Report 2012,' 2012.

380. For the technology-based forecast, the report gives a little insight into the methodology and assumptions it uses. Mainly, it assesses the advantages and challenges of each technology and makes judgment on their further exploitable potential.[589] However, as was discussed in the WEO section, there is a rising criticism regarding the forecasts the Agency does on renewable energy technology,[590] requiring a more transparency on the methodology and the reasons behind the assumptions used in the report. For the country-level forecast, it states the same assumptions as for WEO, such as the GDP and population growth, power demand growth, country-level issues of economic attractiveness and power system integration. The forecast focuses on baseline case scenario, which is carried out in the context of the current policy context, according to the year the report is written.[591]

381. Another important source of information is the diverse TCPs,[592] which consist of independent, international groups of experts that enable governments and industries from around the world to lead programmes and projects on different energy technologies.[593] For instance, the Solar Paces TCP[594] aims to promote the development of Concentrated Solar Power technology through publication, conferences, research task programmes and other activities. Also, it provides the first-hand information on the CSP technology development for the renewable energy report, due to its large experts' network.

382. The last to be added to the market report series is the *Energy Efficiency Market Report (EEMR)* launched in 2013 by the Energy Efficiency Unit.[595] This was an important step towards a further global integration of energy efficiency practice and acceptance of it as an energy source. Indeed, many governments encouraged all sorts of energy production, but fewer encourage energy efficiency.[596] The authors of the EEMR face many challenges regarding data collection, as mentioned in the report. For instance, it is difficult to measure the level of investment in energy efficiency and its value of resultant energy savings.[597]

383. While previous reports had more country-focused perspective, the recent EEMR prepared in 2018[598] had more global perspective with a clear division of

589. *Ibid.* at 16.
590. S. Evans, *Analysis: How have the IEA's Renewable Forecasts Changed?* | Carbon Brief (2016), https://www.carbonbrief.org/analysis-how-have-iea-renewable-forecasts-changed accessed 13 April 2019.
591. IEA, *supra* n. 589 at 17.
592. For more information, please visit the link: https://www.iea.org/tcp/ accessed 13 April 2019.
593. IEA, 'Frequently Asked questions,' Paris, 2018.
594. For more information please visit: https://www.solarpaces.org/csp-research-tasks/about-the-solarpaces-tcp-with-iea/ accessed 13 April 2019.
595. IEA, 'Energy Efficiency Market Report 2013,' 2013.
596. B. Somberg, 'IEA: Energy Efficiency is 40 Percent of the Climate Answer, but Major Economies Still Significantly Underinvest | Alliance to Save Energy,' *Alliance to save energy*, 2018, https://www.ase.org/blog/iea-energy-efficiency-40-percent-climate-answer-major-economies-still-significantly-underinvest accessed 13 April 2019.
597. IEA, *supra* n. 596. .
598. IEA, *supra* n. 520.

Energy Efficiency (EE) possibilities by sectors, such as transport, building, industry, including the usual investments overview. Also, the 2018 *Market Report Series: Energy Efficiency* incorporates a new EWS based on the analysis from the IEA *WEO*. This scenario pictures the world energy mix, in which the government adopts all the available cost-effective energy efficiency potential between now and 2040. The results show that energy efficiency could provide more than 40% of the abatement required by 2040 to be in line with the Paris Agreement.[599] Prior to 2018, the IEA has not done any forecast on EE market, but rather focused on the market overview and country-focused market snapshots. Therefore, it 'is an important step to show policymakers the potential of EE to contribute to their national energy systems and climate goals'. The most recent EE World Scenario projection as of the 2018 WEO depicts projections to 2040 and maps out the particular regulatory and policy strategies to accomplish this. For instance, it proposes 're-allocating spending to efficiency from other subsidies that discourage the efficient use of energy. This has the potential to provide a policy "win-win" because energy efficiency and subsidy reform are mutually reinforcing'.[600]

384. Methodology for EE scenario: The EWS is based on similar WEO assumptions, yet the main difference is the condition that all policies are implemented to allow the market to realize the potential of all known energy efficiency measures that are economically viable. Yet, the report recognizes that the view adopted is rather conservative, as it does not include the potential for technological advances between 2018 and 2040. This means that if further cost reduction would be in place, the integration of EE measures will be even more radical. In determining which energy efficiency measures are economically viable, payback periods have been chosen in line with the literature and in consultation with experts. Also, the value of other benefits, such as improved air quality and the social cost of carbon, are not included in the economical choice.[601] These are conditions, which are important to note, analysing the results of the EE scenario.

IV. World Energy Investment

385. The investment data were in a constant observance under the IEA watch, but usually were a part of the WEO. In 2014 the special report for the WEO focused on the Investment outlook picture to 2035 – a first full update since the 2003 *WEI Outlook*.[602] Since then the new series of *WEI Report* started to be published annually, looking closer in the investment made worldwide and recognizing the importance of mobilizing the investments for the energy sector. The report is provided as a free publication and explores the general data and analysis on global energy investments, financing and funding trends, investments in R&D and new technology, and implications of the investments, with a breakdown by industry sector and

599. *Ibid.* at 13.
600. *Ibid.* at 43.
601. *Ibid.* at 26.
602. IEA, 'World Energy Investment Outlook. Special Report of World Energy Outlook series', 2014.

geography. According to the IEA, this analysis is intended to complement other IEA publications such as the *WEO, TCEP* and *Annual Market Reports*.[603] Moreover, the WEI looks in the future, as how much investment is needed to meet the demand growth and compensate the declining oil and gas fields, as many of them are retiring.

A. *Methodology*

386. The report covers mainly investments in three sectors: 1) energy efficiency; 2) oil, gas and coal; and 3) electricity and renewables. In most cases, investments are defined as overnight capital expenditure on new assets; however, depending on the sector the definitions might vary. The definitions which are used by the authors vary according to the sector and could be found in the *World Energy Investment: Methodology Annex* for each respective year, together with the detailed methodology on investment calculations.[604] The IEA annually adjusts its data to reflect the inflation and integrate the updated data from the previous year in the new reports. Given the difficulties in collecting the data, which are not always complete or transparent, the IEA warns readers to interpret the results on trends as guidelines. Yet the results remains an important source of information for governments, energy industry and financial institutions to set policy frameworks, implement business strategies, finance new projects and develop new technologies.[605] Before launching the final version of the report, the IEA organizes a special workshop to discuss the findings with relevant experts. In 2018, more than eighty participants gathered to provide insights for the report at the IEA Roundtable on Energy Investment held in March 2018 in Paris. This WEI Roundtable was structured around three sessions, each with a particular thematic focus:[606]

(1) The ongoing transformation of the oil and gas industry.
(2) Changing business models and the financing of electricity sector investments.
(3) Investing in the future: New technologies and business models.

387. In drafting the report, surveys and questionnaires are sent to various private sector and intergovernmental entities, including regional development banks and export credit agencies, which are intended to represent various perspectives along the energy supply chain.[607] Following this, a preliminary draft is circulated to various experts at both public and private institutions for peer review and comments, who are acknowledged in each report. Following the initial 2015 report, the main framework stays the same starting with a broad overview of trends affecting

603. IEA, 'World Energy Investment', Paris, 2017.
604. IEA, 'World Energy Investment 2018: Methodology Annex', Paris, 2018.
605. *Ibid.* at 9.
606. IEA, *World Energy Investment Roundtable 2018, Workshop held in Paris 9 March 2018* (2018), https://www.iea.org/workshops/world-energy-investment-roundtable-2018.html accessed 13 April 2019 accessed 13 April 2019.
607. IEA, 'World Energy Investment', Paris, 2017.

energy investments, both global and sector specific, which affect particular types of energy investments. For instance, in the 2018 WEI, energy investment trends were assessed for electricity and renewable networks and storage, as well as oil, gas and coal supply.[608] The report also covers market-level developments including mergers and acquisitions and upstream implications of factors such as currency valuation and trends in financing and lending. Finally, the WEI covers emerging technologies, such as batteries for EV and Hydrogen, focusing on its investment potential.

388. As for the investment in renewable energy sources, a similar report is prepared by Bloomberg New Energy Finance (BNEF). When both reports were compared by Joshua S Hill,[609] the IEA's report again demonstrated a lower potential of the investment in renewables, representing less than USD 300 billion of total investments in 2018 against USD 333.5 billion reported by BNEF. The reason is the difference in the calculation approach: 'Angus McCrone describes IEA's as "more backward-looking" compared to BNEF's "more forward-looking approach"' – which, is important to note, is not a criticism of one over another, but simply an internal choice made by each organization. According to McCrone, '*the IEA simply takes figures for the amount of capacity that came online in a particular year and then multiplies that by estimated capital costs per megawatt, to come up with investment estimates. The IEA renewable investment numbers represent the overnight cost of the renewables capacity that came online in a given year. This is an important measure because it indicates the actual turnover of the energy asset base rather than just the flow of money*'. As well noted by Fatih Birol '*Investment made today determines the future.*'[610] This report actually tells an important story on where the energy investments went and how our short-term future would look like. The story for now: while investments in renewable energy occupy a big share of new investment, it continues to decline threatening energy security, climate change and air pollution goals.[611]

V. Special Reports

389. While the majority of the reports, which the IEA produced since the beginning of its existence, were mainly about the statistics, as well as the overview of the energy sector and its forecast, data often would indicate a specific trend behind it. Thus, the need for reports with more in-depth focus emerged. More than four hundred special reports and insights series can be found online on the IEA's website on different topics: from very specific, such as the district energy system in China, to

608. IEA, 'World Energy Investment 2018', 2018.

609. J. S. Hill, *BNEF vs. IEA Clean Energy Investment Numbers – Who To Believe?* (*Cleantechnica*, 2018), https://cleantechnica.com/2018/07/31/trends-vs-activity-understanding-the-differences-between-bnef-iea-investment-figures/ accessed 13 April 2019.

610. F. Birol, 'Presentation – Energy Investment Outlook. Presentation Online,' *IEA*, 2014. [Online]. Available: https://www.youtube.com/watch?v=awwVbAG0eig accessed 13 April 2019.

611. A. Vaughan, IEA Warns of 'Worrying Trend' as Global Investment in Renewables Falls (The Guardian, 2018), https://www.theguardian.com/business/2018/jul/17/iea-warns-of-worrying-trend-as-global-investment-in-renewables-falls accessed 13 April 2019.

broader topics, as the EV outlook. In addition to the technology, country or sector-specific focus, which the report usually takes, the latter covers as well often climate change-related issues, such as the emission trading system and climate development mechanisms.

390. The choice of the topic for the report could be either internal or external. The IEA itself might deem a specific topic important to be covered and then prepare a special report on it. For example, the *Global Gas Security Review* published in 2018[612] was prepared by IEA, as authors would like to bring additional attention to the energy security problem in the gas market. Also, the *WEO* has special issues every year on different topics, which the Agency considers to be important to investigate in more details. For instance, in 2017 the *WEO* had several special reports: *South East Asia Energy Outlook, Energy Access, and Natural Gas*[613] – all these topics were highlights of the WEO 2017 findings.

391. The report could be also prepared upon the request of the specific agency, government or for a specific international meeting, often cooperating with another agency. For example, the 2018 *Global Status Report* was prepared by the IEA and UNEP[614] for the Global Alliance for Buildings and Construction and translated to various languages.[615] The report provided guidelines to minimize the carbon footprint of building materials, as well as reducing the vulnerability and increasing the resilience of buildings to climate change. The first special report, which is possible to find online, dates back to 2005 concerning 'saving oil in a hurry' prepared as a response to the high price in the oil market and increasing instability of oil supply. The report provided the quantitative assessment of the potential oil savings and policy alternatives to conventional fuel rationing, as establishing the demand restraint measures. Since then, many other reports have been published, yet the findings and trends shown in these reports are usually in line with data provided in the WEO.

VI. Country Reports

392. The IEA has been conducting in-depth peer reviews of its member countries' energy policies since 1976. These reports serve not only to support national energy policy development but also to encourage other countries to learn from international best practices and experiences. For instance, the report prepared for Finland focuses on its initiative to halve oil consumption in the transport sector by 2030

612. IEA, 'Global Gas Security Review', 2018.
613. All other WEO and its Special Reports could be found here https://webstore.iea.org/world-energy-outlook accessed 13 April 2019.
614. United Nation Environmental Program.
615. IEA and UNEP, '2018 Global Status Report: Towards a ZeroEmission, Efficient and Resilient Buildings and Construction Sector', 2018.

through the use of biofuels. The report provides important recommendation for policymakers in Finland and also brings more transparency to the topic so other countries could learn from this experience.[616]

393. Generally, Country Reports aim to provide more in-depth overview of the IEA's member and non-member countries' energy sector. The analysis is carried out using the IEA's methodology, such as surveys, which highlights the challenges each subsector faces. Then, the Agency proposes recommendations and observations regarding each problem. While all IEA member countries had at least one in-depth country report, the Agency conducts the analysis for non-members occasionally and often upon the government's request. Yet, the methodology of the analysis remains the same. For instance in case of Chile, 'the IEA was invited to conduct the energy policy review, as stated in the report', and in the acknowledgement.[617] This could be explained by the fact that Chile as well as other non-member countries participate in the IEA activities on a voluntary basis and the IEA could conduct the research in these countries upon the request of the government. More than 144 country reports are available online with the oldest one online dating back to 2003, and dedicated to the Russian energy system, where a survey on all subsectors of the energy system was conducted. The survey was timely, as the new Energy Strategy of the Russian Federation to 2020 was just approved by the government in October 2001.[618] As at the time, in Russia, there was little renewable energy developed, the second report followed up investigating the potential of Russian renewable energy sector, as well as many other reports after this one.[619]

394. In general, country reports would start with an overview of the energy sector, main institutions, legal system and energy balance. Then they would highlight the main energy sources a country relies on, such as oil, gas and coal going into details regarding the supply and demand as well as market assessment. Then, they examine renewable energy, energy efficiency, electricity, heating, nuclear power and energy technology research development. Generally, the main focus of the reports is to draw the overview of the whole sector, identify the challenges and propose recommendations on how to tackle them. The questionnaire used to prepare the individual country reviews (In-Depth Review, IDR and Emergency Response Review, ERR) is available online.[620] It consists of Part I (Energy System Transformation) and Part II (Energy Security) with eleven sections. Also, the geographical reach of the analysis has expanded considerably. Since 2005, the scope of non-member countries participated in the in-depth analysis has been growing, starting that year with the Middle East and North Africa, and since then included China and India (2007), Russia (2011), Iraq (2012), Brazil (2013), sub-Saharan Africa (2014), India (2015)

616. EA, 'Energy policy of IEA countries: Finland 2018 Review', 2018.
617. IEA, 'Chile Energy Policy Review 2009', 2009.
618. IEA, 'Russian Electricity Reform', 2003.
619. IEA, 'Renewables in Russia: From Opportunity to Reality', 2003.
620. IEA, Questionnaires, https://www.iea.org/statistics/resources/questionnaires/ accessed 13 April 2019.

and Mexico (2016). Underlining the importance of Asia to the future of global energy, the geographic focus again turned to China in 2017, ten years after the 2007 analysis.[621]

VII. Energy Technology Perspectives (ETP)

395. The comprehensive summary of various technologies development and related policy measures could be found in the annual publication: *Energy Technology Perspectives*.[622] The report started to be published in 2006[623] and since then, looks at the technology and policy opportunities available for accelerating the transition to sustainable urban energy systems[624] and highlights the overall status and recent progress in developing and deploying key clean energy technologies. The report brings together broad IEA expertise, integrating the analysis from the *ETP* as well as the *Market Report Series*. The report covers mainly the technologies, which have usually achieved the commercial scale deployment or could achieve this scale shortly. Moreover, the cost of these technologies is expected as well to decrease.[625] The ETP model, used for the analysis, 'supports integration and manipulation of data from four soft-linked models: energy conversion, industry, transport, buildings (residential and commercial/services). The model explores outcomes that reflect variables in energy supply (using the energy conversion model) and in the three sectors that have the greatest demand, and hence the largest emissions (using models for industry, transport and buildings)'.[626] The recent ETP model 2017 generates different visions based on three scenarios for the technology roadmap:[627]

(1) The Reference Technology Scenario (RTS) – baseline scenario, which takes into account the current and planned energy and climate policies.
(2) The 2°C Scenario (2DS) – 50% chance of limiting future global average temperature increases to 2°C by 2100.
(3) The Beyond 2°C Scenario (B2DS) – to approach carbon neutrality by 2060 and limit temperature increases to 1.75°C by 2100.

396. The scenarios are presented with different energy technology and policy pathways for a low-carbon energy system in the period up to 2060. Each scenario has a different implication for technology deployment and energy policy, which are

621. IEA, World Energy Outlook, https://www.iea.org/weo/aboutweo/ accessed 13 April 2019.
622. IEA, Data and Publications https://webstore.iea.org/energy-technology-perspectives accessed 13 April 2019.
623. K. Ben Naceur, 'The Energy Technology Perspectives 2016. Webinar online', *Grantham Imperial*, 2016. [Online]. Available: https://www.youtube.com/watch?v=8InMHCxqazA. accessed 13 April 2019.
624. IEA, Data and Publications, https://webstore.iea.org/energy-technology-perspectives-2016, accessed 13 April 2019.
625. More on the technology approach https://www.iea.org/etp/etpmodel/technologyapproach/, accessed 13 April 2019.
626. More on the analytical approach and ETP model: https://www.iea.org/etp/etpmodel/, accessed 13 April 2019.
627. IEA, 'Energy Technology Perspectives (ETP) 2017', 2017.

discussed in the report. All scenarios, including the most ambitious one B2DS, are possible to achieve from the technical point of view, but require higher economic and political resources. The ETP publication has two parts: the first is 'Tracking Clean Energy Progress' and the second is the global outlook 'Catalysing Energy Technology Transformations'.[628] The report has four sector-specific chapters: electricity, industry, transport and building; and two cross-cutting chapters: CCS and bioenergy.[629] While the first part gives an overview of the progress of the technology, the second part proposes policy recommendation on how to accelerate the technology transformation. For example, in 2017, the report suggested that while the energy system is evolving, policy signals are needed to accelerate and steer its transformation.[630] These recommendations are important, especially for policymakers, to close the gaps identified in the TCEP.

397. The first TCEP report was done in 2011, and since then, the report covers different clean energy technology and sectors, providing not only the latest number and trends on what happens but also a benchmarking analysis on where these technologies should be in order to achieve climate change goals.[631] Since 2018, the benchmark of technology progress is not done any more to 2DS scenario, but towards a more complex SDS, used in WEO.[632] The progress is divided into three categories: green, which indicates that this technology is on track, yellow – making some progress, but not enough – and red – not making progress at all. The TCEP in 2018, for example, showed that only three of the twenty-six identified clean energy technologies are on track to meet a sustainable energy transition (one more than last year), while fifteen technologies showed only some progress, and eight are significantly off track and in need of renewed action to achieve the SDS goals.[633]

398. TCEP 2017 also included a special section on Tracking Clean Energy Innovation Progress, containing unique information on public and private investment in research, development, and demonstration. The Special Section highlights that total innovation investment needs to pick up to fulfil its important role of achieving secure and sustainable energy systems and delivering economic growth and reducing air pollution.

VIII. Technology Roadmaps

399. While the ETP gives a more general outlook of all low-carbon technology, the technology roadmaps provide a more detailed overview of each technology in

628. https://www.iea.org/etp/ and P. Janoska, Tracking Clean Energy Progress (TCEP). Webinar online (*IEA*), https://www.youtube.com/watch?v=dOrH44aUtGw accessed 13 April 2019.
629. E. Levina, Energy Technology Perspectives 2017 – Catalysing Energy Technology Transformations. Webinar online (*IEA*, 2017), https://www.youtube.com/watch?v=YMZmMPrIdEY accessed 13 April 2019.
630. IEA, 'Energy Technology Perspectives (ETP) 2017', 2017.
631. IEA, Tracking Clean Energy Progress, https://www.iea.org/tcep/ accessed 13 April 2019.
632. Janoska, *supra* n. 629.
633. *Ibid.*

focus, starting from its development, current state of art and future perspectives. The analysis identifies drivers and barriers of technology and provides a practical tool, as well as a conceptual framework to support policymakers to pursue the desired level of technology deployment, as well as to better inform the decisions of key stakeholders, from the industry to the financial sector. The main questions the publications are focused on are the following:[634]

– Where is the technology today?
– Where would we want it to go in the long term?
– What are the priority actions, which are needed to accelerate the development and deployment of a given technology?

400. First, it identifies the technology baseline based on cooperation with different experts, and then the authors would use the IEA's modelling tool to identify the growth pathway to achieve the required technology contribution for the low-carbon transition. Finally, authors identify a set of milestones to guide the implementation of the required steps.[635] The technology roadmaps programme started in 2008 and provides an overview mainly of the low-carbon technologies, which are in line with the general objectives of transition to the low-carbon economy. There are many roadmaps on renewables, but as well, on nuclear energy, and low-carbon transition in industries.[636] The energy technology policy division, which elaborates the reports, is mainly responsible for not only all technology and policy-related analysis but also all the multilateral collaboration work with the network of over six thousand scientists working in forty different fields under the IEA umbrella.[637] These are experts from academia, the public and private sectors from member and non-member countries.

401. Roadmaps can be developed for different levels of deployment, including global, national and regional levels, and can be sector or technology specific. Between 2010 and 2016, a first cycle of thirty-two IEA Technology Roadmaps were produced, covering twenty-one different technology areas, such as Wind, PV, Bioenergy and others. The second cycle was endorsed at the G7 Energy Ministerial Meeting in May 2016 (Kitakyushu) and aims to set out a long-term vision for up to

634. D. Houssin, Energy Storage Technology Roadmap. Webinar Online, *Clean Energy Solutions* (2014), https://youtube/pzmSnaeVA0g accessed 13 April 2019.
635. Check for instance the Technology roadmap on Hydrogen and Fuel cells, 2015. https://www.iea.org/publications/freepublications/publication/ TechnologyRoadmapHydrogenandFuelCells.pdf 13 April 2019.
636. For instance, the Agency has done one report on the Hydrogen and Fuel Cells in 2015. From the recent issues, the report was dedicated to Low-Carbon Transition in the Cement Industry, which the Agency has done together with Cement Sustainability Initiative (CSI). All the reports are possible to find following the link: https://webstore.iea.org/technology-roadmaps?pagenumber=2 accessed 13 April 2019.
637. J.-F. Gagné, 'The IEA's Energy Technology Perspectives 2015 (ETP). Presentation online', *The CSIS Energy and National Security*, 2015. [Online]. Available: https://www.youtube.com/watch?v=OA7MUoNPdRI&t=539s accessed 13 April 2019.

2060[638] and uses the IEA ETP 2DS for guidance.[639] The scenarios mentioned for ETP publication are also used in the technology roadmap. Authors place a particular technology in the framework of these scenarios and analyse which steps should be done in order to achieve the aims of each scenario. If both RTS and 2DS scenarios are compared, there is a significant gap between them. According to the 2DS scenario, all the energy sector need to contribute to achieve the scenario's goal; therefore the report, focused on the particular technology, demonstrates how it could contribute to the overall goal mentioned in the ETP. For instance, the hydrogen technology report highlights that it has the potential to facilitate significant reductions in energy-related CO_2 emissions and increase the energy security.[640] Recently, the IEA started to publish a series of manuals under the IEA Technology Roadmap programme – the *How2Guides* – that offer guidance on the key steps to developing and implementing a national or regional roadmap for some of the most important technologies. The guides provide the required information and tools for government and companies to design, manage and implement an effective energy technology roadmap process relevant to their own local circumstances and objectives.[641]

§2. Interim Conclusion

402. The IEA produces many different publications on various topics and it 'is easy to get lost in the overwhelming amount of these reports'. This chapter aimed to provide an overview of the main publications produced by the IEA divided by category, as the readers can find it on the IEA's website. The publications cover many different aspects of the energy sector from fossil fuel to the development of technology, emissions and energy access. These publications are crucial for the increasing transparency in the energy sector and drawing a global picture on where the energy sector stands and where it heads to. While for some reports and analysis, it was easy to find information on the methodology it used, for others it was a bit more challenging. Therefore, a greater transparency on how the scenarios are made and what kind of assumptions and why they were used is important for a better legitimization of the reports among the scientific community and society in general. Through the development of the publications since the foundation of the IEA till now, the Agency undertook a significant shift in terms of its vision moving from traditional fossil fuel towards delivering more reports and data on clean energy sources. Despite that, the Agency is still viewed as a conservative institution, with

638. The Ministry of Economy, Trade and Industry hosted the G7 Kitakyushu Energy Ministerial Meeting on 1 and 2 May 2016 and adopted the 'Kitakyushu Initiative on Energy Security for Global Growth'. For more details please visit: http://www.meti.go.jp/english/press/2016/0502_04.html accessed 13 April 2019.

639. IEA, 'Technology Roadmap. Delivering Sustainable Bioenergy', Paris, 2017., page 21.

640. IEA, 'Technology Roadmap Hydrogen', 2015.

641. https://webstore.iea.org/technology-roadmap-a-guide-to-development-and-implementation accessed 13 April 2019.

constantly failing projections of renewable energy development. Data and reports are important products which attributed a weight to the IEA's scenarios. With this, it has an increasing responsibility on which kind of story it tells and what kind of energy sector we will have in the future.

Chapter 7. Network-Addresses-Relations with Other Organizations

§1. International Organizations and the IEA

403. Most studies concerning international organizations deal with the reasons why states decide to create or join international organizations.[642] What is less studied is the evolution of international organizations.[643] Few international organizations in the world deal with energy. Many of them are active in the fields of trade, security, and environmental protection. If we consider the energy sector, the most advanced multilateral energy organization is undoubtedly the IEA; it is worth noting that it is not only one of the oldest institutions in the world, but also the most advanced energy organization. An analysis of the evolution of this agency is really interesting. It was originally created to help countries to coordinate themselves in the energy field, after the oil crisis of 1973/1974. The US Secretary of State Henry Kissinger played a leading role in the creation of the Agency; he noticed that there was the need to react together in light of the Arab oil embargo of 1973. The functions of the Agency were, on the one side, maintaining and improving systems for coping with oil supply disruptions and, on the other side, the desire to act as a body for the development of policy, information sharing and technology transfer. The nature of the Agency, however, has changed with the passing of time. The new goal of the Agency became 'helping governments to support their economies with secure, environmentally acceptable energy', as Tanaka, Executive Director, described the IEA's core mission during a speech.[644] By looking at the changes of the IEA, what needs to be born in mind, first of all, is that changes in the wider international environment do not automatically conduct to a change in the institutional design of an international organization.[645] Many hypotheses have arisen regarding this evolution of the IEA. Three of them are here reported. A first hypothesis states that the Member States of the Agency have determined the institutional evolution of the IEA by taking 'deliberate choices',[646] collectively or individually taken, in response to changing conditions. According to this point of view, international organizations are considered as 'glorified permanent conferences'.[647] A second hypothesis, based on the concept of historical institutionalism, posits that the evolution of the Agency is linked to the principles of the IEP Agreement. In this way, there is a sort of 'path dependence' by which it is meant 'previous institutional arrangements

642. Kenneth Abbot and Duncan Snidal, *Why States Act Through Formal International Organizations*, 42(1) Journal of Conflict Resolution 3-32 (1998).
643. Simon Hug & Thomas König, *Domestic Structures and Constitution-Building in an International Organization: Introduction*, 2(2) The Review of International Organizations 105, 105-113 (2007).
644. Nobuo Tanaka (2009). *Shifting Gears in the Global Dialogue on Energy Security and Climate Change*, The Brookings Institution, 13 February.
645. Graaf and Lesage, *supra* n. 34 at 296.
646. Barbara Koremenos, Charles Lipson & Duncan Snidal, *The Rational Design of International Institutions*. 55(4) International Organization, 761, 767 (2001).
647. Buzan, B., & Little, R. (2000). International Systems in World History: Remaking the Study of International Relations. Oxford: Oxford University Press, 266.

affect subsequent changes'.[648] International organizations, however, cannot be considered simply passive actors; they can be active. A third hypothesis, based on the concept of sociological institutionalism, states that the Secretariat of the IEA can be considered an actor with its own interests. In this way, international organizations can be considered bureaucracies with rational authority, trying to increase their budget, independence and staff.[649] This short description of the evolution of the IEA and the main theories concerning this process are of interest also in the perspective of the Agency's attitude towards member and non-member countries. The Agency has made quite big efforts to develop its relationship with many countries beyond its member countries. The global perspective of the Agency was stressed during the 2009 IEA Ministerial Meeting during which China, India and Russia joined the twenty-eight IEA members. On that occasion, IEA released joint statements with each of the three countries. The IEA Secretariat was asked to expand the training and workshops it offers to partner countries in order to bolster the capacity to formulate sound energy policy. The goals identified on that occasion were access to energy and the reduction of energy poverty,[650] especially in Africa and Asia. In particular, the IEA, starting from its knowledge and experience, had the duty to address energy poverty in developing countries. The IEA Secretariat was asked to convene senior officials from IEA member countries and from some other countries and international organizations in order to discuss an international partnership on energy and sustainability. Making the influence of the Agency wider obviously needed an expansion of its membership. The IEA was created first to support the consuming countries, but, with the passing of time, half of the energy consumption was located in non-member countries.[651] This is the reason why the Agency had to focus on its external relationships. An interesting issue is also about the opportunity for new

---

648. John S. Duffield, *The Limits Of 'Rational Design'*, 57(2) International Organization. 411, 418 (2003).

649. Yoram Haftel & Alexander Thompson, The Independence of International Organisations, 50(2) Journal of Conflict Resolution 254 (2006).

650. As Nobuo Tanaka told the Financial Times: '*Our relevance is under question because half of the energy consumption already is in non-Organisation of Economic Cooperation and Development countries. And for oil it is soon coming that the majority of consumption is happening in non-OECD countries.*' He added: '*In many ways they [the Chinese] are already working closely with us. But eventually we wish they would join us.*'

651. The IEA Executive Director Nobuo Tanaka explained in a speech of 2009 that: '*The member countries of the IEA no longer dominate world energy markets, as consumers or as producers, to the extent they once did ... And their share will continue to diminish: our research shows that non-OECD countries will account for 87% of global energy demand growth between 2006 and 2030, taking their share of world primary energy demand from 51% to 62% over the same period. ... on top of this, our very notion of "energy security" is broadening ... we must also now consider gas security ... as well as the reliability of renewable energy sources and ensuring stable electricity markets. At the same time, we are today confronting a phenomenon that might barely have been thought possible 35 years ago. And one that is inextricably linked to our energy production and use – that of climate change. As part of this challenge, we see that an increasing share of energy related CO2 emissions will come from non-IEA members ... there is a third and related factor that is vitally important to consider in the context of a global energy dialogue. And that is the need for continued investment in the energy sector.*' He then continued '*It is my view that the IEA can and must remain at the centre of such a global dialogue. The IEA is the only international energy organization with expertise across the entire energy field. We have a philosophy of open markets and diversity of supply. We have a reputation for objective and independent analysis. And we provide*

players to join the Agency. If we consider the case of China, for example, it was invited to join the Ministerial meeting of 2009 and it responded positively to this invitation, sending its deputy director general of the National Administration of Energy Industry (NAEI). On that occasion, China showed interest in deepening the relationship with the IEA in terms of energy efficiency, new energy production and carbon capture. Even if the behaviour of China was clearly positive, this does not mean the Chinese Government plans to join the Agency.

404. This example shows why the IEA is expanding its influence. The IEA is developing policy relationships with non-member countries through its various dialogues, workshops and training sessions. The cooperation with the G8 has particularly facilitated the process of expansion of the Agency, giving the opportunity of forming forums such as the Networks of Expertise in Energy Technology (NEET).

405. It also organizes workshops and training seminars for members and non-members alike. The IEA fosters collaboration through the technology-IAs on a variety of issues such as solar power, clean coal and wind energy, which include Signatories from IEA member and non-Member States. The Agency is focusing in particular on the 'big three' non-members (China, India and Russia), planning meetings that will bring together all three, along with perhaps a dozen of other non-Member States, in the hope of developing stronger multilateralized ties even in the absence of formal membership.

I. Goals of the IEA

406. The IEA aims at creating conditions to make its member countries developing in a sustainable way, for the sake of people and the environment.[652] While shaping energy policies, the Agency highlights the importance of free and open markets in order to favour environmental protection and assure energy security. Among the principles of the activity of the Agency, diversity, efficiency and flexibility are considered as a starting point for energy security. Energy systems should be flexible and ready to face energy emergencies. The shared goals of the Agency should be achieved through a sustainable use of energy sources and the impact of energy production should be minimized as much as possible. As a consequence, not only more environmentally friendly sources, such as non-fossil sources, should be developed and favoured, but also efficiency in the use of energy should be considered. Governments are asked to support energy opportunities concerning its entire cycle, through research, development and investment. Dialogue and cooperation are of crucial importance. The idea of cooperation, after all, is part of the roots of the IEA. This is glaringly shown in the goals of the Agency, which are included in the I.E.P.

---

a range of forums in which governments – both IEA and non-IEA, as well as researchers and industry experts, can come together to solve common problems in a practical and cooperative environment.'

652. *IEA Shared Goals*, document available at https://www.iea.org/about/history accessed 13 April 2019.

Agreement. In the Preamble of the Agreement, it is clearly said that the organization aims at the promotion of secure oil supplies, basically throughout the ESS. This system is based on two obligations for member countries: 1) they must hold oil emergency reserves of ninety days of net imports; 2) they must conceive a programme of demand restraint measures which can be implemented in the hypothesis of oil supply disruption.[653] This scenario happens if any member, or the entire group of member countries, has an oil supply shortfall of at least 7%. In this case, the Secretariat declares that the emergency and the measure become mandatory. Clearly, this mechanism highlights the importance of the role of the Secretariat. In the event of activation, if member countries fail to comply, they can be punished receiving less from the allocation system. This system also includes oil companies. When it was created, forty-five oil companies with business operations in the IEA's area agreed to share their oil in case of emergency.[654] The idea to face oil shortfalls with a cooperative attitude was not new for oil companies. In this way, the insurance function was shared and based on an agreed mechanism.

II. Autonomy of the IEA

407. In order to carry out its functions, the IEA has been provided with a proper set of internal and external dynamics and support. The Agency, thanks to its relationship with the OECD, retains full autonomy.[655] It is worth noting that many provisions of the I.E.P. Agreement state that OECD rules do not apply to the IEA. Moreover, it is highlighted that there is no dependence of the IEA on the OECD. The IEA has simply been created in the framework of the OECD; this means that, first of all, in order to become a member of the IEA, a state is required to be part of the OECD.[656] Second, quick references to the OECD principles are recalled when dealing with the IEA scales of contributions.[657] The link between the two institutions dates back to 1974, when, during the negotiations on the I.E.P. Agreement, important contributions were made by the OECD representatives. These contributions were focused on the structure of the Agency and its instruments.[658] Thanks to this cooperation between the IEA and the OECD, the IEA helped the OECD with its long-term energy assessment.[659] This assessment dealt with energy statistics and economic analysis, making the IEA itself being enriched by the OECD's contributions. Furthermore, the OECD worked to guarantee the support necessary for the IEA. A proper analysis of this relationship is necessary.

---

653. Scott, R. (1994). IEA – *The First Twenty Years. The History of the International Energy Agency, 1974-1994*. Paris: IEA/OECD.
654. Badger, D. B. (1988). International Cooperation During Oil Supply Disruptions: The Role of the International Energy Agency. In G. Horwich & D. L. Weimer (eds), Responding to international oil crises (pp. 1-16). Washington: American Enterprise Institute for Public Policy Research.
655. The autonomous status of the IEA in the OECD was a stated objective in the negotiation stage.
656. Art. 71.1 I.E.P. Agreement.
657. Art. 64.1 I.E.P. Agreement.
658. *Ibid.* 129.
659. OECD, *Energy Prospects to 1985.*

408. By looking at Article 1 of the Council Decision,[660] the IEA could be considered as part of the OECD for some purposes. In these cases, the Agency can exploit the legal personality of the OECD, even if keeping its independence. Moreover, the IEA could use OECD services. By considering the history of the two organizations, the relationship looks quite harmonious. In sectors with a specific framework, no problems have arisen. Some issues have been created by general rules, especially in the fields of personnel and financing. Clearly, cooperation needs a good attitude by both organizations.

409. The I.E.P. Agreement, the decisions of the Governing Board and of the Council are at the base of the link between the two institutions. The I.E.P. Agreement, which is a treaty under international law, deals with the structure of the Agency, the obligations of the member countries and the Agency goals in the energy sector. Including all the elements of the Agency, the Agreement represents a real achievement of autonomy.

410. The decision of the Council, on the other hand, deals with the relationship of the Agency with the OECD. The Program is regulated by the I.E.P. Agreement. The mechanism to develop, adapt and modify the Program is included.

411. Regarding the process to adopt the I.E.P. Agreement, it was a two-step procedure. First an OECD Council Decision was necessary; second, the I.E.P. Agreement had to be signed. The Council Decision was adopted in the form it had been negotiated at the ECG meetings in Brussels. Some arrangements were made by the two institutions in a dynamic form of cooperation.

412. Concerning the current cooperation of the two organizations, Article 9 of the Council Decision says that 'The Agency shall co-operate with other competent bodies of the Organisation in areas of common interest. These bodies and the Agency shall consult with one another regarding their respective activities.' The bodies involved in this cooperation are the Governing Board and the Standing Groups and Committees, on the side of the IEA, and the Council and the Executive Committee on the OECD side.

III. The IEA Membership (Once Again)

413. First of all, some terms used in the I.E.P. Agreement need to be explained. According to Article 1.2, this agreement is among 'States'.[661] By looking at Chapter X of the Agreement, the role of states as parties of the Agreement is confirmed. States are included in the Agreement both with their names, for example on the signature pages of the Agreement, and with the term 'Governments'. A second term is also often used: 'governments'; even if it is not specifically defined, it is adopted in

660. Art. 1 Council Decision, 'An International Energy Agency . . . is hereby established as an autonomous body within the framework of the Organisation.'
661. This term is here used in the sense of international law.

the Preamble of the Agreement. Moreover, by looking at the Preamble, the governments 'have agreed' concerning the Agreement. In this sense, the meaning of governments may be identified in the idea of 'member countries' of the Agency.[662] After all, the obligations of the members of the IEA are taken in the name of 'participating countries'. What can be said concerning this various terminology is probably the simple need to avoid repetitions. Article 1.2 gave a detailed definition concerning the meaning of 'participating countries' as 'States to which this Agreement applies provisionally and States for which the Agreement has entered into and remains in force'.[663] The idea of membership, despite the use of different terms, is clear. The IEA's membership has expanded a lot over the years. Such a change has also influenced the IEA's institutional design. In 1974, the starting year of the Agency, there were sixteen signatory states. They were Austria, Belgium, Canada, Denmark, Germany, Ireland, Italy, Japan, Luxembourg, the Netherlands, Spain, Sweden, Switzerland, Turkey, the UK and the US.[664] These states, called Signatories, had to apply the Agreement on a provisional basis.[665] According to Article 68.1, '(...) this Agreement shall be applied provisionally by all Signatory States, to the extent possible not inconsistent with their legislation, as from 18th November, 1974 following the first meeting of the Governing Board'. This kind of application was necessary to give the states enough time to give their consents to be bound. Thanks to this mechanism, the first meeting of the Governing Board was made on the same day of the signature of the Agreement. Such an application under I.E.P. Agreement was planned to continue until one of three events took place: 1) the Agreement definitively entered into force for the State concerned by deposit of the definitive consent to be bound, 2) the depositary received notification that the State concerned would not 'consent to be bound' by the Agreement, or 3) if the time limit for notification of consent to be bound by the State concerned expired. For each IEA member, the provisional application terminated upon the definitive entry into force of the Agreement for the State concerned. The provisional period lasted from 18 November 1974 until the Agreement entered into force on 19 January 1976 and each Signatory had deposited its definitive consent to be bound.[666] In order to enter into force, an agreement requires the states' consent to be bound. Article 67.1 of the I.E.P. Agreement states that: 'each Signatory State shall, not later than 1st May, 1975, notify the Government of Belgium that, having complied with its constitutional procedures, it consents to be bound by this Agreement'.[667] What is worth noting is that Article 67 does not give a detailed definition of how this consent should be expressed. The answer to this issue is given in Article 11 of the Vienna Convention on the Law of Treaties. It makes clear that the consent of a State to be bound by a treaty 'may be expressed

662. It is worth noting that the term 'Members' is often used in I.E.A. documentation, although, in reality, it is never employed in the Agreement to refer to IEA countries.
663. Scott, *supra* n. 400 at 66.
664. These countries are defined as Signatories. Since no provision was made for later signatures, the other countries which joined the Agency are not Signatories in a technical sense; they can be defined as 'acceding States'.
665. Application is specifically provided for in Art. 25 of the Vienna Convention on the Law of Treaties.
666. Scott, *supra* n. 400399 at 69.
667. Belgium had a role of depositary of the Agreement.

by signature, exchange of instruments constituting the treaty, ratification, acceptance, approval or accession, or by any other means if so agreed'. In the case of the I.E.P. Agreement, most of the members gave the consent to be bound by the deposit with the Government of Belgium, as depositary of the I.E.P. Agreement, of their respective instruments of ratification. As stated in Article 29 of the Vienna Convention on the Law of Treaties, also the I.E.P. Agreement includes the general rule according to which a treaty is binding in respect of the entire territory of each party. However, the Agreement gives to the Member States the possibility to broaden the territorial scope of its commitments by extending its application to areas within its frontiers. Concerning reservations, the Agreement never mentions this concept, which is part of international law.[668]

414. With the passing of time, the number of member countries has grown, reaching twenty-eight in 2009. The actual member countries of the IEA are thirty.[669] In 2018, Lithuania became a member of the OECD. During the same year, South Africa became an IEA Association country, and it is now included in the IEA and Accession/Association countries aggregate. The IEA continues to expand the coverage of its statistics reports and encourages more countries to collaborate on data exchange. Along with the participation of countries, also eight association countries are included.[670] This participation deals with the fact that the Agency tends to adopt an inclusive policy. This means the number of the IEA member countries can always change: at the moment, the process to be admitted is currently open for Chile and Lithuania. The steps in order to be admitted to the Agency deal with showing evidence of various requirements: 1) all the IEA member countries should be part of the OECD; 2) the prospective member countries should have crude oil and/or product reserves equivalent to ninety days of the previous year's net imports. These reserves should be of immediate access in the event of disruptions of global oil supply; 3) the countries should have a restraint programme in order to reduce by 10% the national oil consumption; 4) the CERM should be adopted and organized by the countries to be ready and efficient in the event of an emergency; each state should demonstrate its capacity to ensure its contribution to an IEA collective action. A collective action of the IEA is put in place in case of global oil supply disruption; this means that the IEA member countries should make available more vol umes of crude oil on the market, by reducing demand or increasing the oil supply. All these requirements are checked by the IEA Executive Director, who makes a finding to verify the potential of the country. During the process, the candidate country works with the IEA Secretariat in order to favour and accelerate the process. The final decision of admission or no admission is taken by the Governing Board.

---

668. Art. 19 of the Vienna Convention on the Law of Treaties deals with the possibility for a State to formulate reservations when signing or ratifying a treaty unless the reservation is prohibited or excluded by the treaty or is 'incompatible with the object and purpose of the treaty'.
669. The list of all the member countries is available at: https://www.iea.org/countries accessed 13 April 2019.
670. To know the Association countries in detail: https://www.iea.org/countries accessed 13 April 2019.

415. Being a Member State of the IEA means that the I.E.P. Agreement has an influence on both the internal and the external dimension of the state. Historically, the I.E.P. Agreement was created to be effective at the international level, more than at the national one. By looking at the Agreement, it is worth noticing that it focuses on the international dynamics of the Agency and of its organs.[671] According to the Vienna Convention, international law is considered as a different system and national law cannot be used as justification in case of failure of performing a treaty.[672] By focusing on the facts linked to the I.E.P. Agreement, however, since the Agreement is not self-executing, the bridge had to be covered in order to make the Agreement effective. This means that every member country has a role in implementing the Agreement. No commitment of the Agreement has ever been defined as subordinate to national law in any provision of the Agreement, once the member country has approved it. The provisional application of the I.E.P. Agreement, stated in Article 68.1, confirms this perspective. According to this principle, there was a provisional period according to which, in case of inconsistent actions, Member States could be excused because of national legal requirements. Once the Agreement entered into force, no legislative defences were available in case of actions against the Agreement covered by the national legislation.[673] This is clearly stated in Article 66,[674] which tells that each member country must take the necessary measures to implement both the I.E.P. Agreement and the decisions of the Governing Board. By analysing the practice, according to Article 66, a member country must not only have all the implementing measures *ex ante* but also maintain them and shape the following measures. The readiness of the legislative measures at the national level is constantly monitored; in fact, all the IEA member countries must report to the Secretariat.[675]

IV. Activities Towards Non-member Countries

416. The IEA, along with organizing its own activities, has also coordinated itself with non-member countries. According to the I.E.P. Agreement, the Agency had the power to have external relations. This means not only with non-member countries but also with other international organizations, individuals and entities. In particular, the goal of cooperation is included in several paragraphs[676] of the Preamble to the I.E.P. Agreement which state that: 'Desiring to promote co-operative relations with oil producing countries and with other oil consuming countries, including those of the developing world, through a purposeful dialogue, as well as

671. Scott, *supra* n. 400 at 64.
672. Art. 27, Vienna Convention on the Law of Treaties, 1969: 'A party may not invoke the provisions of its internal law as justification for its failure to perform a treaty.'
673. *Ibid.*
674. Art. 66 I.E.P. Agreement: 'Each Participating Country shall take the necessary measures, including any necessary legislative measures, to implement this Agreement and decisions taken by the Governing Board.'
675. Scott, *supra* n. 400 at 65.
676. I.E.P. Agreement, par. 3-5.

through other forms of co-operation, to further the opportunities for a better understanding between consumer and producer countries, Mindful of the interests of the other oil consuming countries, including those of the developing world, Desiring to play a more active role in relation to the oil industry by establishing a comprehensive international information system and a permanent framework for consultation with oil companies.' By considering Article 11 of the Agreement, it is clear that non-participating countries are included in the perspectives of the Agency.[677] This article makes clear that the Agency aims at including individual non-participating countries in its dynamics. A constructive approach is adopted both internally and externally. This kind of cooperation was to be exercised in total autonomy from the OECD.[678] Even if this external perspective was warmly recommended, during the first years of the Agency there were no good results.[679] The Office of Global Energy Dialogue was created in 1993. It was basically where the dialogue with non-member countries was put in place. Most of the activity of the Office was focused on cooperation with China, India and Russia. The reason why these three countries were at the centre of the attention does not only lies in their importance in the energy field. The IEA had the goal to develop relations also with Africa, Latin America and other countries but, since financial resources were not enough to cover all these areas of interest, it had to prioritize. During the 1990s, the Agency signed bilateral agreements with these countries.[680] This policy has been particularly developed, thanks to a project whose executive director was Robert Priddle. During those years, even if member countries showed interest in external relations, they were reluctant to provide additional financial resources. However, many indirect outreach activities were sustained by the Agency. Non-member countries were involved in IAs, which are operational networks in order to deepen research in the field of energy technology. Moreover, many IEA publications got attention in non-member countries, thanks to the seminars and conferences organized by the Agency, along with free and unconditional advice. In this sense, the IEA can be considered a research centre. The Agency has embodied a role of authoritative source of information concerning energy. In particular, the annual *WEO* has become a fundamental source for governments to be informed concerning energy trends, data and energy markets.

417. If we look at, for example, the years 2006-2008, the Agency organized meetings of the NEET. Another activity of the IEA has a crucial role: reviewing

677. *I.E.P. Agreement, Article 11*: 'Article 11 1. It is not an objective of the Program to seek to increase, in an emergency, the share of world oil supply that the group had under normal market conditions. Historical oil trade patterns should be preserved as far as is reasonable, and due account should be taken of the position of individual non-participating countries. 2. In order to maintain the principles set out in paragraph l, the Management Committee shall make proposals, as appropriate, to the Governing Board, which, acting by majority, shall decide on such proposals.'
678. Scott, *supra* n. 654.
679. MacNaughton, J. (2007). *Cooperating on Energy Policy: The Work of the International Energy Agency.* In N. Bayne & S. Woolcock (eds), The New Economic Diplomacy: Decision-Making and Negotiation in International Economic Relations, 290.
680. Bamberger, C. (2004). IEA – The First Thirty Years. The History of the International Energy Agency, 1974-2004.

energy policies of non-member countries. In 2009, Russia, China and India were invited to take part in the Ministerial meeting of the Agency.

418. Looking at the relationship of the IEA with OPEC, it is worth noting that until the end of 1990s communications between them had been not easy. The only way of communication during that time was indirect, through media. Thanks to a common effort and good diplomatic skills of both parties, a first meeting happened in 1995, in Vienna.[681]

A. *Right of Accession to the European Union*

419. By accession to the I.E.P. Agreement, it is meant that the procedure by which a state which is not a Signatory becomes bound by the Agreement. Such a procedure is included in Article 15 of the Vienna Convention on the Law of Treaties. This procedure is provided by Article 71.1 of the I.E.P. Agreement. It states that 'This Agreement shall be open for accession by any Member of the Organisation for Economic Co-operation and Development which is able and willing to meet the requirements of the Program. The Governing Board, acting by majority, shall decide on any request for accession.'

420. The European Communities have always been part of the I.E.P. Agreement. Its importance is included in Article 72 of the Agreement. According to it, the Agreement is open for accession by the European Communities and there is no possibility to impede this accession. Moreover, this attitude towards the European Communities was highlighted in Article 3 of the Council Decision, which states that 'this Decision will be open for accession by the European Communities upon their accession to the Agreement in accordance with its terms'. The mechanism of accession by the European Community is quite different from the one provided for states. While, regarding states, the procedure is based on the invitation of the Governing Board and the necessity for the candidate state to meet the requirements of the Programme, no requirements are requested for the European Community. Such a decision may derive from a political tendency to favour the accession of the European Community. The possible accession of the EU, however, is not an easy step. Many questions have arisen concerning this accession and the relationship of European countries with the IEA. The role of every single European Member State is particularly in doubt. On the one side they may remain an active part of the IEA; on the other side, this accession of the EU may cause a withdrawal of the single states, causing many institutional questions for the IEA concerning the applicability of the Agreement to the Union, the real proof of the Union's ability to carry out the programme, the mechanism to vote and the financial adjustments necessary to adapt the

681. This meeting was secret and informal, in a hotel in Vienna. When Robert Priddle, director of the IEA, asked to organize a meeting with Rilwani Lukman, secretary general of OPEC, many were surprised. To know more, *see*: Willenborg, R., Tönjes, C., & Perlot, W. (2004). *Europe's oil defences: An analysis of Europe's oil supply vulnerability and its emergency stockholding systems*, 40.

current contributions.[682] Furthermore, some adjustments to the IEA institutional arrangements may be necessary. The authority of the Member States concerning oil stock, demand restraint and allocation may be transferred to the Union. By looking at the practical development of the IEA, the European Communities have always had an active role, especially if we consider that the European Commission had an active role in the Washington Energy Conference. Moreover, sometime after the Conference, the Energy Co-ordinating Group (ECG) convened in Brussels to develop the programme in detail along with the OECD and the European Commission. Since that moment, the Commission has been having an active role in the daily work of the Agency. This participation deals with the Supplementary Protocol No. 1 to the OECD Convention, which allows the Commission to 'take part in the work' of the Organization.[683] In this way, the Commission can access the meetings of the IEA, make proposals and receive agendas and documents. On the other side, along with no right to vote, the Commission does not contribute financially and cannot prevent the Agency from taking actions.

B. The IEA and the Concept of Cooperation

421. It is worth noting that the IEA has to care not only about its internal organization but also external perspectives. As made clear at the moment of creation of the Agency, its role has an incredible potential to influence non-member countries. Hence, the original goal of controlling the oil consumption was obviously linked to all the energy consumers (not only the member ones); this means that the idea of cooperation was considered in a wide sense: not only among the Agency member countries but also between them and the rest of the energy-consuming countries. Such an idea, concerning the value of cooperation, was first included in the Communiqué of the Washington Energy Conference, which details the means to fight against the oil crisis.[684] This document, which dates back to the preparatory phase of the IEA, was the occasion to agree that 'there was need to develop a cooperative multilateral relationship with producing countries, and other consumer countries that takes into account the long-term interests of all'.[685] On that occasion, the importance of cooperation, the role of international oil companies and consultation with

682. Scott, *supra* n. 400 at 77-78.

683. On 20 November 1974 the Governing Board Chairman Davignon sent a letter to the Commission President Ortoli stating: 'I have the honour to inform you that, after having discussed the matter, the Governing Board of the Agency, referring to Supplementary Protocol No. 1 to the OECD Convention, which states that the Commission of the European Communities shall take part in the work of the OECD, has instructed me to invite your Institution to take part from now on in the work of the various bodies of the Agency. This invitation, of course, in no way commits the Community with regard to the decision that it may take on the basis of Article 3 of the Decision establishing the Agency. This Article states that This Decision will be open for accession by the European Communities upon their accession to the Agreement in accordance with its terms.'

684. A description of the oil crisis of the time is available in: Schmidt H. (2014) Washington Energy Conference, 11 February 1974 Statement by the German Federal Minister of Finance, Helmut Schmidt. In: Soell H. (eds) Helmut Schmidt. SpringerBriefs on Pioneers in Science and Practice, vol 20, Springer, Cham.

685. Communiqué of the Washington Energy Conference, Paragraph 14, 11 February 1974.

developing countries were described as fundamental. All these values were then included in the I.E.P Agreement, the founding document of the Agency.[686] By looking at the I.E.P. Agreement,[687] it is clear that a common goal of the member countries is the promotion of cooperative relations, both with producing and consuming oil countries. Means to do so are a proper dialogue among the member countries and a deep understanding of the dynamics of oil production and consumption. In particular, the member countries aim at creating an international information system. Article 11 of the I.E.P. Agreement underlines that 'historical oil trade patterns should be preserved as far as is reasonable, and due account should be taken of the position of individual non-participating countries'.

422. A proper consideration of the external dynamics of the Agency is clearly recommended, with a constructive and proactive approach. If we analyse the I.E.P. more in detail, many mandates and a grant of external relation powers refer to this goal of cooperation. Chapter VIII of the I.E.P. is entitled 'Relations with Producer Countries and with Other Consumer Countries'.

423. By looking at Article 44,[688] which states that the member countries have the goal to promote cooperative relations with oil-producing countries and with other consuming countries, the importance of cooperation is clear. The principle of 'promoting a purposeful dialogue' is underlined in the article, along with other kinds of cooperation. It is worth noting that the needs of developing countries[689] and the importance of exchanging views on the relations with producer countries[690] are included as fundamental in the I.E.P. Agreement. Other important principles included in the I.E.P. are encouraging stable oil trade and secure supplies and considering different fields of cooperation. Cooperation, in particular, is crucial in fields of common interest regarding energy; not only the production but also its conservation and development is of importance.[691]

---

686. Jacoby KD., *supra* n. 392.
687. I.E.P. Agreement 1974, Par. 3-5.
688. Art. 44 I.E.P. states that 'The Participating Countries will endeavour to promote co-operative relations with oil producing countries and with other oil consuming countries, including developing countries. They will keep under review developments in the energy field with a view to identifying opportunities for and promoting a purposeful dialogue, as well as other forms of co-operation, with producer countries and with other consumer countries.'
689. Art. 45 I.E.P. Agreement, 'To achieve the objectives set out in Article 44, the Participating Countries will give full consideration to the needs and interests of other oil consuming countries, particularly those of the developing countries.'
690. According to Article 46 I.E.P., 'The Participating Countries will, in the context of the Program, exchange views on their relations with oil producing countries. To this end, the Participating Countries should inform each other of co-operative action on their part with producer countries which is relevant to the objectives of the Program.'
691. Art. 47 I.E.P.

424. The external potential role of the IEA has been shaped and conferred on two plenary bodies of the Agency: first, the Standing Group on Relations with Producer and other Consumer Countries[692] and second the Ad Hoc Group on International Energy Relations, known as the Committee of Non-Member Countries.[693]

425. The Standing Group on Relations with Producer and other Consumer Countries is the first body empowered of the external cooperation of the Agency. According to Article 48, it had the duty to analyse and report to the Management Committee and to carry out the functions delegated by the Governing Board.[694] Article 48 I.E.P. states first that 'The Standing Group on Relations with Producer and other Consumer Countries will examine and report to the Management Committee on the matters described in this Chapter' and follows saying that 'The Management Committee may make proposals on appropriate co-operative action regarding these matters to the Governing Board, which shall decide on such proposals.'

426. This body was decided to be replaced some years later when the Governing Board realized that there was the need of members' officials directly linked to their capitals for international energy relations. In 1977, the Board created an informal Ad Hoc Group on International Energy Relations. The first chairman was Mr R. A. Burrows, from the United Kingdom; for this reason, the group was called the 'Burrows Group'. This group had the duty to report to the Governing Board concerning the international energy relations.[695] With the beginning of the activity, the Ad Hoc Group and the Standing Group started to become less important. By the passing of time, all the functions of the Standing Group, which formally continued to exist,[696] flew to the Ad Hoc Group which became the Committee of Non-Member Countries. The Committee of Non-Member Countries has continued to have a crucial role for exchanging information. Since the world's share of energy consumption of non-OECD members is growing, the importance of this Committee, which usually meets three times per year, has increased. Many activities of the Agency involving non-member countries are the primary responsibilities of Secretariat Directorates other than the Office of non-member countries and are reviewed by the pertinent Standing Groups and Committees.[697] The work of the Committee has focused during the years on hot areas, such as China, India and Russia. Concerning Russia, the IEA was invited to present a paper during a G8 Ministerial Energy Meeting in Moscow in 1998. The preparation of the meeting was reviewed by the Committee. Some years later, in 2001, a second energy policy review of the

692. I.E.P. Agreement Arts 44-48 and 58.
693. IEA/GB(90)46, Item 6.
694. Scott, *supra* n. 400 at 281.
695. IEA/GB(77)33, Item 8.
696. According to Article 49.1 of the I.E.P. Agreement, the Standing Group was still existing, even if all its functions were absorbed by the Committee of Non-Member Countries.
697. Bamberger, *supra* n. 420 at 281.

Russian Federation was made. It represented the basis for the Agency's 2002 *Russia Energy Survey*. A couple of years later, the 'Joint Measures for Co-operation during 2003-2005' were signed by the IEA and Russia. Opportunities for renewables were then discussed by the Committee.

427. China was also of great importance for the Agency. During the meeting of the Committee during April 1996 the Secretariat asked the Committee concerning a possible cooperation with China. On that occasion a conference on energy efficiency was organized with the consent of the Committee. China has represented a key topic for the Committee, in relation to different issues, including emergency oil stock, the development of Chinese natural gas and clean coal technology deployment.[698] Some publications of the Agency dealt with this country: *Coal in the Energy Supply of China* (1999), *China's Worldwide Quest for Energy Security* (2000) and *Developing China's Natural Gas Market* (2002).

428. A relationship with India was also identified as valuable in 1996.[699] The IEA-India policy cooperation agreement was signed in 1998. A workshop on data requirements for energy policy was then organized. The situation of India was of interest for the Agency, and the Committee of Non-Member Countries was involved in a workshop to accelerate the renewable energy market,[700] a review of the Indian power market development[701] and a conference on coal and electricity.[702] Also some publications concerning India have been made; among them, there are: *Electricity in India* (2002) and *Coal in the Energy Supply of India* (2002). During the meeting of the Committee of 2003, an update of the Indian programme was made by the Agency. This programme was particularly important, especially considering that India was not part of any multilateral framework.[703] Some other initiatives were put in place: a conference on oil stocks and emergency response measures, an analysis of the development of gas to replace coal, a conference on power and coal, and an energy efficiency conference[704] on standards and labels.[705]

V. Some Policy Considerations

429. The number of members of the IEA can obviously change. In 1994, for example, the Executive Director has been invited to discuss the possible membership of the Czech Republic, Hungary, the Republic of Korea, Mexico, Poland and the Slovak Republic. Hungary joined the IEA in 1997, followed by the Czech Republic, in 2001, and the Republic of Korea, in 2002.

---

698. *Ibid.*
699. IEA/NMC/M(96)3.
700. IEA/NMC/ M(2000)3/REV1.
701. IEA/NMC/M(2001)2.
702. IEA/NMC/M(2002)3.
703. Bamberger, *supra* n. 420 at 283.
704. IEA/NMC/M(2003)1.
705. Bamberger, *supra* n. 420 at 283.

430. During a meeting, in 1995, the ministers of the Agency realized how the economic interdependence of the IEA with non-member countries was becoming more and more important. The Secretariat was asked, on that occasion, to consider new forms of cooperation with non-member countries and organizations. In particular, the ministers aimed at a closer cooperation with the Russian Federation, which had signed a Joint Declaration of Co-operation, for its evident importance in the energy field. Some years later, in 1997, ministers focused on the need to strengthen the relations with countries with a strong role in the energy market, like Russia, China and India. The goal of deepening the Agency's relations with major non-member countries, also considering the idea to bring them into IEA membership, was highlighted once again during the meeting of 1999.[706] Russian interest in joining the IEA, in 2003, was seen by the Governing Board as the occasion to make Russia become part of the OECD. Discussions on the idea to create an IEA/Russia coordination committee started on that occasion.[707] The participation of the Russian Energy minister during the meeting of 2003 was particularly welcomed by the Governing Board, with the goal of involving more intensely Russian and other key countries in the energy policy net. On that occasion, the Russian minister signed a 'Joint Measures for Co-operation during 2003-2005'. Furthermore, during the meeting, a world perspective was strongly stressed.[708]

431. Concerning the People's Republic of China, a 'Memorandum of Policy Understandings in the Field of Energy' was signed with the Agency in 1996.[709]A 'Framework for Energy Technology Co-operation' with the Chinese Ministry of Science and Technology was approved in 2001. Also, India took part in this net of non-binding agreements, signing a 'Declaration of Co-operation' with the IEA in 1998.[710]

VI. The IEA and External Relations

432. Since the origins of the IEA, it was clear that the Agency had control over both its internal operations and its external relations. A deep involvement in the net of powers and corporations at the international level was obviously necessary. There was no possibility for the member countries of the Agency to isolate themselves from the rest of the globe since energy is consumed and produced worldwide.[711]

433. The necessary cooperation has always been not only between the member countries but also between them and the Agency itself. This idea of cooperation has been included in the early preparatory stages of the Agency, in the Communiqué of the Washington Energy Conference on 13 February 1974. Participants 'agreed that there was need to develop a cooperative multilateral relationship with producing

706. IEA/GB/C(99)3/ANN1.
707. IEA/GB/C(2003)2, Item 4.
708. IEA/GB/C(2003)4, Item (iii) and Annex 1.
709. IEA/GB(96)43 and IEA/GB/C(96)4, Item 6.
710. Bamberger, *supra* n. 420 at 25.
711. Scott, *supra* n. 400 at 143.

countries, and other consumer countries that takes into account the long-term interests of all'. Also, the relationship with oil companies was included in the I.E.P. Agreement. Considering the importance of this sector, a permanent framework for consultations with oil companies and information requests has been established within the Agency. According to Article 37, 'The Participating Countries shall establish within the Agency a permanent framework for consultation within which one or more Participating Countries may, in an appropriate manner, consult with and request information from individual oil companies on all important aspects of the oil industry, and within which the Participating Countries may share among themselves on a co-operative basis the results of such consultations.' The 'Procedures for Consultations with Oil Companies'[712] were drafted by the Standing Group on the Oil Market in February 1975.[713] These procedures represent the basis to make oil company consultation take place. The idea to consult with oil companies is also included in Article 58.3 of the Agreement,[714] which consents the Standing Group on Relations with Producer and other Consumer Countries to consult with oil companies. The inclusion of oil companies is also part of the IEA EES, in relation to the Special Section of the Oil Information System and the Oil ESS. Concerning the information system, the participation of oil companies derives from Article 35 of the I.E.P.,[715] which aims at assuring that the system is in line with industry operations. Consulting with oil companies is also part of the ESS.[716] Article 19.7 states that 'an international advisory board from the oil industry shall be convened, not later than the activation of emergency measures, to assist the Agency in ensuring the effective operation of such measures'.

434. Along with the cooperation with oil companies, the Agency is empowered to enter into the external relation in order to realize the objectives of the Agreement. This goal was established in Article 63 of the I.E.P. Agreement establishing that 'In order to achieve the objectives of the Program, the Agency may establish appropriate relations with non-participating countries, international organisations, whether governmental or non-governmental, other entities and individuals.' What is worth noting is that the objectives of the Programme represent the limits of the power of the Agency on external relations. This means that there is the need of a link between the external powers exercised and the objectives which should be reached with appropriateness. The power of the IEA, in other words, is quite wide. Such a wideness has been shaped in order to make the Agency as much flexible as

712. IEA/GB(75)8, Item 8(a).
713. IEA/SOM(75)2.
714. I.E.P. Agreement, Art. 58.3: 'The Standing Group may consult with oil companies on any matter within its competence.'
715. I.E.P. Agreement, Article 35 'In preparing its report under Article 34, the Standing Group on Emergency Questions shall: – consult with oil companies to ensure that the System is compatible with industry operations; – work out precise standards for the harmonization of the required information in order to ensure comparability of the data; – work out procedures to ensure the confidentiality of the information.'
716. I.E.P. Agreement, Art. 19.6: '6. In making its finding under this Article, the Secretariat shall consult with oil companies to obtain their views regarding the situation and the appropriateness of the measures to be taken.'

possible in defining its scope and form in external relations. What needs to be underlined concerning this power is the autonomy of the Agency from the OECD. There is no link between the OECD and the external relations of the IEA. In order to act externally, the IEA does not need any authorization. In other words, there is no dependency on the OECD Council and the Agency can freely exercise its power. The fact that Article 63 of the Agreement is parallel to Article 12 of the Council Decision does not cause any doubts concerning the autonomy of the IEA. This represents simply a way to assure that there is no doubt about the independence of the IEA from both the OECD Council and the Secretary.

435. Concerning the future of the Agency, it is clear that the IEA has tried to get a crucial role in order to make the world move to an energy transition. Such a goal has been developed through publishing technology road maps and improving capacity building. What is clear is that the Agency has extensively evolved from its original design.

Chapter 8. Conclusions

436. The world of energy still presents multiple challenges to governments, international organizations, private stakeholders and consumers. Constantly growing energy demand, problems of scarcity and environmental impact are all pressing issues of today, which require the contribution of scientists, public and private entities, as well as ordinary people in order to secure sustainability for future generations.

437. According to the World Energy Council (WEC),[717] the most important topics, which will certainly resonate in the upcoming decade on a global level, are digitalization, storage of electricity, the need for securing constant economic growth, potential volatility of commodity prices influenced by various factors, and dynamically developing market design aiming more and more on decentralization. All these topics go hand in hand with high uncertainty regarding their future perspectives – including policy (regulatory) uncertainties,[718] uncertainties in investments/ costs, as well as technological uncertainties of R&D results and their pace in general, all able to shape the designing acceptable solutions. Besides these uncertainties, climate uncertainty (i.e., uncertainty in the evolution of climatic conditions) can also influence tackling these future challenges. In particular with a significantly lower uncertainty level, but with the same impact, the monitoring report of the WEC mentions issues like growing energy needs and related economic power of China, balancing electricity prices, subsidization of energy (primarily clean energy, mainly from renewable sources), renewables in general and the related energy efficiency.[719]

438. In comparison, the latest energy outlook of the IEA (WEO 2019) also underlines some of the issues mentioned earlier (i.e., increasing energy demand, the evolution of renewable energy, the importance of electricity, energy efficiency), but also adds energy security and emphasizes Africa as one of the energy consumers on the rise, primarily in relation to oil demand. These challenges are put into perspective under the various scenarios the IEA operates with, in particular the 'Stated Policies Scenario' (STEPS) and the 'Sustainable Development Scenario' (SDS) and the 'Current Policy Scenario' (CPS) (already described throughout this monograph[720]). Under the STEPS, the mentioned increase of energy demand (mainly satisfied by fossil fuel supply, due to its flexible and relatively cheap deployment) will go on, while under the SDS, the WEO models would need to have a 50% chance of limiting warming to 1.65°C – which is fully in compliance with the Paris Agreement.

---

717. The report of the World Energy Council is based on survey responses from nearly 2,300 energy leaders from a total of eighty-six countries. *See*: WEC, *World Energy Issues Monitor 2019: Global and Regional Perspectives* https://www.worldenergy.org/assets/downloads/3.-World-Energy-Issues-Monitor-2019-Interactive-Executive-Summary.pdf (accessed on 20 January 2020).

718. *See e.g.* the impact of uncertain policy development on the transition to renewable energy sources – IEA, *Policy Uncertainty Threatens to Slow Renewable Energy Momentum* https://www.iea.org/news/policy-uncertainty-threatens-to-slow-renewable-energy-momentum (accessed on 22 of January 2020).

719. WEC, *supra* n. 718 at p. 4.

720. *See* in particular Chapters 3 and 6.

Although these scenarios do sound like forecasts of future energy development, the WEO stresses that '[t]he World Energy Outlook does not aim to provide a view on where the energy world will be in 2030 or 2040. This will depend on hugely important choices that lie ahead. What the WEO-2019 does aim to do is to inform decision-makers as they design new policies or consider new investments or shape our energy future in other ways. It does so by exploring various possible futures, the ways that they come about, the consequences of different choices and some of the key uncertainties'.[721] This approach is one of the key features to underline about the IEA's existence and goals in general, which have been attempted to elaborate on throughout this monograph.

439. The IEA has come a long way since the mid-1970s, while the world changing significantly around it, shifting from fossil fuel (mainly oil) security to energy security in general, widened with other important goals reacting on the changing global conditions overall.

§1. Emergency Response to Energy Crises: Is It Still Necessary to Focus on Oil?

440. Multiple chapters within this monograph[722] have dealt with the description and analysis of the main goal of the IEA originally – responding to energy crises through its members maintaining energy reserves, without the necessity of being dependent on a particular source, both in the sense of utilization (energy source) and supplies (source of imports). The issue of energy solidarity is still resonating intensely on a national and international level, even though shortages and disruptions of a global level comparable with the oil crises at the end of the 20th century are more and more scarce. Naturally this does not mean that leading economic powers do not have to deal with temporary shortages, which further underline the importance of maintaining and sharing supplies.[723] The concept of energy solidarity is therefore still valid, mainly for the EU and other supranational organizations, wherein the rules can set a clearer and broader group of obligations for states without authoritatively interfering with their sovereignty.

441. In case of the IEA, the CERM and ESS systems set ground rules regarding this process in case of a disruption on the energy (most importantly oil) markets,

721. IEA, World Energy Outlook 2019, *supra* n. 381; cf. Simon Evans, *'Profound Shifts' Underway in Energy System, Says IEA World Energy Outlook* https://www.carbonbrief.org/profound-shifts-underway-in-energy-system-says-iea-world-energy-outlook (accessed on 22 January 2020).

722. *See* in particular Chapters 1, 2, 5 and 6.

723. According to a survey conducted by the Gallup Organization upon the request of the European Commission in 2007, the majority of EU citizens are in favour of sharing reserves of oil and natural gas among Member States in case of a sudden shortage. *See*: The Gallup Organization, *Attitudes on Issues Related to EU Energy Policy* (ec.europa.eu, 2007) https://ec.europa.eu/commfrontoffice/publicopinion/flash/fl206a_en.pdf (accessed on 22 January 2020).

and in this sense a cardinal question arises related to future development: are such systems still necessary? Are the countries and smaller regional clusters of states better equipped to react to such shortages?

442. Reasons for posing such questions in the first place in relation to the IEA are multiple, stemming also from the challenges previously listed: (i) IEA member countries aiming at being less and less dependent on oil and natural gas; (ii) countries, where the demand for oil and natural gas are on the rapid rise not being IEA members; (iii) the widespread of renewables more and more balancing the energy mix; and (iv) technologies increasing energy efficiency and making electricity storage possible combined with the increased pace of electrification within certain industries.

443. In fact, less and less dependency on oil and natural gas has to be taken with some reservations, and although it looks good as a trend being part of various national and supranational policies, the oil market still has its say in the global energy picture. One thing is that the developed countries are deploying larger and larger amounts of clean energy and alternative sources in their energy mix (solar, wind and hydropower being the common alternatives), but another thing to be considered is that the so-called 'oil peak'[724] is nowhere near in sight in the next couple of years. On the contrary, emerging economies and developing countries continue to be at the top of the (currently slower) growing fossil fuel demand. In 2020 the oil consumption growth is expected to be 1.4 million barrels per day, stemming presumably mainly as the result of the US/ China trade war.[725] Furthermore regardless of what various statistics of, e.g., the OPEC says, the total amount of existing oil reserves being available on the planet is still difficult to estimate. It is a similar situation in case of natural gas too, demand mainly centred in Asia powering the growth of demand in the upcoming five years, presumably rising by more than 10% reaching more than 4.3 trillion m^3 in 2024.[726]

444. The emergency response measures applied by the IEA are obviously built around oil due to the fact that it is one of the most easily transportable and deployable energy sources, requiring minimum infrastructure to get from production to consumption. It is obvious from the statistics and also from all the data related to energy transition, sustainable development and electrification that oil as an energy source is undoubtedly under pressure, and will eventually be on the descent similarly to coal, but it is more resistant to the ongoing changes on the global energy

724. On more details regarding this concept *see* Chapter 3.
725. Julianne Geiger, *How Much Crude Oil Has the World Really Consumed?* (Oilproce.com, 2019) https://oilprice.com/Energy/Crude-Oil/How-Much-Crude-Oil-Has-The-World-Really-Consumed.html# (accessed on 22 January 2020). This prediction was made before the corona crisis.
726. IEA, *Demand from Asia is Set to Power the Growth of the Global Gas Industry over the Next Five Years* (iea.org, 2019) https://www.iea.org/news/demand-from-asia-is-set-to-power-the-growth-of-the-global-gas-industry-over-the-next-five-years (accessed on 23 January 2020).

scene. Therefore, oil security still remains an issue for the decades to come – practically until the total depletion of all reserves. What all these energy trends are changing is only the pace of oil demand growth.[727]

445. In the light of these conclusions, also shared by the latest WEO from the IEA, in order to prepare for potential future oil market disruptions reserves will have to be maintained by IEA members. However, a slow expansion of the variety of reserves should also be considered opening from sole oil reserves, towards introducing requirements of natural gas or other utilizable energy storage at least to cover domestic demand. Indeed, it is true and common that states already have these emergency plans and scenarios in case of a sudden shortage, and that the IEA has originally been assigned the task of tackling a widespread global shortage with potential devastating consequences, perhaps natural gas (even LNG) or other resources could also be added to the energy reserve mix. Energy crises can have an effect wider than just the oil market; therefore, other energy sources could be looked for and added as a flexible replacement for oil, as technological development proceeds. Naturally one has to consider the limitations stemming from difference between energy sources, which cannot be stored – resources like solar power, wind power, hydropower generating direct electricity, which is also difficult to store, but there are battery technologies and methods of turning electricity to storable hydrogen.[728] If we add additionally emerging sources like shale gas, methane hydrates,[729] etc. to the equation, the difficulties of maintaining oil reserves for some countries (e.g., net oil importers, with low or no exports at all) will ease. As a result, more countries will be able to fulfil accession conditions of the IEA (of course this is only possible via the OECD, as elaborated in Chapter 3), eventually broadening the range of Member States, including more and more energy intensive economies of the second and third world.

446. Notwithstanding, we are aware that these changes do not happen overnight, neither concerning the global energy structures nor concerning the IEA. However, as more time passes and we move closer to hour zero regarding climate change, energy leaders, including organizations like the IEA, will have to reconsider and potentially update requirements having roots in the last century/ millennia. This means that in other words technology will certainly reach a level, when alternatives of oil, natural gas and fossil fuels in general will become a market force

727. cf. Tim Gould, Tae-Yoon Kim, *The World Can't Afford to Relax about Oil Security* (iea.org, 2019) https://www.iea.org/commentaries/the-world-cant-afford-to-relax-about-oil-security (accessed on 22 January 2020).

728. IRENA, *Hydrogen from Renewable Power: Technology Outlook for the Energy Transition* (September 2018) https://www.irena.org/-/media/Files/IRENA/Agency/Publication/2018/Sep/IRENA_Hydrogen_from_renewable_power_2018.pdf (accessed on 24 January 2020); US Department of Energy, *Hydrogen Production: Electrolysis* (energy.gov) https://www.energy.gov/eere/fuelcells/hydrogen-production-electrolysis (accessed on 22 January 2020).

729. These crystalline molecular complexes are estimated to have high, but somewhat uncertain reserves underwater sediments, with more and more R&D 'spotlight' shedding on them for a relatively long time. Cf. Sang-Yong Lee, Gerald D. Holder, *Methane hydrates potential as a future energy source*, 71 Fuel Processing Technology 181-186 (2001).

to be seriously reckoned with, and a reliable source, which can be efficiently utilized in the event of a crisis. Therefore, building a wide consensus about the cooperation on and between various platforms/ stakeholders in this matter cannot start early enough.

§2. IEA Membership: Freeriding on the Shoulder of Giants?

447. The requirement of oil reserves and emergency response systems of the IEA bring us directly to another issue, which is necessary to underline after analysing all the aspects of this multinational intergovernmental organization more in detail – the problematic membership and why is it necessary to expand it in the upcoming future.

448. The two largest difficulties to overcome and to solve in this regard are: membership criteria (besides maintaining oil reserves already discussed) and problem of freeriding. As dissected in detail throughout Chapters 3 and also 6 of this monograph, the IEAs membership is, was (questionable though, but for now definitely also will be), conditioned to the membership in the OECD.

449. The criteria of OECD membership are by themselves quite extensive and for some of the countries currently not fulfillable. They include a system of values, principles and policies, which the candidate country has to support, apply and stand for. Most of them are naturally the classic legal, policy and governance-related axiological notions, which civilized countries already have in common – in particular: pluralistic democracy, respect for human rights and competitive market economy. Beyond these values shared by OECD countries, the potential new candidate country also has to be able to contribute to the advancement of the organization (including mutual benefits) and maintain the regional balance of membership.[730] Why are these criteria important to mention reflecting mainly on the chapter dealing with IEA membership? Mainly due to the fact that many currently significant energy players are on the sidelines of the OECD, which keeps them also out of the IEA.

450. Of course the solution was to consider them as partner countries (Association countries) via signing a Joint Declaration since 2013 (with China, India, Brazil – just to mention the countries with the highest potential to impact future energy development), but this declaration did not make them full members. Through this partnership, these countries participate in the data sharing and are committed also

730. These criteria were laid down in the 1990s and also via the Noburu report in 2004. *See*: OECD, *Strategy for Enlargement and Outreach (Report by the Chair of the Heads of Delegation Working Group on the Enlargement Strategy and Outreach, Ambassador Seiichiro Noboru)* (oecd.org, 2004) http://www.oecd.org/global-relations/globalrelationsstrategy/37434513.pdf (accessed on 16 January 2020).

to be involved in sharing of energy reserves and improving quality of their data together with accessing their national policies for analysis, as well as opening up for external influence from the IEA.[731]

451. These contributions are beneficial for the development of the global energy market and are increasing the reach of the energy statistics, analyses and monitoring; therefore one can start to question where would this balance of benefits shift to after, e.g., China and India become full members. Would a successfully finished accession process be more useful for the IEA or the particular country?

452. At this point it is worth to examine this question from both sides. We will consider China as an example to gain some perspective, but we could have easily picked any of the emerging countries currently being in the status of a non-member/ partner of the Agency.[732]

453. On the one hand, the IEA would benefit from an extended membership base including China primarily due to the economic capacity of the country and its key role in energy development. The IEA members moreover pay obligatory and voluntary contributions to the organization to support and maintain its general functionality. This is not something to ignore, since: (i) contributions are paid based on the size of economy of the country (which in case of China is remarkable[733]) and (ii) non-members are technically not part of this obligation, which is also derived from OECD structures.[734] In the light of this, the indicated freerider problem becomes a reality.

454. It is mainly because, on the other hand, non-members having a status of Association countries have technically most of the benefits coming with membership. Although they cannot directly influence the course of decisions the IEA takes via its organizational structure, they can participate in meetings, be part of information and know-how sharing, get policy advice from the IEA, access databases, stay in the loop of analyses and future forecasts, etc., all helping them to improve their energy planning and build connections with other, more developed countries via diplomatic channels. These are the main things China was basically struggling to

731. For the various types of cooperation between countries and the IEA (including countries of different status of accession) and for more related details *see* Chapters 3 and 6 of this monograph.

732. Nevertheless, China can also serve as a good example since it has been the most urged country to become an IEA member, which puts its leaders into a peculiar negotiating position. The IEA is still considered by some leaders as the 'club of the rich'; therefore China's approach is not surprising, considering the challenges it had to overcome since the 1990s in order to gain its current status on the global scene. cf. Carola Hoyos, *China invited to join IEA as oil demand shifts* (ft.com, March 2010) https://www.ft.com/content/0f973936-3beb-11df-9412-00144feabdc0 (accessed on 10 January 2020).

733. China has currently the 2nd largest GDP in the world directly after the United States, and according to future outlooks, it has huge potential to continue its economic growth. *See*: IMF, *Gross Domestic Product (Current Prices)* (imf.org, 2020) https://www.imf.org/external/datamapper/NGDPD@WEO/OEMDC/ADVEC/WEOWORLD/CHN (accessed 29 January 2020).

734. Regarding the details of the IEA finances and budget (including the process of its creation) we would like to point to Chapter 5 of this monograph.

achieve since the 1990s. The energy crises hit hard also in Asia, and the nations have dealt with the situation the best way they could – energy diplomacy. China's energy imports in the 2000s shifted more and more towards sea lines, from the Persian Gulf, which meant instant diversification of sources and less dependency. The rapidly rising role of Chinese ties wrapped around the whole region reaching across the whole continent (due to its size of course) soon culminated in foreign investments being pumped everywhere,[735] discovering new resource bases (mainly in Africa[736]) and shifting from an underdeveloped economy to a modernized strong state. This being said, it is highly questionable, whether China does even need to fully enter the IEA at all. Let us take a particular look on what would it cost to a country like China to commit to intergovernmental organizations like the IEA and the OECD tied to it.

455. The primary reasons why China is not so eager to rush for IEA membership vary. First and foremost, the international obligations derived from the values, principles and policies necessary for accession simply cannot be fulfilled by China at this moment. There are questions raised regarding its rule of law governance – openly implying more a rule of men; it does not have a fully competitive market economy (although it is a work in progress, with significant results recently); and last but not least, without going into particularities, there are many negative reactions on the way China is complying with respecting human rights and basic freedoms. The second reason comes from the already mentioned contributions to the IEA's budget, which goes hand in hand with contributions to the OECD. To use an example, such contribution, e.g., to the Official Development Assistance,[737] funding sustainable development of developing countries, has to be at least 7% of the country's GDP. Similar obligations can mean economic loss for China in order to gain access to benefits, part of which it already has from the IEA. Last but not least, mainly the OECD membership being the gate to the IEA also comes with the necessity to enter into various bilateral agreements (e.g., in the field of taxes and customs) with other members, which can skew China's current revenue from imports.[738] So the dilemma in case of China lies mainly between the need to further

---

735. The Belt and Road Initiative was the main milestone of these investments becoming the most dominant worldwide, including not only poor regions but also developed clusters, like the European Union. For related databases *see*: The Green Belt and Road Initiative, *Databases for the Belt and Road Initiative (BRI)* (green-bri.org, 2019) https://green-bri.org/databases-for-the-belt-and-road-initiative-bri?cookie-state-change=1580429198198 (accessed on 14 January 2020).
736. For related data about the Chinese presence in Africa via investments, loans and foreign aid, please refer to: China-Africa Research Initiative website (http://www.sais-cari.org) (accessed on 22 January 2020).
737. OECD, Official Development Assistance – Definition And Coverage (oecd.org, 2019) http://www.oecd.org/development/financing-sustainable-development/development-finance-standards/officialdevelopmentassistancedefinitionandcoverage.htm (accessed on 29 January 2020).
738. Consider China being, e.g., in a customs union with some of the OECD members, all parties trading completely duty free. This still requires some mutual policy development and alignment of interests, mainly due to the past experience with Chinese free-trade agreements, being rather imbalanced in the sense of abolishing quotas and duties faster on Chinese products leaving the country, than on products entering China. cf. MOFCOM, *China FTA Network* (mofcom.gov.cn, 2020) http://fta.mofcom.gov.cn/list/chinageorgiaen/chinageorgiaennews/1/encateinfo.html (accessed on 30 January 2020).

tighten the relationship and collaboration with the world major oil import countries to make oil markets more stable, and losing energy independence together with becoming (in a real or only assumed way) vulnerable due to more extensive data sharing.[739] Speaking of data sharing in relation to China, and going back to the IEA perspective of benefits, it is indeed questionable how accurate Chinese data are currently mainly due to the fact that sometimes they can be closely exposed to various 'statistical requirements' or even governmental propaganda.

456. Regardless from all these interests, agendas and potential gains, new members joining the IEA could be mutually beneficial even from a perspective beyond the OECD: from a global perspective another country would opt to align its internal governance and economic system with values dominant in the developed world, while the country itself would become a large network of countries sharing not only technology, knowledge or perhaps even resources eventually but also challenges to tackle, goals to pursue and a common future to foster. This is true as for China as for India,[740] Brazil, South Africa and any other country currently outside of the IEA's club of energy 'elite'. Nevertheless, the same question remains linking us back to the beginning of this part: how to make it happen to overcome freeriding?

457. There are currently several ideas on how to overcome the difficulty of fulfilling some of the outdated accession criteria, or just make the existing, still up-to-date ones easier for non-member countries to fulfil. According to the research of Neil Hirst and Yufeng Yang, there are four broad options for opening up the IEA to wider membership:

(1) Creating a new organization with a completely new legal basis.
(2) Amending the IEP[741] in a non-extensive way.
(3) Membership without becoming a party to the IEA founding treaty.
(4) The institute of Association gaining key importance within the IEA.[742]

458. Each of these options would have their benefits and disadvantages too. Creating a new organization would of course be the easiest and most comprehensive method: leaving out all the outdated provisions from the original founding documents of the OECD and the IEA, and completely separating the two. A new system of conditions could be set up reflecting the needs and real interconnections of the modern energy world, based on a wider consensus of developed, developing and

---

739. Yuwa Wei, *Issues Decisive for China's Rise or Fall: An International Law Perspective* Chapter 3.3, 44-45 (Springer, 2019).
740. It well reflects the current efforts of these countries to gain more and more proximity to IEA members and to the Agency itself. *See*: Takeo Kumagai, Eric Yep, *India Moves Toward IEA Membership with 'Strategic Partnership'* (S&P Global, December 2019) https://www.spglobal.com/platts/en/market-insights/latest-news/oil/120919-india-moves-toward-iea-membership-with-strategic-partnership (accessed on 27 January 2020).
741. For details on the Agreement on an International Energy Program please refer back to Chapter 2 of this monograph.
742. Hirst & Yang, *supra* n. 71.

perhaps even least developed countries. This would on the other hand take a significant amount of time, while full of uncertainties how the different interests, sometimes being totally misaligned, can compromise.

459. Amending the existing founding documents (the IPE) in a minimal way would keep most of the existing conditions, changing only those, which are the biggest obstacles for current Association countries to overcome. This would send candidate countries the signal from the IEA to meet them somewhere in the middle. Once again, the setting of the conditions could already face different ideas, while putting the result through the formal decision-making mechanisms is also time-consuming – less so than in case of a complete renewal.

460. Membership without signing the IEP would not be completely uncommon (*see* the case of Norway not ratifying it shortly after the IEA was founded),[743] which clearly underlines that IEA membership does not really have strong legal barriers, rather than political ones. The downside in this case would be creating a precedent ignoring the basic foundations on which the IEA has been built, and degrading the existing memberships completely.

461. The cited discussion paper of Hirst and Yang suggests one more potential solution, which can be considered, and which is also more aligned with the first pointed out conclusion of this monograph (and many others indeed) – the maintenance of oil reserves as a requirement. The fourth option ignores it and makes the IEA stand for an International Energy Association, instead of an agency.

462. In a simplified way, this fourth option combined with, not the complete abandonment of the energy reserve concept, but with its expansion, could mean the future solution to include a wider range of countries under the IEAs aegis, closely working together equally towards energy security, as towards sustainability. The feasibility of these solutions remains questionable for now and will depend mainly on how close can long-term interests of countries get without too much imbalance and potential exploitation of weaker participants by more dominant energy players. In the light of this, the initial question in the title regarding the giants seems to require a slight change, since giants are both within and outside of the IEA's circles.

§3. Financing Energy Development: What Projects Get the Funding and How Much Independence to Aim For?

463. We have already touched upon the fact of the IEA being closely merged and interconnected with the OECD, and so did multiple chapters of this monograph, including its implications mainly on financial independence. The IEA's budget set on a biannual basis consists of covering the expenses of the main activities and also contributions of members funding various projects, mainly aiming on promotional

743. Neil Hirst, *The Energy Conundrum: Climate Change, Global Prosperity, and the Tough Decisions we Have to Make* Chapter 10, 284 (World Scientific, 2018).

activities. The IEA naturally does not directly invest into energy-related projects having the characteristics of building infrastructure and developing existing energy-related processes (e.g., generation), but its finances are spent primarily on data collection, processing, analysis, communication, fostering cooperation with other organizations and countries.[744] It has to be emphasized that IEA members make up 4/5 of its whole budget, while the rest is covered from sales of publications (e.g., WEO and other extensive statistical analyses, as well as monitoring reports).

464. Promotion activities and international collaboration projects are consuming vast amounts of funds, the allocation of which is primarily in the hands of the IEA, despite its dependency on the OECD. The promotion projects align with the activity aims of the IEA (as listed in Table 2 within Chapter 4) – energy security, energy access, energy transition, mitigation & adaptation of climate change and technological development.

465. The TCPs, but also various other collaboration projects promoting, e.g., solar power (SHC Program of the IEA[745]), energy efficiency (e.g., in relation to buildings – IEA EBC[746]), etc. are funded (co-funded) and launched on a regular basis. Their aim is to share best practices from around the world, support R&D. This is besides the specific projects carried out between IEA members mutually, as well as between members and non-members. Such projects receive specific funding only from participating countries, but are implemented under the aegis of the IEA (particularly IAs).[747]

466. Obviously, although the IEA is inside the organizational framework of the OECD, it can exercise control over its budget and where to spend it without large influence practically from the non-IEA members of the OECD. Nevertheless, the OECD has still some control over its budget and financial management via appointing a Supreme Audit Institution[748] of a member country to carry out external auditing.[749] Therefore it is necessary for the IEA to keep maximum transparency regarding its finances, in order to avoid mismanagement resulting potentially in individual or even collective international liability.[750]

744. These activities are analysed in more detail throughout Chapters 4 and 6 of this monograph.
745. IEA, *Solar Heating & Cooling Technology Collaboration Programme (SHC)* https://www.iea-shc.org (accessed on 30 January 2020).
746. IEA, *Energy in Buildings and Communities Programme (EBC)* https://www.iea-ebc.org/projects (accessed on 30 January 2020).
747. *See* Chapter 5 of this monograph.
748. OECD, *External Audit – Supreme Audit Institutions* (oecd.org, 2019) https://www.oecd.org/gov/external-audit-supreme-audit-institutions.htm (accessed on 23 January 2020).
749. IEA, *Structure: The IEA is an autonomous inter-governmental organisation within the OECD framework, headed by its Executive Director* https://www.iea.org/about/structure (accessed on 4 January 2020).
750. It is worth considering what would the international liability scheme under DARIO look like in case of an internationally punishable conduct of the IEA. For details on DARIO *see*: Mirka Moldner, *Responsibility of International Organizations – Introducing the ILC's DARIO*, 16 Max Planck Yearbook of UN Law 281-328 (2012).

467. The direct financial independence of the IEA being strong, the OECD still has indirect control over it via limiting membership and through it also the scope of financial contributions. Making strong economic players, which have the potential to grow even more in the future (e.g., China), the OECD is risking a separation scenario to take place and the IEA becoming independent (referring to the study of Hirst and Yang above). The struggle has been real for quite a long time now, the IEA opening discussions about separation with the OECD exactly because of the issue with China.[751] However in reality, membership expansion being necessary, neither of the parties (OECD nor IEA) are being committed enough in the present to go on separate tracks and becoming completely independent from each other: keeping their own staff, managing and ensuring all the necessary capacities and resources to fulfil the goals they have taken on. It would be specifically difficult in case of the smaller IEA relying on the technical and personal background of the OECD. Needless to say, this does not rule out the current approach changing significantly in the future. In any case, the eventual transformation process would bring new challenges, making the continuation of high reliability, reputation and fulfilled complexity expectations very uncertain.

751. Felix & Lewis, *supra* n. 159.

No Ultimate Conclusion

468. It is impossible to phrase such a conclusion in case of the IEA. The aim of this monograph was not to provide it either. It was more an attempt to collect, to understand, to interconnect and to organize data and knowledge available about this Agency largely contributing to the shape of our energy world.

469. Some of the challenges of energy security, access and transition will be hard to overcome, perhaps a full transition to clean energy will never take place, but the way should always be paved towards sustainability and environmental conservation via economic development. The IEA is one of the pioneers of this process. Its activities although mostly aiming at theoretical, statistical and not always tangible work, its importance lies in the strong background it provides for countries (not only members) on the way to satisfy their energy needs without compromising the same possibility for other countries.

470. Overall obviously the added value of the IEA's results in the field of global energy governance overlaps with other institutions, and at the end with even the OECD itself. Though considering the areas, where these overlaps are missing, the sudden realization is that, true value starts right there, where uniqueness does. As a result, the IEA and other international organizations being present, contributing to solving the problems with energy supplies should not be competing with each other in the reached and disseminated results. Instead they should keep collaborating, sharing and joining forces covering specific areas of the seemingly endless net interconnecting energy with sustainability and environmental awareness. Only an approach like this can save the planet and stop any energy crisis. To refer to the thoughts of Jimmy Carter at the end, energy is indeed the ultimate test of our ability to unite on a global scale and it will also be a standard around which we rally. Energy is the battlefield on which we can win ourselves new confidence, and seize control again of our common destiny.

Bibliography

Abbot, Kenneth & Snidal, Duncan. 'Why States Act Through Formal International Organizations'. Journal of Conflict Resolution 42(1) (1998): 3, 32

African Union. 'Agenda 2063: The Africa We Want (Overview)'. https://au.int/agenda2063/overview

Agnew, John. 'The Tragedy of the Nation-State'. Territory, Politics, Governance 5(4) (2017): 347, 350

Agreement on an International Energy Program signed in Paris on 18 November 1974 [C(74)203(Final) Annex II]

Agreement on an International Energy Program signed in Paris on 18th November 1974, deposited with the Government of Belgium

Akande, Dapo. 'The Competence of International Organizations and the Advisory Jurisdiction of the International Court of Justice'. European Journal of International Law 9 (1998): 437, 467

Aksu, Esref. 'What, Then, Is Global about Global Governance'. Chinese Journal of Global Governance 1(2) (2015): 105, 132

Aleklett, Kjell et al. 'The Peak of the Oil Age – Analyzing the World Oil Production Reference Scenario in World Energy Outlook 2008'. Energy Policy 38(3) (2009): 1398, 1414

Alliance to Save Energy. 'IEA: Energy Efficiency is 40 Percent of the Climate Answer, but Major Economies Still Significantly Underinvest'. https://www.ase.org/blog/iea-energy-efficiency-40-percent climate-answer-major-economies-still-significantly-underinvest 19 October 2018

Amadeo, Kimberly. 'OPEC and Its Goals, Members, and History'. https://www.thebalance.com/what-is-opec-its-members-and-history-3305872

Asgeirsdottir, Aslaug. Who Gets What?: Domestic Influences on International Negotiations Allocating Shared Resources. Albany, NY: SUNY Press, 2008, 144

Association of Southeast Asian Nations. 'Overview'. https://asean.org/asean/about-asean/overview/

Badger, D. B. 'International Cooperation During Oil Supply Disruptions: The Role of the International Energy Agency' in *Responding to International Oil Crises*, edited by George Horwich & David L. Weimer. Washington DC: American Enterprise Institute for Public Policy Research, 1988, 1-16

Bahgat, Gawdat. *Energy Security: An Interdisciplinary Approach*. Hoboken: John Wiley & Sons, 2011

Bamberger, Craig S. *The History of the International Energy Agency, 1974-2004: IEA the first 30 years*. Paris: OECD/IEA, 2004

Bibliography

Barnsley, Ingrid, Ahn, Sun-Joo. Mapping Multilateral Collaboration on Low-Carbon Energy Technologies. Insight Series 2014. Paris: IEA, 2014

Ben Naucer, K. 'Towards Sustainable Urban Energy Systems: Energy Technology Perspectives 2016'. Presentation for the Grantham Institute for Climate Change, 2016

Bernstein, Steven. 'Grand Compromises in Global Governance'. Government and Opposition 47(3) (2012): 368, 394

Bexell, Magdalena, Tallberg, Jonas & Uhilin, Anders. 'Democracy in Global Governance: The Promises and Pitfalls of Transnational Actors'. Global Governance 16(1) (2010): 81, 101

Birol, F. 'Energy Investment Outlook'. Presentation available online https://www.youtube.com/watch?v=awwVbAG0eig IEA, June 2014

Birol, Fatih. 'India's Rise on the Global Energy Scene'. https://www.iea.org/commentaries/indias-rise-on-the-global-energy-scene 14 January 2020

Bryan Pasquier, Sara & Sassay, Aurelien. Progress Implementing the IEA 25 Energy Efficiency Policy Recommendations: 2011 Evaluation. IEA Energy Papers 2012/9. Paris: OECD Publishing, 2012

Buzan, Barry & Little, Richard. *International Systems in World History: Remaking the Study of International Relations*. Oxford: Oxford University Press, 2000

Carin, Barry & Thakur, Ramesh. Global Governance for a Global Age: The Role of Leaders in Breaking Global Deadlocks. CIGI Policy Brief No. 7. Waterloo, Ontario, Canada: Centre for International Governance Innovation, 2008

Carrington, Gerry & Stephenson, Janet. 'The Politics of Energy Scenarios: Are International Energy Agency and Other Conservative Projections Hampering the Renewable Energy Transition?'. Energy Research & Social Science 46 (2018): 103, 113

Chapman, Andrew, McLellan, Benjamin & Tezuka, Tetsuo. 'Strengthening the Energy Policy Making Process and Sustainability Outcomes in the OECD through Policy Design' Administrative Sciences 6(9) (2016): 1, 16

Chimni, B.S. International Institutions Today: An Imperial Global State in the Making'. European Journal of International Law 15(1) (2004): 1, 37

China and Africa Research Initiative. *Official website.* http://www.sais-cari.org

Clayton, Blake C. *Market Madness: A Century of Oil Panics, Crises, and Crashes.* Oxford: Oxford University Press, 2014

Clean Cooking Alliance. 'How We Are Funded'. https://www.cleancookingalliance.org/about/how-we-are-funded/index.html

Clean Energy Ministerial. 'About the Clean Energy Ministerial'. http://www.cleanenergyministerial.org/about-clean-energy-ministerial

Clean Energy Solutions Center. 'IEA Policies and Measures Database'. https://cleanenergysolutions.org/resource/pams

Cohen, Ariel. 'Is Fusion Power Within Our Grasp?'. https://www.forbes.com/sites/arielcohen/2019/01/14/is-fusion-power-within-our-grasp/ 14 January 2019

Colgan, Jeff, Keohane, Robert O. & Van de Graaf, Thijs. 'Punctuated Equilibrium in the Energy Regime Complex'. The Review of International Organizations 7(2) (2012): 117, 143

Colgan, Jeff. The International Energy Agency: Challenges for the 21st Century. GPPi Policy Paper Series 6/2009. Berlin: Global Public Policy Institute, 2009

Collins, Anna. *The Climate Change Crisis.* New York: Lucent Press, 2019
Communiqué of the Washington Energy Conference, 11 February 1974
Conclusions of the 124th Meeting of the Governing Board on 11 May 1992 [IEA/GB(92)25]
Conclusions of the 16th meeting of the Governing Board on 20-21 November 1975 [IEA/GB(75)94]
Conclusions of the 203rd Meeting of the Governing Board on 18-19 October 2006 [IEA/GB/C(2006)3/REV1]
Conclusions of the 30th Meeting of the Governing Board on 27-28 June 1977 [IEA/GB(77)33]
Conclusions of the 44th meeting of the Governing Board held on 11 July 1979 [IEA/GB(79)49] as amended on 3 April 2003 [IEA/GB/C(2003)3] and 7-8 March 2007 [IEA/GB/C(2007)1]
Conclusions of the first meeting of the Governing Board on 18-19 November 1974 [IEA/GB(74)9(1st Revision)]
Costello, Kenneth W. 'Why Natural Gas has an Uncertain Future'. The Electricity Journal 30(7) (2017): 18, 22
Cozzi, Laura, Chen, Olivia, Daly, Hannah & Koh, Aaron. 'Population Without Access to Electricity Falls Below 1 Billion'. https://www.iea.org/commentaries/population-without-access-to-electricity-falls-below-1-billion 30 October 2018
de Jong, Sijbren & Wouters, Jan. 'Institutional Actors in International Energy Law' in *Research Handbook on International Energy Law*, edited by Kim Talus. Cheltenham: Edward Elgar Publishing, 2014, 18-43
Decision of the Council Establishing an International Energy Agency of the Organisation [C(74)203(Final)]
Decision of the OECD Council Establishing an International Energy Agency of the Organisation
Decision on an International Energy Program adopted by the Governing Board at its 1st meeting on 18-19 November 1974 [IEA/GB(74)9(1st Revision); IEA/GB/DOC.74/5, Annex]
Deere-Birkbeck, Carolyn. 'Global Governance in the Context of Climate Change: The Challenges of Increasingly Complex Risk Parameters'. International Affairs 85(6) (2009): 1173, 1194
Dixon, Richard Lewis. 'The Challenge & Complexities of Nation-State Sovereignty in the Era of 21st Century Internationalism'. SSRN Electronic Journal (2011): 1, 68
Downie, Christian. 'Global Energy Governance in the G-20: States, Coalitions, and Crises'. Global Governance 21(3) (2015): 475, 492
Duan, Fei, Ji, Qiang, Liu, Bing Yue & Fan, Ying. 'Energy Investment Risk Assessment for Nations along China's Belt & Road Initiative'. Journal of Cleaner Production 170 (2018): 535, 547
Dubreuil, J-B. 'IEA's Gas 2018 Medium Term Market Report and Global Gas Security Review 2018'. Presentation for the Center on Global Energy Policy, October 2018
Duffield, John S. 'The Limits of Rational Design'. International Organization 57(2) (2003): 411, 430

Bibliography

Elkind, Jonathan. Modernizing the International Energy Agency: A Task Worthy of US Leadership. New York: Colombia SIPA Center on Global Energy Policy, 2017

Energia no Mundo. Brasilia: Ministério de Minas e Energia (MME), 2017

Energy Research Institute/Grantham Institute. Global Energy Governance Reform and China's Participation. Final Report. London: Imperial College London, 2014

Energy Watch Group. 'New EWG study: International Energy Agency Holds Back Global Energy Transition'. https://energywatchgroup.org/new-ewg-study-international-energy-agency-holds-back-global-energy-transition 22 September 2015

European Commission. 'International Energy Agency'. https://ec.europa.eu/energy/topics/international-cooperation/international-organisations-and-initiatives/international-energy-agency_en

European Parliament Resolution of 12 June 2012 on Engaging in Energy Policy Cooperation with Partners Beyond our Borders: A Strategic Approach to Secure, Sustainable and Competitive Energy Supply (2012/2029(INI))

Evans, Simon. 'Analysis: How have the IEA's Renewable Forecasts Changed?'. https://www.carbonbrief.org/analysis-how-have-iea-renewable-forecasts-changed 26 October 2016

Evans, Simon. 'Profound Shifts Underway in Energy System, says IEA World Energy Outlook'. https://www.carbonbrief.org/profound-shifts-underway-in-energy-system-says-iea-world-energy-outlook 13 November 2019

Farah, Paolo Davide. 'Trade and Progress: The Case of China'. Columbia Journal of Asian Law 30(1) (2017): 51, 112

Farand, Chloé. 'IEA World Energy Outlook Outlines 1.5C Scenario'. https://www.climatechangenews.com/2019/11/13/iea-world-energy-outlook-outlines-1-5c-scenario/ 13 November 2019

Fattouh, Bassam & van der Linde, Coby. *The International Energy Forum. Twenty Years of Producer-Costumer Dialogue*. Riyadh: IEF, 2011

Felix, Bate & Lewis, Barbara. 'OECD and IEA Ponder Divorce After Years of Friction: Document'. https://fr.reuters.com/article/us-iea-oecd-split-idUSKCN0Y20O1 11 May 2016

Ferreira-Snyman, M.P. & Ferreira, G.M. 'Global Good Governance and Good Global Governance'. South African Yearbook of International Law 31 (2006): 52, 94

Florini, Ann & Dubash, Navroz. 'Introduction to the Special Issue: Governing Energy in a Fragmented World'. Global Policy 2(S1) (2011): 1, 5

Florini, Ann & Sovacool, Benjamin K. 'Who Governs Energy? The Challenges Facing Global Energy Governance'. Energy Policy 37 (2009): 5239, 5248

Florini, Ann. 'The International Energy Agency in Global Energy Governance'. Global Policy 2(1) (2011): 40, 53

Forgó, Katrin. 'Die Internationale Energieagentur, Grundlagen and aktuelle Fragen'. EI Working Papers / Europainstitut 36 (2000)

G20 Principles on Energy Collaboration. Brisbane: G20, 2014

G7 Kitakyushu Energy Ministerial Meeting. Kitakyushu Initiative on Energy Security for Global Growth Joint Statement. Kitakyushu: G7, 2014

Gadowski, Marek. 'Międzynarodowa Agencja Energetyczna (MAE), Wybrane zagadnienia organizacyjno-prawne'. Urząd Regulacji Energetyki 4 (2011): 9, 16

Gagné, J-F. 'The IEA's Energy Technology Perspectives 2015'. Presentation for the CSIS Energy and National Security Program, July 2015

Gallarotti, Giulio M. 'The Limits of International Organization: Systematic Failure in the Management of International Relations'. International Organization 45(2) (1991): 183, 220

Geiger, Julianne. 'How Much Crude Oil Has the World Really Consumed?'. https://oilprice.com/Energy/Crude-Oil/How-Much-Crude-Oil-Has-The-World-Really-Consumed.html 20 August 2019

Gould, Tim & Kim, Tae-Yoon. 'The World Can't Afford to Relax about Oil Security'. https://www.iea.org/commentaries/the-world-cant-afford-to-relax-about-oil-security 19 September 2019

Green Belt and Road Initiative Center. Databases for the Belt and Road Initiative (BRI). https://green-bri.org/databases-for-the-belt-and-road-initiative-bri?cookie-state-change=1580429198198

Greenpeace. Energy [R]evolution: Towards a Fully Renewable Energy Supply in the EU 27. Amsterdam, Brussels: Greenpeace International/ European Renewable Energy Council, 2010

Guzman, Andrew T. 'The Design of International Agreements'. The European Journal of International Law 16(4) (2005): 579, 612

Haftel, Yoram & Thompson, Alexander. 'The Independence of International Organisations' Journal of Conflict Resolution 50(2) (2006): 253, 275

Haghighi, Sanam S. *Energy Security: The External Legal Relations of the European Union with Major Oil – and Gas – Supplying Countries*. Oxford: Hart Publishing, 2007

Halabi, Yakub. 'The Expansion of Global Governance into the Third World: Altruism, Realism, or Constructivism?'. International Studies Review 6(1) (2004): 21, 48

Halff, A. 'The IEA's Medium-Term Oil Market Report 2014'. Presentation for the CSIS Energy and National Security Program, July 2014

Heubaum, Harald & Biermann, Frank. 'Integrating Global Energy and Climate Governance: The Changing Role of the International Energy Agency'. Energy Policy 87 (2015): 229, 239

Hill, Joshua S. 'BNEF vs. IEA Clean Energy Investment Numbers – Who to Believe?'. https://cleantechnica.com/2018/07/31/trends-vs-activity-understanding-the-differences-between-bnef-iea-investment-figures/ 31 July 2018

Hillebrand, Evan. 'What is Energy Security? Definition and Scenarios'. https://judithcurry.com/2016/03/03/what-is-energy-security-definitions-and-scenarios/ 3 March 2016

Hirst, Neil & Yang Yufeng. Next Steps of Modernisation of the International Energy Agency. London: Imperial College London, 2017

Hirst, Neil. *Energy Conundrum: Climate Change, Global Prosperity, And the Tough Decisions We Have to Make*. London: World Scientific Publishing Europe Ltd, 2018

Hoekman, Bernard. 'Proposals for WTO Reform: A Synthesis and Assessment'. Minnesota Journal of International Law 20(2) (2011): 324, 364

Hoffmann, Stanley. 'The Role of International Organization: Limits and Possibilities'. International Organization 10(3) (1956): 357, 372
Houssin, D. 'Energy Storage Technology Roadmap'. Webinar for the Clean Energy Solutions Center, 19 March 2014
Hoyos, Carola. 'China Invited to Join IEA as Oil Demand Shifts'. https://www.ft.com/content/0f973936-3beb-11df-9412-00144feabdc0 30 March 2010
Hug, Simon & König. 'Domestic Structures and Constitution-Building in an International Organization: Introduction'. The Review of International Organizations 2(2) (2007): 105, 113
Hulsman, John C. 'The Shale Revolution and Donald Trump'. Aspen Review 4 (2018): 30
Hurd, Ian. 'Legitimacy and Contestation in Global Governance: Revisiting the Folk Theory of International Institutions'. The Review of International Organizations 14 (2018): 1, 13
IEA Bioenergy. 'Task 37: Energy from Biogas'. http://task37.ieabioenergy.com/about-task-37.html
IEA Coal Industry Advisory Board. The Role of Coal for Energy Security in World Regions. Paris: IEA, 2016
IEA/GB(2000)27
IEA/GB(2002)21
IEA/GB(75)8, Item 8(a)
IEA/GB(77)33, Item 8
IEA/GB(90)46, Item 6
IEA/GB(92)25, Item 11
IEA/GB(92)45, Item 7(a)(ii) and (iii)
IEA/GB(93)65, Item 2(f)(xviii)
IEA/GB(94)15
IEA/GB(94)25
IEA/GB(94)28
IEA/GB(95)1
IEA/GB(96)13, Item 3(a)(viii)
IEA/GB(96)43 and IEA/GB/C(96)4, Item 6
IEA/GB/C (2002)1, Item 9(c)
IEA/GB/C(2000)5, Item 8
IEA/GB/C(2002)2, Item 6
IEA/GB/C(2003)2, Item 4
IEA/GB/C(2003)4, Item (iii) and Annex 1
IEA/GB/C(2003)5, Item 6(c)
IEA/GB/C(2003)6, Item 5(a)(v)
IEA/GB/C(99)3/ANN1
IEA/NMC/ M(2000)3/REV1
IEA/NMC/M(2001)2
IEA/NMC/M(2002)3
IEA/NMC/M(2003)1
IEA/NMC/M(96)3
IEA/SOM(75)2

International Atomic Energy Agency. Energy Indicators for Sustainable Development: Guidelines and Methodologies. Vienna: IAEA, 2005

International Energy Agency & United Nation Environmental Program. 2018 Global Status Report: Towards a Zero-Emission, Efficient and Resilient Buildings and Construction Sector. UNEP, 2018

International Energy Agency. '3rd Universal Meeting of IEA Technology Collaboration Programmes'.https://www.iea.org/events/3rd-universal-meeting-of-iea-technology-collaboration-programmes

International Energy Agency. 'About the WEO'. https://www.iea.org/weo/aboutweo/

International Energy Agency. 'Amsterdam City Subsidies for Electric Commercial Vehicles'. https://www.iea.org/policies/7222-amsterdam-city-subsidies-for-electric-commercial-vehicles

International Energy Agency. 'Analysis'. https://www.iea.org/analysis/all?topic=world-energy-outlook

International Energy Agency. 'Asian Development Bank and IEA Hold Joint Workshops on Low-Carbon Energy'. https://vipo.iea.org/newsroom/news/2012/october/asian-development-bank-and-iea-hold-joint-workshops-on-low-carbon-energy.html 31 October 2012

International Energy Agency. 'Broadest Ever Participation in IEA Emergency Response Exercise'. https://www.iea.org/news/broadest-ever-participation-in-iea-emergency-response-exercise 12 February 2018

International Energy Agency. 'Carbon Capture, Utilization and Storage'. https://www.iea.org/fuels-and-technologies/carbon-capture-utilisation-and-storage

International Energy Agency. 'Clean Energy Ministerial Secretariat Finds New Home at the IEA'. https://www.iea.org/news/clean-energy-ministerial-secretariat-finds-new-home-at-the-iea 15 June 2016

International Energy Agency. 'Climate Change'. https://www.iea.org/topics/climate-change

International Energy Agency. 'Climate-Energy Policies for Low-Carbon Transitions'. https://vipo.iea.org/topics/climatechange/climate-energypoliciesforlowcarbontransitions/

International Energy Agency. 'Communiqué of the 2019 Meeting of the IEA Governing Board at Ministerial Level'.https://www.iea.org/news/communique-of-the-2019-meeting-of-the-iea-governing-board-at-ministerial-level 6 December 2019

International Energy Agency. 'COP21'. https://www.iea.org/cop21/

International Energy Agency. 'Countries and Regions'. https://www.iea.org/countries

International Energy Agency. 'Cross-cutting'. https://www.iea.org/areas-of-work/technology-collaboration/cross-cutting

International Energy Agency. 'Data and Publications: Energy Technology Perspectives'. https://webstore.iea.org/energy-technology-perspectives

International Energy Agency. 'Data and Statistics'. https://www.iea.org/data-and-statistics?country=WORLD&fuel=Energy%20supply&indicator=TPESbySource

International Energy Agency. 'Data Centres & Networks'. https://www.iea.org/fuels-and-technologies/data-centres-networks

Bibliography

International Energy Agency. 'Demand from Asia is Set to Power the Growth of the Global Gas Industry over the Next Five Years'. https://www.iea.org/news/demand-from-asia-is-set-to-power-the-growth-of-the-global-gas-industry-over-the-next-five-years 7 June 2019

International Energy Agency. 'Electricity Security'. https://www.iea.org/areas-of-work/ensuring-energy-security/electricity-security

International Energy Agency. 'Emergency Response Training and Outreach'. https://vipo.iea.org/topics/energysecurity/emergencyresponse/

International Energy Agency. 'Energy Access'. https://www.iea.org/topics/energy-access

International Energy Agency. 'Energy Business Council, Dialogue among the IEA, the Business Community and Policymakers'. https://www.iea.org/areas-of-work/industry-engagement/energy-business-council

International Energy Agency. 'Energy Efficiency Policies and Measures Database'. https://www.iea.org/topics/energyefficiency/policies/

International Energy Agency. 'Energy Efficiency Training Week for Southeast Asia 2018'. https://www.iea.org/events/energy-efficiency-training-week-for-southeast-asia-2018

International Energy Agency. 'Energy Efficiency Training Week for Southeast Asia 2019'. https://www.iea.org/events/iea-energy-efficiency-training-week-for-southeast-asia-2019

International Energy Agency. 'Energy Efficiency Training Week for Sub-Saharan Africa 2019'. https://www.iea.org/events/energy-efficiency-training-week-for-sub-saharan-africa-2019

International Energy Agency. 'Energy Efficiency. The First Fuel of a Sustainable Global Energy System.' https://www.iea.org/topics/energy-efficiency

International Energy Agency. 'Energy Efficiency. Training Week for Brazil 2017.' https://www.iea.org/events/energy-efficiency-training-week-for-brazil-2017

International Energy Agency. 'Energy in Buildings and Communities Programme (EBC)'. https://www.iea-ebc.org/projects

International Energy Agency. 'Energy Ministers set Course for New Era at IEA'. https://www.iea.org/news/energy-ministers-set-course-for-new-era-at-iea 18 November 2015

International Energy Agency. 'Energy Technology Perspectives'. https://www.iea.org/topics/energy-technology-perspectives

International Energy Agency. 'Events. Energy Efficiency Training Week for India 2018'. https://www.iea.org/events/energy-efficiency-training-week-for-india-2018

International Energy Agency. 'Financing Energy Access'. https://www.iea.org/energyaccess/financingenergyaccess/

International Energy Agency. 'Frequently Asked Questions'. https://vipo.iea.org/classicstats/resources/questionnaires/faq/

International Energy Agency. 'Fusion Power'. https://www.iea.org/areas-of-work/technology-collaboration/fusion-power

International Energy Agency. 'G20. A Global Forum of Major Economies'. https://www.iea.org/areas-of-work/international-collaborations/g20 29 September 2020

International Energy Agency. 'G7. An Informal Group of Seven Industrialised Economies'. https://www.iea.org/areas-of-work/international-collaborations/g7

International Energy Agency. 'Global Energy Demand Rose by 2.3% in 2018, Its Fastest Pace in the Last Decade'. https://www.iea.org/news/global-energy-demand-rose-by-23-in-2018-its-fastest-pace-in-the-last-decade 26 March 2019

International Energy Agency. 'Global Engagement'. https://www.iea.org/countries/cooperation/

International Energy Agency. 'Glossary'. https://vipo.iea.org/about/glossary/e/

International Energy Agency. 'History'. https://www.iea.org/about/history

International Energy Agency. 'How does the IEA Respond to Major Disruptions in Oil Supply?'. https://vipo.iea.org/newsroom/news/2011/march/how-does-the-iea-respond-to-major--disruptions-in-the-supply-of-oil-2011-03-10-.html 10 March 2011

International Energy Agency. 'How Solar Energy Could be the Largest Source of Electricity by Mid-Century'. https://www.iea.org/news/how-solar-energy-could-be-the-largest-source-of-electricity-by-mid-century 29 September 2014

International Energy Agency. 'IEA @ COP24'. https://www.iea.org/cop24

International Energy Agency. 'IEA and Argentina Agree to Cooperate on Energy Statistics'. https://www.iea.org/news/iea-and-argentina-agree-to-co-operate-on-energy-statistics 20 March 2017

International Energy Agency. 'IEA and Asian Development Bank Commit to Step Up Co-Operation'. https://www.iea.org/news/iea-and-asian-development-bank-commit-to-step-up-cooperation 29 March 2017

International Energy Agency. 'IEA and the UNFCCC'. https://www.iea.org/topics/climatechange/ieaandtheunfccc/

International Energy Agency. 'IEA Celebrates the 10th Anniversary of the Energy Business Council with its Largest Gathering ever in Paris'. https://www.iea.org/news/iea-celebrates-the-10th-anniversary-of-the-energy-business-council-with-its-largest-gathering-ever-in-paris 17 April 2019

International Energy Agency. 'IEA Holds Energy Efficiency Training Week in Singapore' https://www.iea.org/news/iea-holds-energy-efficiency-training-week-in-singapore 3 July 2017

International Energy Agency. 'IEA Holds High-Level Workshop on the Future of Electricity'. https://www.iea.org/news/iea-holds-high-level-workshop-on-the-future-of-electricity 24 April 2018

International Energy Agency. 'IEA Holds Meeting with Energy Business Council'. https://www.iea.org/news/iea-holds-meeting-with-energy-business-council 22 November 2018

International Energy Agency. 'IEA Launches Climate Change and Renewable Energy Websites'. https://www.iea.org/news/iea-launches-climate-change-and-renewable-energy-websites 14 May 2003

International Energy Agency. 'IEA Launches the Clean Energy Transitions Programme to Support Clean-Energy Development'. https://www.iea.org/news/iea-launches-the-clean-energy-transitions-programme-to-support-clean-energy-development 7 November 2017

Bibliography

International Energy Agency. 'IEA Sees Global Demand Rising to 2022 as US Drivers Market Transformation'. https://www.iea.org/news/iea-sees-global-gas-demand-rising-to-2022-as-us-drives-market-transformation 13 July 2017

International Energy Agency. 'IEA Sees Renewable Energy Growth Accelerating Over Next 5 Years'. https://www.iea.org/news/iea-sees-renewable-energy-growth-accelerating-over-next-5-years 5 July 2012

International Energy Agency. 'IEA, Association of Southeast Asian Nations (ASEAN) Agree to Strengthen Co-Operation'. https://www.iea.org/news/iea-association-of-southeast-asian-nations-asean-agree-to-strengthen-co-operation 20 September 2011

International Energy Agency. 'Innovation'. https://www.iea.org/topics/innovation

International Energy Agency. 'Leadership. The IEA Secretariat is headed by Executive Director Dr Fatih Birol'. https://www.iea.org/about/leadership

International Energy Agency. 'Market Flexibility is Improving Thanks to LNG and Markets Currently Well Supplied Bus Gas Security Remains a Concern'.https://www.iea.org/news/market-flexibility-is-improving-thanks-to-lng-and-markets-currently-well-supplied-but-gas-security-remains-a-concern 18 October 2017

International Energy Agency. 'Market Report Series'. https://webstore.iea.org/market-reports?pagesize=24&viewmode=list

International Energy Agency. 'Member and Key Partner Country Emergency Policies'. https://vipo.iea.org/topics/energysecurity/memberandkeypartneremergencypolicies/

International Energy Agency. 'Methodology – Defining Energy Access'. https://vipo.iea.org/energyaccess/methodology/

International Energy Agency. 'Monthly OECD Electricity Statistics'. https://www.iea.org/reports/monthly-electricity-statistics

International Energy Agency. 'Natural Gas Security'. https://www.iea.org/areas-of-work/ensuring-energy-security/natural-gas-security

International Energy Agency. 'New IEA-IRENA Partnership Will Heighten Co-Operation and Policy Collaboration'. https://www.iea.org/newsroom/news/2012/january/new-iea-irena-partnership-will-heighten-co-operation-and-policy-collaboration.html January 2012

International Energy Agency. 'Nuclear'. https://www.iea.org/fuels-and-technologies/nuclear

International Energy Agency. 'Oil Market Report'. https://www.iea.org/topics/oil-market-report

International Energy Agency. 'Oil security'. https://www.iea.org/areas-of-work/ensuring-energy-security/oil-security

International Energy Agency. 'Only 4 Out of 38 Clean-Energy Technologies are on Track to Meet Long Term Climate Goals'. https://www.iea.org/news/only-4-out-of-38-clean-energy-technologies-are-on-track-to-meet-long-term-climate-goals 23 March 2018

International Energy Agency. 'Our Mission'. https://www.iea.org/about/mission

International Energy Agency. 'Policies Database'. https://www.iea.org/policies/about

International Energy Agency. 'Policy Uncertainty Threatens to Slow Renewable Energy Momentum'. https://www.iea.org/news/policy-uncertainty-threatens-to-slow-renewable-energy-momentum 28 August 2014

International Energy Agency. 'Questionnaires'. https://www.iea.org/areas-of-work/data-and-statistics/questionnaires

International Energy Agency. 'Renewable Capacity Growth Worldwide Stalled In 2018 After Two Decades of Strong Expansion'. https://www.iea.org/news/renewable-capacity-growth-worldwide-stalled-in-2018-after-two-decades-of-strong-expansion 6 May 2019

International Energy Agency. 'Renewables'. https://www.iea.org/fuels-and-technologies/renewables

International Energy Agency. 'Solar Heating & Cooling Technology Collaboration Programme (SHC)'. https://www.iea-shc.org

International Energy Agency. 'Statistics Resources'. https://www.iea.org/areas-of-work/data-and-statistics

International Energy Agency. 'Structure. The IEA is an Autonomous Inter-Governmental Organization within the OECD Framework, headed by its Executive Director'. https://www.iea.org/about/structure

International Energy Agency. 'Technology Collaboration Programme'. https://www.iea.org/areas-of-work/technology-collaboration

International Energy Agency. 'Tracking Clean Energy Progress'. https://www.iea.org/topics/tracking-clean-energy-progress

International Energy Agency. 'Training. Establishing Ongoing Working Relationships with Participating Countries for Continual Capacity Building'. https://www.iea.org/areas-of-work/training

International Energy Agency. 'United States to Lead Global Oil Supply Growth, While No Peak in Oil Demand in Sight'. https://www.iea.org/news/united-states-to-lead-global-oil-supply-growth-while-no-peak-in-oil-demand-in-sight 11 March 2019

International Energy Agency. 'Update to the IEA Energy Efficiency Indicators Database'. https://www.iea.org/news/update-to-the-iea-energy-efficiency-indicators-database 7 December 2018

International Energy Agency. 'What is Energy Security?'.https://www.iea.org/areas-of-work/ensuring-energy-security

International Energy Agency. 'Will System Integration of Renewables be a Major Challenge by 2023?' https://www.iea.org/articles/will-system-integration-of-renewables-be-a-major-challenge-by-2023 7 January 2020

International Energy Agency. 'World Energy Investment 2018'. Paris: IEA, 2018

International Energy Agency. 'World Energy Investment Roundtable 2018'. https://www.iea.org/events/world-energy-investment-roundtable-2018

International Energy Agency. Africa Energy Outlook 2019. Paris: IEA, 2019

International Energy Agency. Annual Statistical Supplement to the Oil Market Report. Paris: IEA, 2017

International Energy Agency. Annual Statistical Supplement to the Monthly Oil Market Report. Paris: IEA, 2006

International Energy Agency. Are We Entering a Golden Age of Gas?. Paris: IEA, 2011

Bibliography

International Energy Agency. Chile Energy Policy Review 2009. Paris: IEA, 2009
International Energy Agency. COAL 2017: Analysis and Forecast to 2022. Paris: IEA, 2017
International Energy Agency. Digitalization and Energy. Paris: IEA, 2017
International Energy Agency. Energy Access Outlook 2017. Paris: IEA, 2017
International Energy Agency. Energy and Climate Change. Paris: IEA, 2015
International Energy Agency. Energy Efficiency 2018. Paris: IEA, 2018
International Energy Agency. Energy Efficiency 2019. Paris: IEA, 2019
International Energy Agency. Energy Efficiency Indicators 2019. Paris: IEA, 2019
International Energy Agency. Energy Efficiency Indicators: Fundamentals on Statistics. Paris: IEA, 2014
International Energy Agency. Energy Efficiency Market Report 2013. Paris: IEA, 2013
International Energy Agency. Energy Policies Beyond IEA Countries. https://webstore.iea.org/search?q=energy+policies+beyond+IEA+countries&adv=false&cid=0&isc=false&pf=&pt=&sid=false
International Energy Agency. Energy Policies of IEA Countries. https://webstore.iea.org/search?q=energy+policies+of+IEA+countries
International Energy Agency. Energy Policy of IEA countries: Finland 2018 Review. Paris: IEA, 2018
International Energy Agency. Energy Technology Innovation Partnerships. Paris: IEA, 2019
International Energy Agency. Energy Technology Perspectives 2016. Paris: IEA, 2016
International Energy Agency. Energy Technology Perspectives 2017. Paris: IEA, 2017
International Energy Agency. Energy Technology RD&D Budgets 2019: Overview. Paris: IEA, 2019
International Energy Agency. Energy Technology RD&D Budgets. Paris: IEA, 2020
International Energy Agency. Gas 2017. Paris: IEA, 2017
International Energy Agency. Gas 2019. Paris: IEA, 2019
International Energy Agency. Global Gas Security Review 2018. Paris: IEA, 2018
International Energy Agency. International Low-Carbon Energy Technology Platform. Frequently Asked Questions. Paris: IEA, 2011
International Energy Agency. Medium-Term Coal Market Report 2015. Paris: IEA, 2015
International Energy Agency. Medium-Term Oil Market Report. Paris: IEA, 2007
International Energy Agency. Medium-Term Renewable Market Report 2015. Paris: IEA, 2015
International Energy Agency. Medium-Term Renewable Market Report 2012. Paris: IEA, 2012
International Energy Agency. Medium-Term Renewable Market Report 2016. Paris: IEA, 2016
International Energy Agency. Monthly Oil Data Service. https://www.iea.org/monthly-oil-data-service
International Energy Agency. Monthly Oil Market Report: December. Paris: IEA, 2018

International Energy Agency. Natural Gas Market Review 2009. Paris: IEA, 2009
International Energy Agency. Offshore Wind Outlook 2019. Paris: IEA, 2019
International Energy Agency. Oil 2017: Analysis and Forecasts to 2022. Paris: IEA, 2017
International Energy Agency. Oil 2018: Analysis and Forecasts to 2023. Paris: IEA, 2018
International Energy Agency. Oil and Gas Emergency Policy Series. https://webstore.iea.org/search?q=Oil+and+Gas+Emergency+Policy&adv=false&cid=0&isc=false&pf=&pt=&sid=false
International Energy Agency. Oil Market Report. https://www.iea.org/topics/oil-market-report
International Energy Agency. Partner Country Series. https://webstore.iea.org/search?q=partner+country+series&adv=false&cid=0&isc=false&pf=&pt=&sid=false
International Energy Agency. Renewables in Russia: from opportunity to reality. Paris: IEA, 2003
International Energy Agency. Russian Electricity Reform. Paris: IEA, 2003
International Energy Agency. Seven Women Entrepreneurs of Solar Energy. Paris: IEA, 2019
International Energy Agency. Shared Goals. Paris: IEA, 1993
International Energy Agency. Solar Energy: Mapping the Road Ahead. Paris: IEA, 2019
International Energy Agency. Special Briefing for COP21. Paris: IEA, 2015
International Energy Agency. Technology Innovation to Accelerate Energy Transitions. Paris: IEA, 2019
International Energy Agency. Technology Roadmap – A Guide to Development and Implementation. Paris: IEA, 2014
International Energy Agency. Technology Roadmap – Delivering Sustainable Bioenergy. Paris: IEA, 2017
International Energy Agency. Technology Roadmap – Low-Carbon Transition in the Cement Industry. Paris: IEA, 2018
International Energy Agency. Technology Roadmap – Solar Photovoltaic Energy. Paris: IEA, 2014
International Energy Agency. Technology Roadmap – Energy and GHG Reductions in the Chemical Industry via Catalytic Processes. Paris: IEA, 2013
International Energy Agency. Technology Roadmap – High-Efficiency, Low-Emissions, Coal-Fired Power Generation. Paris: IEA, 2012
International Energy Agency. Technology Roadmap – Hydrogen and Fuel cells. Paris: IEA, 2015
International Energy Agency. Technology Roadmap – Solar Thermal Electricity 2014. Paris: IEA, 2014
International Energy Agency. Technology Roadmap Hydrogen. Paris: IEA, 2015
International Energy Agency. The Role of Gas in Today's Energy Transitions. Paris: IEA, 2019
International Energy Agency. Tracking Fuel Supply 2020. Paris: IEA, 2020
International Energy Agency. Water-Energy Nexus. Paris: IEA, 2017
International Energy Agency. World Energy Investment 2017. Paris: IEA, 2017

Bibliography

International Energy Agency. World Energy Investment 2018: Methodology Annex. Paris: IEA, 2018

International Energy Agency. World Energy Investment 2019. Paris: IEA, 2019

International Energy Agency. World Energy Investment Outlook. Paris: IEA, 2014

International Energy Agency. World Energy Model. Paris: IEA, 2018

International Energy Agency. World Energy Model. Paris: IEA, 2019

International Energy Agency. World Energy Outlook 2010. Paris: IEA, 2010

International Energy Agency. World Energy Outlook 2013. Paris: IEA, 2013

International Energy Agency. World Energy Outlook 2017: China. Paris: IEA, 2017

International Energy Agency. World Energy Outlook 2017. Paris: IEA, 2017

International Energy Agency. World Energy Outlook 2018. Paris: IEA, 2018

International Energy Agency. World Energy Outlook 2019. Paris: IEA, 2019. Ù

International Energy Agency. World Energy Statistics 2019. Paris: IEA, 2019

International Energy Forum & Resources for the Future. Introductory Paper: A Comparison of Recent IEA and OPEN Outlooks. Riyadh: IEF, 2018

International Monetary Fund. 'Gross Domestic Product'. https://www.imf.org/external/datamapper/NGDP_RPCH@WEO/OEMDC/ADVEC/WEOWORLD

International Renewable Energy Agency. 'About IRENA'. https://www.irena.org/aboutirena

International Renewable Energy Agency. Hydrogen from Renewable Power: Technology Outlook for the Energy Transition. Abu Dhabi: IRENA, 2018

International Renewable Energy Agency. Remap 2030: A Renewable Energy Roadmap. Abu Dhabi: IRENA, 2014

Iriye, Akira. *Global Community: The Role of International Organizations in the Making of the Contemporary World*. Berkeley: University of California Press, 2002

Jacoby, Klaus-Dietmar. 'Energy Security: Conceptualization of the International Energy Agency (IEA)' in *Facing Global Environmental Change*, edited by Hans Günter Brauch et al. Hexagon Series in Human and Environmental Security and Peace book series, vol. 4. Berlin, Heidelberg: Springer, 2009, 345-354

Janoska, P. 'Tracking Clean Energy Progress 2018'. Webinar for the International Energy Agency, 14 June 2018

Johansson, Thomas B., Pathwardhan, Anand, Nakicenovi, Nebojsa & Gomez-Echeverri, Luis. *Global Energy Assessment: Towards a Sustainable Future*. Cambridge: Cambridge University Press, 2012

Joint Declaration by the IEA and Brazil, China, India, Indonesia, Russia and South Africa on the occasion of the 2013 IEA Ministerial Meeting Expressing Mutual Interest in Pursuing an Association. Paris: IEA, 2013

Joint Ministerial Declaration on the Occasion of the 2015 IEA Ministerial Meeting Expressing the Activation of Association. Paris: IEA, 2013

Joint Organisations Data Initiative. 'History'. https://www.jodidata.org/about-jodi/history.aspx

Joint Organisations Data Initiative. 'JODI World Data Bases'. https://www.jodidata.org/about-jodi/jodi-world-databases.aspx

Joint Organisations Data Initiative. Jodi Gas Manual – 1st Edition. Riyadh: JODI, 2014

Joint Organisations Data Initiative. Jodi Oil Manual – 2nd Edition. Riyadh: JODI, 2011

Jones, Kent. 'Green Room Politics and The WTO's Crisis of Representation'. Progress in Development Studies 9(4) (2009): 349, 357

Jørgensen, Birte Holst, Andersen, Katrine Krogh & Wilson, Elisabeth J. *Accelerating the Clean Energy Revolution – Perspectives on Innovation Challenges: DTU International Energy Report 2018*. Kongens Lyngby: Technical University of Denmark, 2018

Junxia, Liu. 'Investments in the energy sector of Central Asia: Corruption risk and policy implications'. Energy Policy 122 (2019): 110912

Kahler, Miles. 'Global Governance: Three Futures'. International Studies Review 20(2) (2018): 239, 246

Kahler, Miles. 'Regional Challenges to Global Governance'. Global Policy 8(1) (2017): 97, 100

Kennedy, Andrew B. 'China's Search for Oil Security: A Critique' in *The New Politics of Strategic Resources: Energy and Food Security Challenges in the 21st Century*, edited by David Steven, Emily O'Brien & Bruce Jones. Washington, DC: Brookings Institution Press, 2015, 23-39

Kennedy, David. 'The Mystery of Global Governance'. Ohio Northern University Law Review 34(3) (2008): 827, 860

Keohane, Robert O. 'The International Energy Agency: State Influence and Transgovernmental Politics'. International Organization 32(4) (1978): 929-951

Khanna, Parag. 'Global Governance and Megadiplomacy'. Brown Journal of World Affairs 18(1) (2011): 25, 34

Kissinger, H. Speech Given at the IEA Ministerial, 14 October 2009

Kohl, Wilfrid L. 'Consumer Country Energy Cooperation: The International Energy Agency and the Global Energy Order' in *Global Energy Governance: The New Rules of the Game*, edited by Andreas Goldthau & Jan Martin Witte. Washington, DC: Brookings Institution Press, 2010, 195-220

Konoplyanik, Andrei. 'Energy Security and the Development of International Energy Markets' in *Energy Security: Managing Risk in a Dynamic Legal and Regulatory Environment*, edited by Barry Barton, Catherine Redgwell, Anita Rønne & Donald N. Zillman. Oxford: Oxford University Press, 2004, 47-84

Koremenos, Barbara, Lipson, Charles & Snidal, Duncan. 'The Rational Design of International Institutions'. International Organization 55(4) (2001): 761, 799

Koronen, Carolina, Ahman, Max & Nilson, Lars J. 'Data Centres in Future European Energy Systems-Energy Efficiency, Integration and Policy'. Energy Efficiency 13 (2020): 129-144

Kruyt, Bert, van Vuuren, D.P., de Vries, H.J.M. & Groenenberg, H. 'Indicators for Energy Security'. Energy Policy 37(6) (2009): 2166, 2181

Kumagai, Takeo & Yep, Erik. 'India Moves Toward IEA Membership with Strategic Partnership'. https://www.spglobal.com/platts/en/market-insights/latest-news/oil/120919-india-moves-toward-iea-membership-with-strategic-partnership 9 December 2019

Lee, Caroline. 'The Energy Sector Is Feeling the Heat'. https://www.iea.org/commentaries/the-energy-sector-is-feeling-the-heat 29 August 2018

Bibliography

Lee, Sang-Yong & Holder, Gerald D. 'Methane Hydrates Potential as a Future Energy Source'. Fuel Processing Technology 71(1-3) (2001): 181, 186

Legros, Gwénaëlle, Havet, Ines, Bruce, Nigel & Bonjour, Sophie. The Energy Access Situation in Developing Countries. New York: United Nations Developing Programme, 2009

Letter of the Governing Board Chairman Etienne Davignon to the Commission President Jean-Xavier Ortoli, 20 November 1974

Levina, E. 'Energy Technology Perspectives 2017 – Catalysing Energy Technology Transformations'. Webinar for the International Energy Agency, 10 July 2017

Liang, Ting, Chai, Jian, Zhang, Yue-Jun & Zhan, Zhe George. 'Refined Analysis and Prediction of Natural Gas Consumption in China'. Journal of Management Science and Engineering 4(2) (2019): 91, 104

Linos, Katerina & Pegram, Tom. 'The Language of Compromise in International Agreements'. International Organizations 70(3) (2016): 587, 621

Macalister, Terry. 'Key Oil Figures Were Distorted by US Pressure, Says Whistleblower'. https://www.theguardian.com/environment/2009/nov/09/peak-oil-international-energy-agency 9 November 2009

MacNaughton, Joan. 'Cooperating on Energy Policy: The work of the International Energy Agency' in *The New Economic Diplomacy: Decision-making and Negotiation in International Economic Relations*, edited by Nicholas Bayne & Stephen Woolcock. Farnham: Ashgate Publishing, 2007, 279-296

Mathiesen, Karl. 'IEA Develops Pathway to Ambitious 1.5°C Climate Goal'. https://www.climatechangenews.com/2019/06/11/iea-develops-pathway-ambitious-1-5c-climate-goal/ 11 June 2019

Matthew, Richard A. & Hammill, Anne. 'Sustainable Development and Climate Change'. International Affairs 85(6) (2009): 1117, 1128

McArthur, John W. & Werker Eric. 'Developing Countries and International Organizations: Introduction to the Special Issue'. The Review of International Organizations 11(2) (2016): 155, 169

McGlade, Christophe E. 'Comment on the Uppsala Critique'. Energy Policy 67 (2015): 154, 158

McGlade, Christophe, Sondak, Glenn & Han, Mei. 'Whatever Happened to Enhanced Oil Recovery?'.https://www.iea.org/commentaries/whatever-happened-to-enhanced-oil-recovery 18 November 2018

McNally, R. 'The Critical Importance of Improving Oil Data'. Presentation given at the 2017 EIA Energy Conference. Washington DC, 26-27 June 2017

Meerts, Paul. *Diplomatic Negotiation: Essence and Evolution.* The Hague: Clingendael Institute, 2015

Millard, D. 'Developing and Enhancing Worldwide Energy Data'. Presentation given at the 2018 EIA Energy Conference. Washington DC, 4-5 June 2018

Millard, Duncan & Quadrelli, Roberta. 'Understanding and Using the Energy Balance'. https://www.iea.org/commentaries/understanding-and-using-the-energy-balance 4 September 2017

Miller, Richard G. 'Future Oil Supply: The Changing Stance of the International Energy Agency'. Energy Policy 39(3) (2015): 1569, 1574

Ministry of Commerce, PRC. 'China FTA Network. News Release'. http://fta.mofcom.gov.cn/list/chinageorgiaen/chinageorgiaennews/1/encateinfo.html

Ministry of Economy, Trade and Industry. Japan hosted the G7 Kitakyushu Energy Ministerial Meeting. https://www.meti.go.jp/english/press/2016/0502_04.html
Mission Innovation. 'Overview'. http://mission-innovation.net/about-mi/overview/
Mohn, Klays. Undressing the Emperor: A Review of IEA's WEO. UiS Working Papers in Economics and Finance. Stavanger: University of Stavanger, 2016
Moldner, Mirka. 'Responsibility of International Organizations – Introducing the ILC's DARIO'. Max Planck Yearbook of UN Law 16 (2012): 281, 328
Moriarty, Patrick & Honnery, Damon. 'Can Renewable Energy Power the Future?'. Energy Policy 93 (2016): 3, 7
Muller, Philippe Sebastian. 'Politicians of Global Governance'. CONfines de relaciones internacionales y ciencia política 1(1) (2005): 51, 66
Muttitt, Greg. 'Oil Change International Responds to International Energy Agency's 2018 World Energy Outlook'. http://priceofoil.org/2018/11/12/oil-change-international-responds-to-international-energy-agencys-2018-world-energy-outlook/ 12 November 2018
Nuclear Energy Agency. 'The Nuclear Energy Agency'. https://www.oecd-nea.org/general/about/
O'Brien, Emily & Gowan, Richard. What Makes International Agreements Work: Defining Factors for Success. New York: New York University Center on International Cooperation, 2012
OECD 50th Anniversary Vision Statement. Paris: Meeting of the OECD Council at Ministerial Level, 25-26 May 2011
Organisation for Economic Co-operation and Development. 'A Solid Partnership Between Thailand and the OECD'. http://www.oecd.org/southeast-asia/countries/thailand/
Organisation for Economic Co-operation and Development. 'External Audit – Supreme Audit Institutions'. https://www.oecd.org/gov/external-audit-supreme-audit-institutions.htm
Organisation for Economic Co-operation and Development. 'OECD and Enlargement'. https://www.oecd.org/about/document/enlargement.htm
Organisation for Economic Co-operation and Development. 'OECD Strengthens Co-Operation with Morocco – Renews Morocco Country Programme Agreement'. http://www.oecd.org/tax/oecd-strengthens-co-operation-with-moroccorenews-morocco-country-programme-agreement.htm
Organisation for Economic Co-operation and Development. 'Official Development Assistance – definition and coverage'. http://www.oecd.org/development/financing-sustainable-development/development-finance-standards/officialdevelopmentassistancedefinitionandcoverage.htm
Organisation for Economic Co-operation and Development. 'Our Global Reach'. https://www.oecd.org/about/members-and-partners/
Organisation for Economic Co-operation and Development. 'Singapore'. https://www.oecd.org/countries/singapore/
Organisation for Economic Co-operation and Development. Energy Prospects to 1985: An Assessment of Long-Term Energy Developments and Related Policies. Paris: OECD Publishing, 1974

Organisation for Economic Co-operation and Development. Report of the Chair of the Working Group on the Future Size and Membership of the Organisation to Council. Framework for the Consideration of Prospective Members. Paris: OECD Publishing, 2017

Organisation for Economic Co-operation and Development. Secretary-General's Report to Ministers 2019. Paris: OECD Publishing, 2019

Organisation for Economic Co-operation and Development. Secretary-General's Report to Ministers 2016. Paris: OECD Publishing, 2016

Organisation for Economic Co-operation and Development. Strategy for Enlargement and Outreach. Report by the Chair of the Heads of Delegation Working Group on the Enlargement Strategy and Outreach, Ambassador Seiichiro Noboru. Paris: OECD Publishing, 2004

Organization for Security and Co-operation in Europe. 'IEA Role in International Cooperation on Clean Energy'. A Paper in support of the Concluding Meeting of the 21st OSCE Economic and Environmental Forum. Prague, 11-13 September 2013

Organization of the Petroleum Exporting Countries. 'Brief History'
https://www.opec.org/opec_web/en/about_us/24.htm

Pisani-Ferry, Jean. Should We Give up on Global Governance?. Brussels: Bruegel, 2018

Raustiala, Kal. 'Form and Substance in International Agreements'. The American Journal of International Law 99(3) (2005): 581, 614

Report of the Commission on Global Security, Justice & Governance: Confronting the Crisis of Global Governance. The Hague: The Hague Institute for Global Justice/the Stimson Center, 2015

Revision of the Mandate of the Committee on Budget and Expenditure, approved by the Governing Board at its 221st meeting [IEA/GB(2010)20 and IEA/GB/C(2010)2]

Roffe, Pedro. 'Reflections on Current Attempts to Revise International Legal Structures: The North-South Dialogue – Clash of Values and Concepts, Contradictions and Compromises'. Georgia Journal of International and Comparative Law 9(3) (1979): 559, 574

Rogan, Fionn, Bolger, Paul & Ó Gallachóir, Brian. Climate Technology – Realising the Potential. EPA Research Report. Wexford: EPA, 2016

Röhrkasten, Sybille. *Global Governance on Renewable Energy. Contrasting the Ideas of the German and the Brazilian Governments.* Wiesbaden: Springer VS, 2015

Santos, Marcelo. 'Global Justice and Environmental Governance: An Analysis of the Paris Agreement'. Revista Brasileria de Política Internacional 60(1) (2017): 1, 18

Sarooshi, Dan. 'Some Preliminary Remarks on the Conferral by States of Powers on International Organizations'. Jean Monnet Working Paper Series, 2003/2004

Schmidt, Helmut. 'Washington Energy Conference, 11 February 1974 Statement by the German Federal Minister of Finance, Helmut Schmidt' in *Helmut Schmidt: Pioneer of International Economic and Financial Cooperation*, edited by Hartmut Soell. New York: Springer International Publishing, 2014, 33-38

Schreuer, Christoph. 'The Waning of the Sovereign State: Towards a New Paradigm for International-Law?'. European Journal of International Law. 3 (1993): 447-471

Scott, Richard. 'Innovation in International Organization: The International Agency'. Hasting International and Comparative Law Review 1 (1977): 1, 56

Scott, Richard. *The History of the International Energy Agency, 1974-1994: IEA, the first 20 years.* Paris: OECD/IEA, 1994

Shimbar, Ali & Ebrahimi, Seyek Babak. 'Political Risk and Valuation of Renewable Energy Investments in Developing Countries'. Renewable Energy 145 (2020): 1325, 1333

SolarPACES. 'About the SolarPACES TCP with IEA' https://www.solarpaces.org/csp-research-tasks/about-the-solarpaces-tcp-with-iea/

Sperling, James. *Handbook of Governance and Security*. Cheltenham: Edward Elgar Publishing, 2014, 369

Talberg, Anita & Swoboda, Kai. Emissions Trading Schemes Around the World. Canberra: Parliament of Australia Department of Parliamentary Services, 2013

Tanaka, N. 'Shifting Gears in the Global Dialogue on Energy Security and Climate Change'. Presentation for The Brookings Institution, 13 February 2009

Tanaka, Nobuo. Speech, 2009

The Gallup Organization. Attitudes on Issues Related to EU Energy Policy. Flash EB Series #206. The Gallup Organization, 2007

UN Department of Economic and Social Affairs (Statistics Division). 'SDG Indicators – Metadata Repository of SDG 3'. https://unstats.un.org/sdgs/metadata/?Text=&Goal=&Target=3.9

UN Department of Economic and Social Affairs (Statistics Division). 'SDG Indicators – Metadata Repository of SDG 7'. https://unstats.un.org/sdgs/metadata/?Text=&Goal=7&Target=

UN Department of Economic and Social Affairs (Statistics Division). 'SDG Indicators – Metadata Repository of SDG 9'. https://unstats.un.org/sdgs/metadata/?Text=&Goal=9&Target=

UN Department of Economic and Social Affairs (Statistics Division). International Recommendations for Energy Statistics (IRES). Statistical Papers Series M No. 93. New York: United Nations, 2017

UNFCCC Technology Executive Committee. Enhancing Financing for the Research, Development and Demonstration of Climate Technologies. Bonn: United Nations Climate Change Secretariat, 2017

United Nations. 'Ensure Access to Affordable, Reliable, Sustainable and Modern Energy'. https://www.un.org/sustainabledevelopment/energy/

United Nations. 'Sustainable Development Goals'. https://sdgs.un.org/goals

US Department of Energy. 'Hydrogen Production: Electrolysis'. https://www.energy.gov/eere/fuelcells/hydrogen-production-electrolysis

US Department of Energy. Secretary's Annual Report to Congress. Washington DC: GPO, 1984

Van de Graaf, Thijs & Lesage, Dries. 'The International Energy Agency After 35 Years: Reform Needs and Institutional Adaptability'. The Review of International Organizations 4(3) (2009): 293-317

Van de Graaf, Thijs & Westphal, Kirsten. 'The G8 and G20 as Global Steering Committees for Energy: Opportunities and Constraints'. Global Policy 2 (2011): 19, 30

Van de Graaf, Thijs. 'Obsolete or resurgent? The International Energy Agency in a Changing Global Landscape'. Energy Policy 48 (2012): 233, 241

Van de Graaf, Thijs. 'The IEA, the New Energy Order and the Future of Global Energy Governance' in *Rising Powers and Multilateral Institutions. International Political Economy Series*, edited by Dries Lesage & Thijs Van de Graaf. London: Palgrave Macmillan, 2015, 79-95

Van de Graaf, Thijs. *The Politics and Institutions of Global Energy Governance*. London: Palgrave Macmillan, 2013

Vaughan, Adam. 'A Century of Global Warming'. New Scientist 242(3228) (2019): 1, 14

Vaughan, Adam. 'IEA Warns of 'Worrying Trend' as Global Investment in Renewables Falls'. https://www.theguardian.com/business/2018/jul/17/iea-warns-of-worrying-trend-as-global-investment-in-renewables-falls 17 July 2018

Vera, Ivan & Langlois, Lucille. 'Energy Indicators for Sustainable Development'. Energy 32 (2007): 875, 882

Vienna Convention on the Law of Treaties, 1969

Wälde, Thomas W. 'International Energy Agency' in *Handbook of Transnational Economic Governance Regimes*, edited by Christian Tietje & Alan Brouder. Leiden: Brill, 2009, 293-313

Watts, Jonathan. 'IEA Accused of Undermining Global Shift From Fossil Fuels'. https://www.theguardian.com/environment/2018/apr/05/iea-accused-of-undermining-global-shift-from-fossil-fuels 5 April 2018

Wei, Yuwa. *Issues Decisive for China's Rise or Fall: An International Law Perspective*. Singapore: Springer Singapore, 2019

Weiss, Thomas G. 'Governance, Good Governance and Global Governance: Conceptual and Actual Challenges'. Third World Quarterly 21(5) (2000): 795, 814

Weiss, Thomas G. *Thinking about Global Governance: Why People and Ideas Matter*. London: Routledge, 2011

Weiss, Thomas G., Seyle, Conor D. & Coolidge, Kelsey. The Rise of Non-State Actors in Global Governance: Opportunities and Limitations. Broomfield: One Earth Future Foundation, 2013

White, William, Lunnan, Andres, Nybakk, Erlend & Kulisic, Bijana. 'The Role of Governments in Renewable Energy: The Importance of Policy Consistency'. Biomass and Bioenergy 57 (2013): 97, 105

Whitman, Jim. 'Disseminative Systems and Global Governance'. Global Governance 11(1) (2005): 85, 102

Whitman, Jim. *The Limits of Global Governance*. London: Routledge, 2005

Willenborg, Robbert, Tönjes, Christoph & Perlot Wilbur. *Europe's Oil Defences: An Analysis of Europe's Oil Supply Vulnerability and its Emergency Stockholding Systems*. The Hague: Clingendael Institute, 2004

Wilson, Alex Benjamin. International Energy Agency: Origins and Development. In-depth analysis. Brussels: European Parliamentary Research Service (EPRS), 2016

Winther Tanja. *The Impact of Electricity: Development, Desires and Dilemmas.* New York: Berghabn Books, 2008

World Energy Council. World Energy Issues Monitor 2019: Global and Regional Perspectives. London: WEC, 2019

Wu, Fuzuo. *Energy and Climate Policies in China and India: A Two-Level Comparative Study*. Cambridge: Cambridge University Press, 2018

Youming, Wang. 'Global Governance versus Harmonious World'. China International Studies 24 (2010): 79, 90

Yuan, Mei-Hua & Lo, Shang-Lien. 'Developing indicators for the monitoring of the sustainability of food, energy and water'. Renewable and Sustainable Energy Reviews 119 (2020): 109565

Zuzhang, Xia. 'Unlocking Financial Resources' in *Energy Poverty: Global Challenges and Local Solutions*, edited by Antoine Halff, Benjamin K. Sovacool & Jon Rozhon. Oxford: Oxford University Press, 2014, 411-440

Index

The numbers here refer to paragraph numbers.

Index

www.ingramcontent.com/pod-product-compliance
Ingram Content Group UK Ltd.
Pitfield, Milton Keynes, MK11 3LW, UK
UKHW021238300926
15471UKWH00013B/586

9 789403 530147